INDIA OF MY DREAMS

Foreign Service Institute

India
of My Dreams

Edited by Surendra Kumar
and Pradeep K. Kapur

Academic Foundation
New Delhi

www.academicfoundation.com

DISCLAIMER: Views expressed in this volume are those of the respective authors and not necessarily those of the Government of India, Foreign Service Institute or the organisation/s to which they belong.

First published in 2008

by : ACADEMIC FOUNDATION
4772-73 / 23 Bharat Ram Road, (23 Ansari Road),
Darya Ganj, New Delhi - 110 002 (India).
Tel : 23245001 / 02 / 03 / 04.
Fax : +91-11-23245005.
E-mail : academic@vsnl.com
www.academicfoundation.com

Published in collaboration with
Foreign Service Institute, New Delhi.

Cataloging in Publication Data--DK
Courtesy: D.K. Agencies (P) Ltd. <docinfo@dkagencies.com>

India of my dreams / edited by Surendra Kumar and Pradeep K. Kapur.
p. cm. Contributed articles.
ISBN 13: 9788171886890
ISBN 10: 8171886892

1. Economic forecasting--India. 2. India—Economic policy--1991- 3. Social prediction--India. 4. India—Politics and government--21st century--Forecasting. I. Kumar, Surendra. II. Kapur, Pradeep K.

DDC 330.954 22

Designed and typeset by Italics India, New Delhi.
Printed and bound in India.

10 9 8 7 6 5 4 3 2 1

Contents

सत्यमेव जयते
प्रणब मुखर्जी
PRANAB MUKHERJEE

जय हिन्द

विदेश मंत्री, भारत
MINISTER OF EXTERNAL AFFAIRS
INDIA

FOREWORD

It is human to dream. Individuals dream about their future all the time. But to dream about the future of the nation is something different. Here, dreams encapsulate not only our hopes, aspirations and expectations, but also our anxieties and concerns about the success and failures of our plans and policies and their impact on the people of our country.

I am glad to note that the Foreign Service Institute, in the 60th anniversary year of India's Independence, initiated the lecture series: "India of My Dreams" and invited eminent personalities from different walks of life to share their dreams about the India of tomorrow. It is, indeed, very heartening that more than two dozen highly respected, qualified and successful individuals responded to FSI's invitation and shared their dreams about India with budding Indian diplomats as well as the foreign diplomats who attended the professional courses. This lecture series deserves to be considered as a crucial course input and the Foreign Service Institute deserves kudos for its efforts for initiating this intellectually stimulating exercise.

India is an ancient country, but a young nation. Proud of its rich cultural heritage, it is poised to take centre stage in the comity of nations as a vibrant and secular democracy. Many of those who have spoken at the FSI lecture series are at the cutting-edge of this effort. On this occasion, I can do

Office : 172, South Block, New Delhi-110011 Tel : 23011127, 23011165, Fax : 23011463
Residence : 13, Talkatora Road, New Delhi-110011 Tel : 23737623, 23323042, 23737658

no better than to recall what Gandhi himself said on board the S.S. Rajput, on 12 Sept 1931 on his way to the Round Table Conference in London:

"I shall work for an India in which the poorest shall feel that it is their country, in whose making they have an effective voice; an India in which there shall be no high class and low class of people; an India in which all communities shall live in perfect harmony. There can be no room in such India for the curse of untouchability, or the curse of intoxicating drinks and drugs. Women will enjoy the same rights as men. We shall be at peace with all the rest of the world. This is the India of my dreams."

I do hope that general readers and serious practitioners of international relations alike will find this volume interesting and thought provoking.

New Delhi

(Pranab Mukherjee)

Introduction

Surendra Kumar

A couple of years back, when the "India Shining" blitzkrieg came crashing and its proponents lost power one wondered why. Many felt, the campaign was overkill; it did not reflect the reality on the ground, it did not connect with the masses; it hyped the gains which, though substantial, left a vast humanity of people unimpressed as they saw nothing much shining in their lives. In a way, the image of India sought to be projected at that time perhaps did not fit the dreams of millions of Indians.

Since then though phrases like India Rising, India Surging, India Marching Forward and Goldman Sach's regularly updated predictions of India becoming the third largest economy in the next 30 years and sustaining a 6 per cent growth rate for it's economy for the next 50 years keep hitting the headlines in the media, there are sober voices as well which include the Prime Minister and the Chairperson of the UPA, advising caution against generating excessive hype about India's progress in the last 20-25 years and stressing the need to make the gains of economic resurgence reach the masses, making them an important stakeholder in India's current progress curve and thus creating an inclusive society.

Apparently, over 1 billion Indians might have 5 billion dreams! While for the burgeoning middle classes, availability of foreign goodies including cars, liquor, electronics, various gadgets, garments, perfumes, lingerie and mushrooming and expanding shopping malls are good news, millions are still mired in abject poverty and face the daily grind to make both ends meet. Their dreams are still filled with *roti, kapda aur makan* (food, clothing and shelter), an engaging and inspiring slogan coined by late Smt. Indira Gandhi in the 60s. But today they also need clean drinking water, health care facilities, schools, roads, regular electric supply and above all receptive and people friendly governance. The dazzling malls do not cheer their hearts. They are more concerned about the price of onions and potatoes and ensuring that their children get two square meals a day. Thus, millions of poor people who somehow eke out a living, also dream, but differently and for different things. They do not give up dreaming; their lives will be that much more difficult to live if they did not conjure up some dreams for their future. The best example of this is Mira Nair's "Salaam Bombay" which epitomises the irrepressible *joie de vivre* of the street children of Bombay.

Apparently, there are countless dreams. While personal dreams might differ drastically depending on the circumstances of one's own life, there is likely to be greater similarity in people's dreams about their motherland. These dreams are more like a vision for one's country, aspirations for its future and hopes, and where you want to see it. In other words, these dreams constitute a virtual wish list which may and may not be fulfilled but are worth pursuing nonetheless.

The lecture series: "India of My Dreams" was triggered off by my desire to pick on the brains of some of the most respected eminent personalities and offer an insight of their vision of the India of tomorrow: where they want it to be, what were the favourable factors which will propel India to rise to their expectations and what hurdles and challenges she is likely to encounter. The broad theme offered them a blank canvas to paint a picture of India of their dreams, to share their thoughts, ideas, hopes and aspirations about the possibility of fulfillment of these dreams and their impact.

As India is renowned for its bewildering diversity, I did not wish to confine to any particular group of personalities but to seek as diverse a group as possible to delineate different contours of India of their dreams. Therefore, in this volume, while on the one hand, you will savour views of senior Ministers of the Government like the Ministers of External Affairs, Home Affairs, Finance, Railways, Social Justice and Empowerment, Panchayati Raj, Youth Affairs & Sports and Development of North Eastern Region and the Chief Minister of the NCT of Delhi, you will also get plenty on your platter from the Captains of industry like Dr. Azim Premji and Sunil Bharti Mittal, economists like Lord Meghnad Desai and Dr. Dipak Jain and journalists like M.J. Akbar and Saeed Naqvi. The readers will also get an inkling of thinking of personalities like Justice J.S. Verma, Chief Election Commissioner of India Shri N. Gopalaswami, and Bharatnatyam and Odissi dance exponent Dr. Sonal Mansingh. Not only this, you also have international inputs from such acclaimed individuals like Dr. Sam Pitroda, Dr. Marshall Bouton and Dr. Shashi Tharoor. Thus, this volume is, as Shashi

Tharoor would say, a "thali of dreams" of different colours, shades, hues, lines, sketches and images, each fascinating in its own way!

The theme is elastic enough to include those who have unfolded and shared their dreams about India as well as those who have addressed certain aspect of India and its future as they perceive it. Dr. Sam Pitroda's two lectures: "From Communication to Knowledge" and "Knowledge for a More Just, Fair, Equitable and Inclusive Society"; Lord Meghnad Desai's lecture of "Emergence of India and China as Major Economic Powers"; Dr. Marshall Bouton's lecture: "India's Rise—What Indians, Americans and Chinese Think" fall in this category. "India at Sixty" was a brainstorming session which has thrown interesting points and counterpoints about what have been India's significant achievements and failures since Independence and where India seems to be heading to in the next decade. Lt. Gen. Nambiar, Prof. Varun Sahni, Sadia Dehlavi and Ms. Mythili Bhusnurmarth used their brain to create a mild storm at the session along with others referred to earlier.

Nobel Laureate Dr. Wangari Maathai was kind enough to visit the Institute and address the budding Indian diplomats. She shared what she thought all diplomats, including Indian diplomats, should be doing wherever they might be serving as their countries' representatives in different parts of the world. We have included her brief comments in appreciation of her special gesture to the Institute and keeping in mind the fact that her views were relevant to the Indian diplomats who will help project India's dreams abroad.

All the dreams about India of tomorrow, mine, yours and theirs are gravely endangered by the menace of internationl terrorism, hence the inclusion of M.J. Akbar's speech: "Islam, Jehad and Global War on Terrorism."

My most sincere thanks and gratitude are due to all the dignitaries who have so generously spared their valuable time to share their visions and comments for India of tomorrow as well as a critique of today's India.

I feel pleased that we were able to host more than two dozen dignitaries of such high calibre and eminence in just 12 months, something which the FSI has not been able to do in the last 20 years! If the volume gives some food for thought, not only to the practitioners of diplomacy but to all decision makers and those who would in some way influence the future of India, our efforts would have served some purpose.

I must thank my colleagues Banbit Roy, Pradeep Kapur, Ranjan Dash, Gusain and Sudha for their unstinted support and valuable cooperation. My special thanks are due to the Academic Foundation for contributing significantly to the concept, design and the layout of the book as it has turned out to be.

PRANAB MUKHERJEE

Pranab Mukherjee is the External Affairs Minister of India. Since 1973 he has held various portfolios and has made significant contributions as Cabinet Minister of India. These include Defence, Finance, Commerce, Steel & Mines and External Affairs. He was adjudged as one of the best five Finance Ministers of the world for 1984 by Euro Money of New York. He also held the position of Deputy Chairman, Planning Commission, Government of India. Mr. Mukherjee is the senior-most Minister in the Council of Ministers and heads 48 Committees of Ministers constituted to deal with important policy and implementation issues. He is also the leader of the House, Lok Sabha, since June 2004. He has authored several books.

1

The World Today

An Indian Perspective

PRANAB MUKHERJEE

Interdependence is the defining characteristic of international relations today. The notion of power, critical to understanding international relations at any time in history, has also evolved significantly and the relatively new construct of "soft power" now attracts significant attention in foreign offices across the world.

The Indian mind is comfortable with change and connectedness. The enabling environment created since the mid-80s, and especially since 1991, has allowed India's entrepreneurs and professionals to leverage change and create wealth and employment on an unprecedented scale. In the same vein, the challenge before the Indian Foreign Service in today's interdependent world is to leverage India's unique soft power to sustain the right external environment and enable India to pursue her national goals successfully. I am confident that with the efforts of the Foreign Services Institute and with the backing of other significant actors in foreign policy, such as Parliament, media and academia, this is eminently possible.

The world today is unfortunately not only about expanding economic and technological horizons. There are dangers and pitfalls such as poverty, environmental degradation, constriction of political freedom and choice, growth of extremism and intolerance, international terrorism, proliferation of weapons of mass destruction and the risk of their falling into the hands of irresponsible actors, pandemics, energy security and climate change. Quite often, the manner of addressing some of these challenges poses a challenge in itself. For a large, diverse, developing democracy located in a region going through many painful transitions, these are not academic concerns, but real, daily issues. We have to respond to them energetically, creatively and in partnership with other actors on the international stage.

From our perspective, the primary challenge for the world today has to be the elimination of poverty and a radical improvement in the living standards of people in the developing world. Much of the industry in the developing world needs significant technology upgrades to become globally competitive. Agriculture faces challenges of productivity, technology, managing scarce water resources and establishing marketing standards. Infrastructure needs a drastic overhaul. Access to predictable, affordable and environmentally sound energy resources, in particular, has emerged as a major bottleneck and must rank foremost in our priorities. A priority task of Indian diplomacy has to be the facilitation of the developmental process, promotion of trade and investment flows, securing predictable and affordable energy supplies and ensuring the widest possible access to technologies. While the primary development effort has to be national, we need to leverage international partnerships to the best possible effect.

The second challenge is institutional. While people are sovereign in choosing how to govern themselves, the Indian experience is that democracy is essential to the management of the diverse aspirations of a plural society. It is also undoubtedly one of the best tools to manage social change without upheaval and violence. As the world becomes more connected and interdependent, the diversity that we see at the level of individual nations will necessarily get more and more reflected at the global level. The management of this global diversity under conditions of interdependence would require the application of democratic principles to global governance as well.

India is not looking for new poles, but rather a pluralistic world order that is reflective of the diversity of the world today and accommodating of new players who can contribute solutions to tomorrow's problems. In this context, the composition of the UN Security Council too needs to come to terms with present reality and reflect future potential. This premier institution of global governance needs to be democratised and India needs to find its rightful place in an expanded Council.

Another priority has to be a significant diminution, if not outright elimination, of the threat of war and conflict. Peace and security are indispensable in confronting challenges that the international community will face in the coming years. In India, we are acutely aware of the ferment in our neighbourhood and the need to ensure a peaceful periphery for our and the region's development. Here again, international priorities blend with our national priorities.

Tighter interlinkages and shared stakes do diminish the prospects of traditional conflict, but old sources of conflict are now being joined by new threats related to proliferation, terrorism as well as natural disasters and pandemics like HIV/AIDS or Avian Flu. Proliferation of weapons of mass destruction and the possibility of their falling into the hands of terrorists must rank among the most critical challenges facing the world today. The issue cannot be addressed merely by focusing on supply-side technology controls. The so-called A.Q. Khan network made a mockery of these controls. A new approach is required, which also prioritises disarmament. India has always pursued the objective of global disarmament, based on the principles of universality, non-discrimination and effective compliance.

Given its record of restraint and responsible behaviour, India's participation as a full partner in a new global consensus on non-proliferation would strengthen global efforts in this arena. Conscious of our responsibilities, we have adopted a comprehensive export control system, harmonised with international best practices, and reiterated our traditional commitment to nuclear disarmament through a Working Paper submitted to the United Nations General Assembly. We believe that a good beginning would be to formalise a no-first use agreement internationally as a step towards delegitimising nuclear weapons. This approach was adopted in 1925 in the Geneva Protocol on chemical and biological weapons and ultimately led to their elimination.

Finally, from my perspective, an essential priority for the world today has to be a new consciousness, not just among the political elites, but also among the peoples of the world, that their choices and their actions affect all others on this planet. This consciousness is what would break down the barriers to greater global cooperation and lead to the structures and processes that are needed to address international challenges such as climate change and energy security. And this is where the voice of India's diplomats can best be heard. However, this is a subtle task. A narrow consciousness can hardly be the best communicator of a global consciousness. Therefore, I would call upon our future diplomats to reflect the best of Indian civilisation when interacting with the world.

In the timeless words of India's best diplomat, Krishna, a diplomat's speech "should not disturb the mind of the listener; it should be precise with correct use of language; and again, if possible, it should be of utility to the listener."

P. CHIDAMBARAM

Palaniappan Chidambaram is the Finance Minister of India since May 2004, a post which he also held from June 1996 to March 1998. He has earlier served with distinction in the ministries of Commerce, Personnel and Internal Security. He has studied at Presidency College, Chennai, Law College, Madras University, and at Harvard Business School. Mr. Chidambaram is a lawyer by profession, and is recognised as one of the leading senior counsels in India, particularly in the area of constitutional and corporate law. He has long experience in international economic diplomacy.

2

India of My Dreams

Abject Poverty can be Eradicated

P. Chidambaram

Like each one of us has dreams, 60 years ago our first Prime Minister Jawaharlal Nehru spoke of a dream in words that have been reverberating within us ever since. He said we have a tryst with destiny, and the time has come for us to redeem our promises substantially, if not in full measure.

During the past 60 years we travelled on a somewhat tortuous road. We have accomplished a lot, but we also know that we have missed some opportunities. We also acknowledge that we have made mistakes. But through all these missed opportunities and mistakes we have stoutly defended our freedom, democracy, the rule of law, liberty and equality for all citizens, and also our proud civilisation and history. Few countries in the world can present such an unbroken record of freedom and democracy as we have—a history of 60 years of democratic traditions and the rule of law.

We are a country with a very large population. We had a large number of poor 60 years ago, and many people are still poor. There is however, a misconception that we are a poor country. We are not a poor country; we are a country where a large number of people are poor. There is no reason why we should have so many poor people even after 60 years of freedom. We are a country endowed with vast natural resources, a nation with an abundance of high quality human resources, and with these we can make a prosperous nation for all our citizens. However, for a variety of reasons this has not happened and it is not an easy task. I, therefore, want to underline some of the major hindrances that are blocking the path to all-round development, and the steps we need to take for the equitable development of our country.

A vast majority of our population is farmers, and many of those are landless because that is how our society is constituted and functions even today. Therefore, a large number of people are poor. This poverty is not something that cannot be wiped out. If I was in the 19th century, perhaps I could have argued that humankind did not have the technological tools to wipe out poverty of a large swathe of people in a short span of time, but here in the beginning of the 21st century, I cannot pretend that a nation is destined to remain poor because there are no tools available to wipe out poverty. More importantly, no nation can afford to live with so many poor people at a time when we have so many enabling tools which can help eradicate poverty. Nations which are smaller than India, and which were poorer than India, have already wiped out poverty long ago. And many poor countries are today determined to do so and are achieving good results too.

Many years ago Jawaharlal Nehru said: "the problem of unemployment is directly related to lower growth in the farm income. And this could be removed only by a considerable increase in the national income. And our economic policy must therefore aim at establishing an equitable distribution of income. And we must achieve that." His words uttered over 50 years ago are true even today. Poverty can be removed only by ensuring an equitable distribution of resources and income. Our economic policy must be based on plenty, but until recently our economic policies were based on scarcity, and the economics of scarcity has no meaning in the world of today.

For 30 years we followed a policy of planned economic model and it had its desired effects. But we missed three decades of available opportunities. The economy was growing at 3.5 per cent while the population was growing at 2.5 per cent, and it left no room for any productive investments and there was no addition to the wealth of the nation. Poverty remained at a stubborn level and it did not decline in the first 30 years at all. The result of this planned economic model was that the consumer paid a huge price. The consumer had the choice between an ambassador car and an ambassador car, the consumer had the choice of flying Indian Airlines and Indian Airlines, and there was a choice between waiting for a fixed telephone connection for nine years and not having one at all!

In 1991, we brought a paradigm shift in our economic policy and the results of this shift were visible from 1995 onwards. The annual growth rate of the economy increased to 5.7 per cent between 1995 and 2000. Between 2000 and 2006 the economy grew by 6.9 per cent annually, and according to the latest available data, the annual economic growth shot up to 8.6 per cent in the fiscal ending March 2007. Our share in international trade in goods grew from 0.6 per cent in 1980 to 1.1 per cent in 2005. Our foreign exchange reserves have increased exponentially from under a billion dollars in 1991 to nearly 225 billion dollars as per the latest data available. These figures reflect both the growth momentum we have built over the past few years as also our production capabilities in addition to our productivity gains.

We have leadership position globally in several sectors such as software, steel, automobiles, telecommunications, refining, textiles, and leather. The *Global Competitiveness Report 2006-07*, brought out by the World Economic Forum, ranks India at 43 out of a list of 125 nations. While we are not the most competitive nation in the world, we have a sharper competitive edge today than we ever had before. In the past 15 years the number of people below the poverty line has declined and, in the past five years, it has declined more sharply. Between the period 1999 and 2004-05, for which the latest data is available, more jobs were created than in any other five-year period. And in the last three-year period, growth has moved up by another percentage point, in fact by two percentage points. During this period, more jobs have been created and more wealth has been added and there has been a sharper decline in poverty too. I can confidently say that we are on the right track when it comes to economic growth. But, of course, there are grey areas. I admit that our roads are really bad. Our roads are not like the German autobahn or the American express ways. We have potholes and unmarked bumps on our roads. But today we are developing four-lane roads and express ways at least in some cities. I am sure that the path that we chose in 1991 and the road that we are travelling today will take us to the right destination—the destination being the removal of abject poverty and deprivation that we have known for the past 5,000 years.

But have we arrived? The answer is no. We have not arrived as yet because of the structure of our economy. And it is this very structure that we are trying to change. Overcoming this challenge is fundamental to what we are doing today and will also determine what we will be tomorrow.

We as a nation have a very peculiar economic structure. Close to 65 per cent of our population still depends on agriculture, 60 per cent of our overall workforce works on the farms, and that is more than 600 million people including children. But this large segment of our population only shares about 18 per cent of the country's GDP. Another 22 or 23 per cent comes from industry and nearly 56 or 57 per cent comes from the services sector. This calls for attention to the state of the farming structure in the country. The average landholding in the country is only a little over two acres of land, in fact to be precise it is around 2.3 acres of land per family. Tell me, how can a farming family with a landholding of 2.3 acres become rich and prosperous? Given that most of the country's cultivable land is rainfed and is fit only for single crop, there is no way in which a farming family from such a background can become rich or prosperous. Therefore, we have to address the structural problems in the farm economy. We have to wean this large portion of population from agricultural activities to industrial, services and other non-farming activities, and at the same time make farming a more viable and profitable activity.

There is yet another problem attached to our agriculture. The overall area under cultivation has stagnated between 120 and 125 million hectares, of this, the area under wheat cultivation has stagnated between 25 and 27 million hectares and the area under paddy cultivation between 41 and 45 million hectares. Within this, the area under pulses has stagnated at around 25 million hectares even as the population in the rural areas have not seen a major decline. Further, the production of wheat has stagnated between 68 and 73 million tonnes, and the production of rice between 85 and 91 million tonnes. Productivity has also stagnated: in case of wheat it is only around 2,700 kg per hectare and in the case of rice, it is 2,000 kg per hectare. The government is fully aware of the situation and is totally focussed on changing the face of our agriculture. On the Independence Day, the Prime Minister announced a massive programme in the form of a new agricultural package. The Cabinet has cleared a massive programme to raise the production of wheat and rice. The Cabinet has also cleared a massive programme envisaging providing Rs. 25,000 crore to the States to help them bring about more farm output through infusing more money into agriculture. I am confident that this new focus on agriculture, new capital being diverted to agriculture, and new technologies such as new hybrid seeds, new micro nutrients, and new water management techniques being adopted in agriculture and new investments in this sector will be able to lift agriculture growth by a minimum of four per cent annually, which will make farming a more viable and profitable activity for our farmers.

The next crucial problem we face is infrastructure. Our roads are inadequate, ports are choked, airports are congested, and production of power is inadequate to meet our needs. There are so many examples of grossly inadequate supply and the demand outstripping the supply. For instance, today we produce 10-times more cement than we were doing 25 years ago. The same story applies to power as also to steel, and virtually in every infrastructure sector this is the case. Keeping this in mind, our next big challenge is infrastructure. The robust growth that we are logging now could have been much higher if we had basic infrastructure in place, if the industry and agriculture got the electricity they needed, if our roads were better, if our airports could handle more cargo planes. Then the economy in fact would have been growing at over 10 per cent during the past four years and not at over 8 per cent as is the case.

The challenges in infrastructure are very huge, and the investment estimates for the sector is humungous. It has been estimated that for the next five-year plan, that is 2007-2012, we will need to invest over $320 billion in infrastructure alone. This includes $130 billion for power, $66 billion for the railways, $49 billion for the national highways, $11 billion for seaports and $9 billion for civil aviation. In fact, the committee on infrastructure that submitted its report in May 2007 has already advised that the target estimates for infrastructure investments be revised upwards from the originally estimated $320 billion to $384 billion at 2005-06 prices, which is equivalent to $475 billion at current prices. I know that the numbers are mind boggling but I can say with confidence that no country save India needs and no country save India can absorb such large funds for the infrastructure sector. But how are we going to obtain such large funds? We intend to fund this through public investments, private investments and through public-private partnerships. In fact, the stakes are more on public-private partnerships.

Savings and investments as a proportion to the GDP for the 2005-06 fiscal (which are the latest figures available) were as follows: the savings ratio was estimated at 32.4 per cent while investment ratio was estimated at 33.8 per cent of the GDP. While we do not yet have the figures for the 2006-07 fiscal, even at an estimated gross domestic capital formation basis, the number stands at 35.1 per cent, which is up by 1.3 percentage points from the previous year. My inference therefore is that the savings and investments ratios have increased by at least 1.3 percentage points to no less than 35 per cent of the GDP. While our inclination would be to increase the funds provided to all sectors, our endeavour would be to channelise a significant proportion of these investments into the infrastructure sector.

The gross capital formation into the infrastructure sector during 2006-07 fiscal was estimated at 4.6 per cent of the GDP, but our endeavour will be to increase the proportion to at least 8 per cent of the GDP in the coming years. Given an economy that is the size of $1 trillion, that is what we are today and still growing very rapidly, and at this rate, next year we will need a minimum of $80 billion for infrastructure annually, and over a five-year period at least $400 billion for investment in the infrastructure sector. I am confident that beginning this year and over the next five years, we will be able to find $400 billion for the infrastructure sector. A portion of this will come from outside sources as multilateral institutions continue to support our efforts. Between 1986 and 2000, we got $1.75 billion and over the past five years $4.7 billion came into the transport sector, $1.38 billion for urban development and $1.5 billion to the energy sector from these lenders. We will find the money internally as well as through our lenders and will invest these monies as productive investments in our infrastructure sector.

So, what do I see for India in the next 5, 10 or the next 20 years? You all know the BRIC report, and every update on that brings us closer, at least by one or two years, to the year when we would be the world's third largest economy. I am not a soothsayer nor am I a futurologist or an astrologer. All I can tell you now is that if we maintain our growth rate of around 9 per cent for this year and at about 8 or 8.5 per cent in the coming years—and am very confident that we will be able to grow at 8 or 9 per cent annually in the next few years—we will surely be the third largest economy in the world in the next 20 or 25 years. And this would make India a large force for peace and stability. This will make South Asia, with India in the lead, a region of peace and prosperity. We will work with smaller nations to help them uplift themselves by sharing our technologies and expertise with them.

What are we attempting in India today? We are attempting to put in place the principles of economics which have raised many nations to the level of prosperous nations. Since we live in an open society, we have many debates on every issue of importance—local politics, local economy or global economy. I firmly believe that only in an open economy can an open society and an open polity framework thrive.

But there are some immediate challenges that we need to overcome. I am sure that we will overcome these challenges. With our passion and attachment to democracy, freedom, the rule of law and to the existence of civil society, we can overcome these challenges with much more ease and certainty. Of course, there are aberrations in our civil society, weaknesses in our polity, there are some people who take extreme measures, but by and large we are a nation that is peace-loving and democratic. We are an open society that is passionately committed to and determined to maintain a democratic and open polity. Second, our large, qualified human resources. I am told, the British system will collapse if our doctors and nurses refuse to work even for a day! Our doctors, engineers, managers, teachers, researchers and software professionals are amongst the best in the world. And we continue to turn out hundreds of thousands of them. Of course, some of them go out of the country for higher studies, but not because we do not have good academic institutions—we also have the best educational institutions in the form of our world class IITs and IIMs. And with all these I am sure we will continue to grow at near 9 per cent and would become the third largest economy in the world sooner than later.

India will live in peace and in friendship, and will find her rightful place in the comity of nations.

"Civilizations have arisen in other parts of the world. In ancient and modern times, wonderful ideas have been carried forward from one race to another... But mark you, my friends, it has been always with the blast of war trumpets and the march of embattled cohorts. Each idea had to be soaked in a deluge of blood... Each word of power had to be followed by the groans of millions, by the wails of orphans, by the tears of widows. This, many other nations have taught; but India for thousands of years peacefully existed. Here activity prevailed when even Greece did not exist... Even earlier, when history has no record, and tradition dares not peer into the gloom of that intense past, even from until now, ideas after ideas have marched out from her, but every word has been spoken with a blessing behind it and peace before it. We, of all nations of the world, have never been a conquering race, and that blessing is on our head, and therefore we live....!"

— Swami Vivekananda

SHIVRAJ PATIL

Shivraj Patil is the Union Home Minister since 2004. He has worked in various capacities, including Speaker of the Lok Sabha (Lower House of the Indian Parliament); Union Minister of Defence; Minister of State: Commerce, Science and Technology, Atomic Energy, Electronics, Space and Ocean Development, Personnel, Defence Production, and Civil Aviation & Tourism. He was Vice-President of the Council for Scientific and Industrial Research (CSIR), and has served on various Committees of the Parliament. Mr. Patil is an author and poet with several books to his credit.

3 Acceptance of *Anekantvada*

Essential for Strengthening India's Democracy

SHIVRAJ PATIL

India is a democracy. The form of democracy it has adopted appears to be foreign, based on the Westminster model. But, the heart of it is indigenous. The most important aspect of democracy is willingness to respect others' points of view, and toleration towards others' way of looking at things, relevant to the state, society, economy, etc.

In India, the people think that an object can be looked at from different angles, and when that is done, it may not appear to be the same to all persons; it may appear to be different to different persons looking at it from different angles. The theory which supports this approach is called the "Anekantvada". The *Anekantvada,* respect of multiplicity of viewpoints, helps the democracy to function without friction and difficulties.

Indian democracy and Indian representatives in the legislatures are not very different from democracies and legislators in other countries. They are as good as other democracies and other legislators. There is a scope for improvement in their working and the manner of discharging their duties. They are meant to provide forums and opportunities to find out what is good for them. If they are used only to find fault with one another, and not to find out what is common in their thinking and desires, the system would continue to fail to produce what is best for them and their countries. There is scope for refining the system, making it less cantankerous, more productive and positive, more capable of solving the problems of the present and those of the future. Steps have to be taken to make the system, better than what it is, more useful, more prompt and more comprehensive and futuristic too. This can be done by looking at the manner in which elections are held, looking at the manner in which the policies, plans and laws are made, budgets are passed and the ruling section is held accountable. This can be done only if the people, all political parties and legislators agree on the principles which should be accepted and used to bring about improvement. It may not be done immediately and at one go. It is being done and maybe in a reasonable time frame, the task would be done to a great extent.

India is a resource rich country. It has good soil, good water resources, good climatic conditions and rich human resources. It was very rich in the past, and this attracted human beings from other parts of the world towards itself. However, today, it is not as rich and developed economically, as some other parts of the world and countries are. The reason for this is that we did not pay enough attention to science and technology, new methods of doing things, and remained contented for long years, with what we had. Since India became Independent, it has begun to pay attention to new concepts, science and technology and new methods of doing things. It has the brain power and human resources to use and develop new technologies, sciences and knowledge. On its own, it is trying to do a lot. With cooperation with other countries of the world, it has embarked on the odyssey of discovery in many new areas on the horizon. It may be able to contribute a great deal, in the area of new knowledge, which is relevant to the land, the oceans, the space and the human mind. It would like to use the strength and intelligence of all citizens in the country to develop the new knowledge and economy of the country, and allow them and the country to cooperate with the citizens of other countries and other parts of the world.

The world has become a small place, in which cooperation is feasible and necessary. We are willing to cooperate not only to use the resources of our planet, but those of other planets also, which are being reached now. India would not fear to work with other countries of the world. It would like to see that in trade and industry, in new knowledge, and in doing justice to all, it would march hand in hand with men and women inhabiting other parts of the world. With cooperation we can achieve most promising results.

Socially, India is a little different from other countries. It has people living on its soil, belonging to different religions, communities and castes. It has been tolerant to different religious concepts and also to the caste system. This tolerance of ours towards different religious concepts has helped us maintain peace and tranquility in the country. Though at times, we have had clashes between people belonging to different religions and castes. The religious concepts and caste system have existed in the country for many years. They are becoming weak in some respects and strong in others. However, attempts are being made by many right-minded people to see that they do not create problems for society and are used to generate understanding and harmony. It is hoped that they do not create divisions in the country and would help in rounding up the angularities to create a homogenous society—politically, economically and socially.

India is a multi-cultural, multi-linguistic, and multi-religious country. Diversity that exists in India is very rich and deep rooted. In its apparent diversity, there is the unity which keeps the country united. If we try to obliterate this diversity, Indian society and culture would become weak and poor. If we nurture this diversity, recognise its uniting factor, our society can become stronger. Attempts are being made to create conditions in which this diversity is protected and unity is strengthened. The task is quite complicated and requires skills of extraordinary nature. However, it appears that Indian people have developed that skill. On occasions, disturbing trends occur on the horizon. But, they do not overpower the basic quality of the people, to understand, tolerate and harmonise. Let us hope that in future, this skill would become more effective and promising.

In the world today, we talk a lot about science and technology and economic development and such other things. Science and technology are needed for material development and well-being of the people. No country can keep pace with the modern time, without paying attention to new knowledge relevant to science and technology. But, there are other things which should also be used to make our lives more livable and meaningful. Without developing the facility to understand the beauty of nature and the things that surround human beings, it is not possible to understand our existence and its importance. All that exists in the cosmos is connected with us. The space connects us, the air connects us, and the earth connects us. In fact, we are parts of the big whole which is a reality. In fact, we come from this reality and we must go back to this reality. It establishes the unity between all things, plants, creatures and human beings. The partitions that we see are artificial, not real. What is real is the unity, the oneness which pervades everywhere. We are however, incapable of easily understanding this principle of unity. Our vision is limited. It divides the reality, the existence, the cosmos and this world. These principles are not unscientific. In fact, they transcend science and technologies. They are the outcomes of super science which can be recognised as spirituality, which means the perception and realisation of unity in the existence. India had thought about it in the past. In fact, it is the basis of its approach towards life. When we forgot this principle, we suffered. When we realised it anew, we came to enjoy true bliss and well being.

This world of ours does not have natural boundaries. At some places, it may have some geographical boundaries, but the land is one and undivided. In many parts of the world, the boundaries are artificial. The divisions are artificial. The way a human being is born, lives and dies at one place of the globe, is the same with respect to the birth, existence and death of other human beings at other places. If this is understood and realised, the human beings will treat themselves as the chips of the same block, members of one family and will not try to dominate, exploit others. Instead, they will try to cooperate with one another and share their joys and sorrows. If this happens, the world may not have wars and conflicts, bloodshed and exploitation. All human beings would be able to cooperate with one another, on the land, on the waves of oceans, in space and outer space, which, in some measures, they are trying to do now.

These dreams may or may not take concrete shape in the near or distant future. But, they are worth having. We may be, at the start of the journey and in different conditions and situations, which would not be very promising and helpful for realising these dreams. Yet, we need to march in this direction. Let us hope that we are able to achieve something which would take us nearer to these goals.

"India is the cradle of the human race, the birthplace of human speech, the mother of history, the grandmother of legend, and the great grand mother of tradition. Our most valuable and most astrictive materials in the history of man are treasured up in India only!"

— Mark Twain

MARSHALL BOUTON

Marshall M. Bouton is President of The Chicago Council on Global Affairs, formerly known as The Chicago Council on Foreign Relations, a position he has held since August 2001. Prior to that, he served for twenty years at the Asia Society in New York, most recently as Executive Vice President and Chief Operating Officer. Previous positions include Director for Policy Analysis in the Office of the Deputy Assistant Secretary of Defence for Near East, Africa and South Asia, Special Assistant to the US Ambassador to India, Executive Secretary for the Indo-U.S. Subcommission on Education and Culture, and Program Director for India Affairs at the Asia Society in New York. Mr. Bouton earned a B.A. (cum laude) in History at Harvard, an M.A. in South Asian Studies from the University of Pennsylvania, and a Ph.D. in Political Science at the University of Chicago in 1980.

4

India's Rise

What Indians, Americans and Chinese Think

Marshall Bouton

I want to share with you some data which have been generated by the Chicago Council for Public Opinion Studies this year. I want to actually broaden the topic from what you see as the bald-headed view to really look at the larger question that we have been investigating in this study, which is how the very important changes, which some would say the tectonic changes, happening in Asia are changing not only Asia itself but the global order.

This year our focus is on the rise of China and India. The study has been conducted in five countries, including the US, South Korea and Australia and we also did focus on the implications of this rise on the Americans. We have interviewed a total of 75,000 people in these five countries and in each of these countries we have carried out this study based on the scientifically selected random sampling method and have done in this collaboration with leading institutions in the US and in these four countries. So the data you see here can be considered as fully representative of the total populations of the countries involved.

I want to share with you one proposal that came out from the study. In the case of India and China, the representatives fully reflect the entire populations of these countries. We did indeed, for the purpose of the objectivity of the analysis, exclude anybody who has no formal education of whatsoever, and the reason for that is not to dismiss the views of those populations but to ensure that the views of the do not know group do not dominate the overall outcome of the survey, as the percentage of the illiterate section of the populace is very high in India and there are a few in China who fall under the 'do not know category', and you know the reasons for that. But the percentage of do not know rises to 30 per cent in India, which makes it really difficult for an objective analysis of the survey outcome. Therefore, it can be said that the data here fully reflect the views of anybody who has at least one year of formal education among the populations of both India and China. And if anyone of you wishes to check up on the data, you can go on to our website and find out the full description of the methodology we used for this survey.

The real overall objective of this study is to analyse the views of these populations to assess the impact of the changes taking place in these countries due to the phenomenal rise of China and India and its impacts in the regional context in particular and the outcome of the great power play of these countries on the rest of the world.

Now, what is the great power relation in Asia? To explain this, first I am going to present to you the responses from the Chinese and how they view their foreign policy and then I will present you the perceptions of the American public on these issues as also those of the rest of the two responding countries. And finally I will present the responses of the Indians on the topic as being looked at not just by the US and China but by the larger world outside.

Of course, the study is more looked at from the US and Chinese angles, but still it has a lot to do with India. So, we started off by asking the respondents in each case: what do you consider to be the main goals of the foreign policy of your country and what should your government be seeking to establish in the foreign policy? And what we see here is interesting, especially when it comes to the responses of Chinese. This is a survey about foreign policy. But the first three main goals for the Chinese are pertaining to their domestic issues only. They are categorical in their response that their country's foreign policy should be about sustaining the ongoing economic growth and how this could benefit the larger mass of the Chinese citizens. National security, or the national security policy, comes only as the fourth goal of the Chinese foreign policy. By the way, strangely, protecting the jobs of Chinese workers is a high priority for our Chinese respondents when it comes to their country's relationship with the US and the rest of the world. Strangely this has exactly been the American response too for the past 30 years—you give them the same list of possibilities, and the Americans have been consistently demanding protection of their jobs for the past three decades—that is since we began this survey. The Americans have been consistently demanding and expecting their successive governments to protect their jobs as the foremost formal goal of their foreign policy.

And this is a significant conclusion and an important perception too that citizens cutting across geographies consider that the top priorities of their governments' international relations should be the protection of their domestic interests rather than larger international issues.

This is, of course, also related to their threat perceptions as you will see from the Chinese respondents. The Chinese consider economic issues as the most powerful potential threat. So, once again there is concern amongst the Chinese about the economic growth and its resultant impact on their wellbeing. So, the avian flu or any other violent epidemics of that nature tops the heap of the Chinese list of high potential threats.

We then asked them, which are the not important, somewhat important and critically important potential threats to their country? And a larger majority consider these health issues to be of critical importance to the majority of Chinese respondents. The problem of public health is a problem that has been exaggerated by the fast economic development in China and you know the reasons for the same. The same is true about energy supply. Remarkably, they also consider global warming to be a critical threat to their security and economic wellbeing—this is strange because none of us expected the Chinese to be concerned about the global issue of warming going by the reactions of the Chinese government so far—we all remember the Chinese's President's I-do not-care reaction in Chicago to the issue of global warming.

Then we asked them how influential the different countries in the world are for China? We gave them a scale of 0 to 10 and then asked them to rate the countries and their influence in the next 10 years. And we got the following responses: The US is at the top of the heap though its position has come down a bit and China obviously comes second and importantly, India comes only at the last of the heap of nine nations when it comes to global influence in the next one decade. When we posed this question to the participating Americans, they too rated India at the end of the list in terms of perceived influence in the world today.

The respondents from the US and Asia were then presented with a question as to how do they feel about China in terms of the warmth of their feeling for that country and its phenomenal rise—whether they feel warm or cold about China's rise, and we gave them a 0 to 100 score scale to rate the kind of their feelings. And you can see that the Australians and South Koreans gave China a 60-point rating, which is a very good rating out of 100 points, while the Indians gave 21 points to the Chinese. But in contrast, the Americans have not even given a pass mark to China.

We asked them about the rise or the potential rise of Chinese military power and following is the response we have received from the public of the participant countries. Surprisingly, the Chinese are positive about this possibility while the Indians do not consider this to be a good possibility as they are very polarised about the outcome of such an eventuality, and surprisingly they are much more negative about the Americans in this regard.

Then we talked about the economic rise of China and India and the impact of the same on Asia. Very surprisingly, a vast majority of the respondents are relatively benign in their thinking about the economic rise of India and China and the resultant positive impact on the rest of Asia. But when we talked about the military power, their concerns are much stronger and higher.

The same question about the economic aspects but just substituting the economic questions from the military power, and without much surprises the Chinese views have not changed. But the South Koreans, the Americans and the Indians have clearly started shifting their views and it is almost mere images of what we saw for as the rise of the Chinese military power.

The overall assessment is that the economic development is something that is binding on this region, while the rise of military development is something that has the potential to divide the region in the years to come. A substantial majority of the Indians view China playing a key role in Asia. And you can read into that what you wish. I think when it comes to Indians, they are a bit divided as a portion of the Indian public view the rise of China with suspicion while another part sees the rise of China as something good for Asia. Similarly, the South Koreans are also happy about the rise of China. However, the Americans are clearly divided as they are not sure what the Chinese role will be in Asia.

We also asked them about their views on the various bilateral relationships. Because today there are many bilateral relationships which are seen primarily as partnerships or as rivalry. And the Indo-China and China-Japan relationship is of very strategic nature as well as very crucial in the sense of geopolitical ties. When it comes to the Japan-China relationship, it is primarily very negative, and you can see both the Chinese and the Americans perceptions in this regard. But Indians are clearly divided about this and this I think is a perceptional gap that is visible in the entire South Asia. This to some extent is understandable as the Japan-China relationship is not particularly relevant or geopolitically important to South Asia. But this gap is not good as the geo-strategic scene in Asia is very central today, not in the relationship that India has with the rest of Asia but the relationship between China and Japan, because the Japan-China relationship is the most important relationship today for the whole of Asia than that of Indo-China, where by the way there is clear and growing tension. The US-China relationship is one of rivalry for the Chinese, and the Chinese perception of rivalry is overwhelming. Again India is divided on this issue. The US apparently places

India in the same place as China. This may be so because the American perception about China is also more or less the same and therefore the perceptions of the Chinese as well as the Americans about the relationship between their countries are more or less clearly balanced. This has something to do with the Taiwanese issue, which is considered today as less threatening than it was earlier. Also, the issue surrounding the Cross Straits is considered to be less threatening for Americans today as less than 20 per cent of the Americans consider the Taiwanese issue posing a threat to American security but a substantial percentage of the Australians and Indians see this as a potential threat to Asian peace. But overall, the US-China relationship is going to be more passive in the near-term than it was in the past. So, the concern about Taiwan has receded and that has created in the region a more passive place.

We then put forth this very critical question: do you think in the next 50 years another country, we did not identify which country, would become at least as powerful as the US or more powerful than the US. We asked this question only to the Indians, Chinese and Americans, and not to the Australians and the Koreans. There will be a perceptible wave of change in the world in the next 50 years and this would, without explicitly saying so, was clear that the question was purely centred on China and India. At the same time there is clearly a widespread perception that since the past 10 years the influence of the US has been on the rise in Asia. This is a shared perception found both among the Chinese and the Indians and that the role of the US has been on the rise here since the past one decade or so. But this is a surprising finding in the sense that there is a widespread criticism in the US that the Bush administration has not been giving enough attention to Asia, but the Asians do not think so, and that is fundamentally good for this region as a whole at the moment.

To add substance to this, we then asked if the US somehow becomes less powerful either economically or militarily would it be a good thing for Asia. And surprisingly, the Chinese think that it will definitely be a bad thing to happen. The Chinese do not want to see the American power decline significantly. My own sense is that this has something to with the general Chinese belief that a powerful US is good for Asia and the whole world as they believe that a powerful US will act as a stabilising force for the Asian region as well as the rest of the world. But Indians are more divided over this and my interpretation for this is that in South Asia the US presence, both militarily and economically, is seen as more contentious unlike in East Asia. Because the role of the US in providing economic stability during the post-war period especially in providing military stability and security during the Cold War period in the East Asian region is widely perceived to be more positive, even by the Chinese, and to be a long-term stabilising intervention throughout the East Asian region. But this is not so when it comes to South Asia. So we are really dealing with two different perceptions in two different regions and in two different contexts. However, there is a perception that it would be good if the US plays a more passive role in Asia and my interpretation on the same is that this is kind of a wishful and forward looking thinking than an actuality.

Now let me get to data especially from the Indian public. And what is most interesting here is that of the five most frequently cited goals, four clearly relate to what I call the dangerous neighbourhood that South Asia has today—terrorism, two rivals having nuclear weapons, tensions between India and Pakistan, Islamic terrorism and religious fundamentalism. In contrast, the Chinese are much more focussed on economic issues that are going to affect their quality of life and the economic substance compared to the Indians. The concern of Indians is more about security in the regional context. Also, the concern about the issue of global warming is much higher amongst Indians than the Chinese which is also much higher than what we expected of the Chinese. This was again reflected and confirmed in the foreign policy goals as is being perceived by the Indians. So, the top two foreign policy goals are related to terrorism and nuclear weapons; and you have to remember again that these are not even a goal in the case of the Chinese. But that is not the case with job security. The public in all these three countries—the US, China and India—are so disparate about their job security, and this is despite having great differences in socio-economic conditions, history and economic parameters. This to me is a great lesson—that is to say that if the governments in these three countries want to keep their public behind their foreign policies they will have to include job security as a top foreign policy goal even as they pursue their economic and political relationships with the outside world.

Then we asked the question about the desirability of influence in the global power game. But again, we do not see Indians, unlike Chinese being more positive about the US being the most desired global power. The Indians however, consider their country to be the second most influential nation in the world in the times to come and place China as fifth in the list of influencers in the current term as well as in the long term. This was expected to be so, considering the way the two nations are marching ahead. But to me I did not think the difference to be so thorough and stoic at the same time.

Then we asked about the increase in India's military power in the region and how it would be perceived by the public in Asia. And not surprisingly, the Indians think that it would be a positive thing. But what is surprising is the Chinese view that says if India's military power increases in the region it will be a positive thing. One of the reasons for the Chinese to think so, we think, is that if India's military power rises, it would help it push the US out of the region. But I personally do not think that it is going to happen in the near future and that the US has any reason to worry about such an eventuality.

However, there is an across-the-board enthusiasm about India's economic progress and this springs from one of the central themes of our survey, which is economic development as a way to bring the region together, as a way of forging mutual bonds between different countries in the region and as a way of building mutual interests, and ultimately as a way of warding off the causes of conflicts in the future. And overall, India is seen as a positive force in Asia by a large majority of populace in all these four countries. This is interesting as for sometime now India has not been acting very diplomatically in Southeast Asia and hence this is a more divided response and is a reflection of the recent Indian diplomacy in the region.

We asked Indians whether countries are mostly rivals or partners. In the case of the US-India relationship, again there is a plurality of views. Surprisingly, the Indo-China relationship is seen as a partnership but the one between India and the US is seen as one of rivalry. The Americans also consider the Indo-China relationship as one of rivalry. We feel that the reason for the public to view the Indo-US relationship as one of rivalry has more to do with the recent Indo-US nuclear deal which is being perceived by a majority of Indians as something being thrust on them by an overarching America.

Only about 22 per cent Indians view the tension between India and Pakistan as a potential threat to their national security and to the region in the future, and this is parallel to the Taiwanese and the Cross Straits issues impacting Asia. So the regional issues are less likely to pose larger regional tension and do not seem to have caught the immediate attention of the respondents. But everybody sees the relationship with US to be improving and I guess this is a positive development. The US seems to be a kind of a pole around which different relationships are moving ahead. However, the China-Japan relationship is seen by the Chinese as distinctly worsening, and I personally feel that if the Sino-Japanese relationship is to worsen that would be the most important threat to the whole of Asia. And this is the one most important cause for worry in the region.

We also asked how the Americans and the Chinese use their mutual relationships, and most of the answers orient towards the other rather than to Japan—Japan is the closest ally of the Americans across the region, whereas for the Chinese, Japan is one of its worst enemies and hence the Chinese regard for the same is at the nadir. But for the Americans, Japan lies very close. But the Chinese do not think so and ranks very low in the order of importance.

Finally we asked about trust—we all know about the comment—that countries have no permanent friends, only permanent interests. So trust is a currency that does not flow very much between the nation states. And by and large I do support that. So even with the relationships between countries and it is partnership and not trust that prevails mostly, and trust does not seem to be in much evidence. So, even when it comes to relationship between the US and China, trust does not seem to be the prevailing thread and then the Indian and the Americans do not trust China to act responsibly in the region at all. This again is evident particularly among the Japanese and the Koreans, who do not trust China and this has more to do with their history. Similarly, the Chinese particularly do not trust India and this is the only specific case where the Chinese do not have a positive feeling about India.

I have given you a lot of information. What I want to underline is that economic forces are really reshaping the regions today and this is understood in the broader terms and supported by the public. This is particularly so when it comes to globalisation—invariably a large number of the respondents in these countries consider globalisation to be an enabler and good, especially in China and India, with the percentage of supporters being above 50 in India.

So I will conclude that in the management of changing bilateral relations in Asia it is going to be critical to keep economics at the centre stage and for the governments to form those policies they need to continue to increase the economic inter-changes among these nations. For instance, the almost failed Doha Round of trade negotiations is being revived mostly by Asian nations today. Secondly, there is not much threat perception about the regional security in the region be it in terms of Taiwan or be it in terms of the lingering Indo-Pak tension but there is a protracted feeling of regional concern regarding terrorism. Thirdly, there is a distinct difference in the concept of regional security in South Asia and East Asia. While the East Asian perception about regional threat is more benign when it comes to South Asia it tends to focus more on regional issues and this is particularly so when it comes to India. And finally there is one bilateral relationship in the region and that causes a lot of constraint and that is the lingering unease between Japan and China.

"If there is one place on the face of earth where all the dreams of living men have found a home from the very earliest days when man began the dream of existence, it is India!"

— Romain Rolland

WANGARI MUTA MAATHAI

Wangari Muta Maathai, recipient of the 2004 Nobel Peace Prize, is internationally recognised for her persistent struggle for democracy, human rights and environmental conservation. She is the first woman in East and Central Africa to earn a doctorate degree. Dr. Maathai has addressed the UN on several occasions and spoke on behalf of women at special sessions of the General Assembly for the five-year review of the earth summit, and has served on the Commission for Global Governance and Commission on the Future. She and the Green Belt Movement have received numerous awards.

5 Dreaming for a Better Society

WANGARI MUTA MAATHAI

India is playing an important role in the world today. It is partly because your representatives are so exceptionally qualified. It is one thing to be a diplomat and defend your country and push the agenda of your country and it is another to be so well educated that you can see and appreciate that the world is much bigger than your own country and that you cannot survive as a single country. You need to work very closely with all the other countries in the world and that your agenda is only one of the many pieces that will make a secure world for you and for your descendents.

Now, I wish to share with you the message that brought me here. First and foremost of course, I came to experience the extraordinary honour and privilege to receive the Jawaharlal Nehru Award. Those of us who have heard of Nehru through history books have admired him and admired the way he was able to impart his leadership to his family, so that his thoughts are continued through his legendary family. I cannot but feel extremely honoured to be given that honour. It was very humbling to see that I was being given that Award in the presence of the power of India.

The other message that I have been passing to the world and I have been hoping that the world would eventually embrace and internalise, is the message that the Norwegian Nobel Committee wanted to pass to the world in the year 2004, and make it as common place as the issue of human rights. Today everybody understands human rights but it was not always like that. When the Nobel Committee was initially formed some 100 years ago, their main focus was to promote peace and there were so many wars that were being fought especially in Europe, that the first thing they did was to honour those people who used to go to the battle field and collected the dead soldiers and buried them with some respect because some of them were just left to the vultures. They also honoured people who collected the soldiers who were not dead and treated them and, sometimes they would plead with the generals that they be given time so that the wounded can be picked and the dead can be buried. Those who used to do that were the first ones to be honoured.

Then they started honouring people who had the vision and the courage to go and bring fighting parties to the table and this is, I am sure, one of the skills that the diplomats are well versed with. If there is one thing that the diplomats eventually carry with them, it is the capacity to listen, the capacity to allow people to speak because sometimes we go to war because we do not want to listen to each other. We hold our position and if someone does not want to subscribe to our position, we fight with them. But diplomats everywhere are trained to encourage people to listen to each other. This is one thing I have seen in all Ambassadors I have come across, they are extremely good listeners rather than talkers. So, those who brought people together to that dialogue were the second category of people that we recognise—people who pre-empted conflict or were able to stop conflict because they could bring people to the table and talk and agree to disagree but stop the guns.

Later on they realised that even if people talk, they can talk all they want but if there is no respect for human rights, you cannot have peace. People sooner or later will fight, as they try to get their rights respected—the right to livelihood, the right to freedom of expression, the right to freedom of information, the right to freedom of movement, the right to freedom of assembling. Now we take these rights for granted. But these are rights that people have died for. Some of us are still fighting for the right to vote—the right to vote for women, the right to receive education. It is only recently that the United Nations passed a charter/ a convention to say that every child has the right to receive education. In many of our countries, including mine, we still have parents who do not want to send their children to school or do not want to send their girls to school.

There is also the right to life, so that people do not kill because you do not look right or you are not the right gender. I know in this country, for example, there are people who are fighting to ensure that especially the girl child is given protection, not to be aborted. So all these rights that we take for granted are rights that were cultivated gradually and people who worked for these rights were recognised by the Nobel Committee. Such is the importance of the human rights issue. Persons like Martin Luther King, who was among the latest that we know was honoured or like Gorbachev, the former President of the Soviet Union, who did a lot to ease the pressure between the two Super Powers and the threat of nuclear war to the world or persons like Kim Dae Jung of South Korea, who has been trying to ease the pressure of nuclear conflicts in that part of the world.

These kinds of people, who really devoted their life, sometimes are completely unknown. They work like diplomats because usually we do not see the work of diplomats because they work behind the scene. But they are very powerful and eventually they can break the wall, like we saw the Berlin Wall fall and many people who saw the fall of the Berlin Wall could not believe it. I personally did not believe that the Berlin Wall would fall in my lifetime. Such people or even people like Nelson Mandela, had to spend 25 years of his life in jail because of what he believed that we are all equal before the law and we should all be given an equal opportunity to exploit our potential and that we should not be discriminated because of our colour, race, religion, or gender. He was supported by many people and he sustained a moral campaign within jail. When he came out, he was honoured by the Norwegian Nobel Committee. I am only giving you examples of what the Committee does with the Peace Prize—bringing to the attention of the world some of the most important issues, which if violated or not respected, can lead to war.

Lately, wars are being fought for control of resources. There are conflicts and wars on resources like oil, water, grazing grounds. Especially in Africa, lot of wars were over grazing ground because we have large number of pastoral communities, the nomadic communities that move from one area to the other. They tend to have their graze and when they have had their graze, they move to greener pastures and sometimes the greener pasture is somebody else's land. When we mention fighting over land, I am sure here in India also you may be hearing about, fighting over settlements, fighting over forests. Sometimes forest areas appear as wasteland, no man's land that can be encroached upon. Yet, we all know that forests are the source of our water, whether it is in the form of rivers or whether it is in the form of ice up there on the mountains and if we do not have forests, ice will melt. And when people try to access or encroach upon forests, it becomes a big issue. In the year 2004, The Norwegian Nobel Committee did warn the world that we have a new frontier of conflict and that is the conflict over resources. As the resources are limited, and are essential for life, unless we learn to manage them properly with responsibility and accountability, and unless we also think about the future generations, most likely, we are going to fight over them. Future generations would be pre-occupied with wars over them.

We need to govern ourselves better and have to respect the rule of law and respect human rights.

In a democratic process, the majority must learn to listen to the minorities. It is very important that all of us feel that we are not excluded and that we are part of the society. Although not easy, but we have to move towards this idealistic society. We have to have a dream and work towards that dream. It is not as if it is going to happen and suddenly everybody on this planet will be respecting human rights and the rule of law and that they will be listening to the minorities, that they are not greedy, selfish, and corrupt. These things do not disappear overnight, but it is a dream for those of us who aspire for better society and we can strive towards that dream. After all, one of the great teachings from this Continent, the Sub-continent of India, is that life is a struggle to perfection. This is the message that the Norwegian Nobel Committee wanted to pass when it decided to give the Nobel Peace Prize to an environmentalist for the very first time. And they gave it to me.

I think the message must also have been to support women because women for a long time have been struggling to have their rights respected, to have space in societies. Every society in the world has been discriminating against its women. Therefore, they wanted to encourage societies to support women and their struggle and that they be given an opportunity to realise their potential. For an African woman, it was another message, to support Africa because Africa has been mistreated and African women have constantly struggled. Thus, this was a message of supporting Africa and of course, to support the grassroots. In Africa it is not an environmental movement at the professional level. We are working with the women at the grassroots. We are planting trees. We are as grassroots as you can get, because we have to dig on our own and get the roots into the ground. So, it was also a way of supporting the struggles of small groups everywhere at the grass root level. This is the message I am very happy to be sharing with you.

As you become diplomats and get posted in different parts of the world wherever you go, you would be confronted by these issues, you would be confronted by the issues of human rights, the issues of people struggling to have their rights respected, you would be confronted by issues of poverty, people wanting to improve their quality of life, you will be confronted by issues of injustices. The issues of equity are everywhere, whether you are in the United States or whether you are in India or Japan or Australia. Wherever you are, you would find people looking for diplomats. Diplomats everywhere are a special class of people who represent hope for the country where they are. They represent hope because they are usually detached from the everyday concerns of the country and they have an ear not only for their country. They are always willing to share with you, advise you and support you to overcome the problems that you would be dealing with. As a diplomat your greatest achievement is the service you can give and that it is not the service to yourself, it is the service to others. And the greatest moment of fulfillment and happiness that you would find is what you can do for others, because there comes a time when you have everything you need.

I have come to the conclusion that the greatest moment of joy is when you serve beyond yourself. Examples are people like Mahatma Gandhi. We think about him all the time and personally he impressed me a lot because he started his career in Africa—in South Africa. Although he was a very successful lawyer, he discarded all material wealth and continued to serve humanity till his death. As a diplomat now when you reach that moment, when you feel you have served, that would be the happiest moment of your life.

ABHISHEK MANU SINGHVI

Abhishek Manu Singhvi is a Member of Parliament (Rajya Sabha); Senior Advocate, Supreme Court of India; former Additional Solicitor General of India (ASG), National Spokesperson, Congress Party, Vice Chairman, Media Department, Congress Party and former (elected) Vice President, Supreme Court Bar Association. He was awarded the Global Leader of Tomorrow (GLT) award by the World Economic Forum (WEF) at Davos, Switzerland. Dr. Singhvi is an eminent jurist, frequent writer, commentator, and a popular media face in both the visual and print media.

6 India of My Dreams

Abhishek Manu Singhvi

India of my Dreams is a very broad topic, so wide; it is indeed as wide as the universe. And anybody who speaks/writes on this subject really cannot do more than perform the role of a fan dancer, which is to draw attention to the subject without really covering it. Thus, what I intend on doing is to draw attention to some aspects of it.

William Dement, a well known writer many decades ago, talked about dreaming. He said dreaming permits each and every one of us to be quietly and safely insane every night of our lives. He said that this is the kind of insanity which can sometimes be very fruitful, sometimes very infectious and sometimes very delectable and delicious. It is in many ways for a country like India a bigger crime not to dream than to dare to dream, because there really cannot be a better subject to dream about than India.

For centuries each one of us has dreamt different dreams for India. We have our individual dreams and our collective dreams. Perhaps the main difference is that for several decades, perhaps for several centuries, we have romanticised India. We have flaunted what some might call its soft attributes. The other day an eminent Harvard professor wrote about India, and how it was a soft power rather than a hard power. She spoke of all the soft attributes of spirituality, tradition, history, our value system, Bollywood, the cuisine, culture, dress, language, the noises, sounds and smells of India, and called it "an iron fist in a velvet glove." So we have at one level, dreamt of these attributes, and romanticised India. This has in a sense led to an imaginary India, conjured up not only in the westerner's mind, which it has been, but also in the Indian mind. It is a tribute to a kind of forgotten era of the past, a kind of a paradise lost, but not necessarily to be regained.

Mark Twain, a remarkable man, was one of the few people who in the late 19th century visited India. He typified that romanticised version of India and said, "India the land of dreams and romance, the country of a 100 tongues, a 1000 religions, two million gods, the cradle of the human race, the birth place of human speech, the mother of history, the grand mother of legend, the great grand mother of tradition, the land that all men desire to see and having seen once even by a glimpse would not give that for the shows of all the rest of the globes combined." This is that very highly romanticised and somewhat exaggerated dream of India. But it is also, in a sense, apologetic. In different hands, it could become somewhat patronising. What is the main difference between these dreams and the ones we have? The main difference between these dreams, in my opinion, is that, for the first time India has given us a reason to have hard dreams and not merely soft dreams. For the first time it has allowed us to dream based on hardcore facts. I think that is a qualitative difference as well as a quantitative difference. Most importantly, it is a difference which needs to be underlined, understood and appreciated.

Look at some of these cold facts. We are now somewhere close to being the world's third largest economy. We are behind Japan at the moment, actually fourth, but we are expected to outstrip them, partly because of our size. We are the second fastest growing economy in the world. We have been growing at 9 per cent now for sometime and we were at 8 per cent a short while ago. But what is more important is that for 25 years we have grown consistently at over 6.5 per cent each year. Very few countries have consistently done that each year for a quarter of a century. For every acquisition a Hindalco makes to become the world's largest aluminum company, you have a steel major like Ispat or Tata acquiring somebody else. Even today after almost five decades, $1/4^{th}$ of all the start-ups in Silicon Valley are by or related to NRIs. We have the world's fastest growing telecom market. In December last year, the monthly figure for net additions was a staggering 60 lakhs! So this is really a dream situation. But more importantly it is a dream situation based on cold hard reality, not merely on subjective adjectives, or the meanderings of somebody's imagination.

But while we must continue to dream, every once in a while we will have to open our eyes, and take stock of the situation. We have to ensure that we are not an ostrich, with our head in the sand and nor are we dreamers in an ivory tower. This brings me to my pet theory of the glass half full and the glass half empty. I will just describe to you a glass seemingly full, but it is actually still only a glass half full. It is the glass half empty, which has to put things into perspective, and those are the challenges which our dreams have to fulfill, those are the challenges which merely dreaming will not meet, but which have to be addressed.

Just as I discussed our achievements, we have on the negative side another list which can go on and on. As far as human development indicators are concerned, India ranks 93 out of 119 developing countries. This is an index of the so-called global hungry index. 48-50 per cent of the world's hungry continue to live in India. 35 per cent of our population, which is a staggering 350 to 400 million plus, gets less than 80 per cent of the stipulated minimum energy requirement. If you take the human indicators and the social indicators such as health, education, etc., we still have that huge glass, hugely half empty. We have a large number of pregnant women between 15 and 49, 90 per cent of whom are malnourished or anaemic. We have 67 per cent out of 1000 babies dying before they are a year old. These are all well above the acceptable international standards. The list could go on. Thus, our dream has to come full circle and fix these problems. Of course, nobody would blame India for trying and failing to achieve these parameters on the right index. What we will be blamed for is failing to try, not for trying and failing.

What then are the challenges, the specific dreams, which we can talk about? The problem with a topic like this is that, in many ways, it is very much diffused. It is also perhaps too idealistic. I could dream about an India where poverty is removed, or an India where criminalisation is gone, but these are mega dreams, macro dreams which are sometimes no more than a slogan or shibboleth. Also, I think Thomas Hardy had a lot of sense when he said, "you take care of the small things and the large things will take care of themselves." You need to have a certain degree of specificity when you turn to the challenges which these dreams are required to fulfill. So, the level at which one looks at is important.

In Edward Luce's, *In spite of the Gods*, he had a wish list in which there are four important challenges for any dreamer of India. He said the four critical problems are: firstly, lifting 300 million odd people out of absolute poverty demarcated by an income of US $ 1 per day. The second was overcoming the dangers of rapid environmental degradation. The third was the HIV-AIDS epidemic, which according to some is at the moment seemingly remote, but in absolute figures in the near future may become a very dangerous figure. The fourth and last was strengthening India's liberal democracy. That is one level at which you might see these challenges and tailor your dreams. Another could be the UNDP wish list on good governance, which again as I said sometimes is so macro and so mega that it really boils down to a slogan. UNDP list of good governance is participation, rule of law, transparency, responsiveness, consensus orientation, equity, effectiveness and efficiency, accountability, strategic vision and respective tolerance. These can all be the ultimate values which systems within any society can aspire to and ultimately also any goal which any dreamer can aspire to.

There are a variety of dreams and formats to choose from. Therefore, I will limit my dreams to four other areas apart from the ones I have listed from Edward Luce. I will deal with education first. Education, in many ways, must be the basic dream. It must receive the highest priority. It is the primary investment in society's human resources, but most importantly it is the lubricant which affects so many other sectors. By affecting one sector or touching one sector you are in fact having a multi-sectoral impact. If you see many of the problems, the social indicators which I read out, the UNDP indicators, the health indicators, behind them and below them, somewhere or the other lie the issues of education. This is because education is not attacking one problem, it is not only solving the education problem but it is solving, at least partially, issues like population crisis, dowry deaths, female infanticide, child labour, etc. Therefore, I think that education really must be part of any basic wish list. I think it is important to plan and aspire and dream moderately and reasonably and not too big. Therefore, in education, we can do one basic thing in the first phase and that is to achieve universal primary education, which has been our constitutionally declared object. Perhaps to that one might add universal secondary education also as far as the girl child is concerned. Of course, we still have a long way to go before we achieve universal primary education. There is a whole gamut of issues related to education like drop out rates, attendance in schools, etc.

As a Member of Parliament I have been to some remote parts of Rajasthan. There, I find that unlike a few decades ago you have some schools with the finest infrastructure. You will go to a place where there is nothing, but you will find a school. The problem is not merely to have that dot on the paper, nor merely to have that physical infrastructure. The problem is to make it operational. The problem is to make it as good as a school to which you and I might want to send our child. Unfortunately on that operational reality we fail because most of these schools have an attendance rate of teachers of below 40 per cent. Most of them have attendance rates of children at dismal levels and of course the big news of the Indian education system at the primary level is the very high drop out rate. So these are issues which need to be addressed in a micro method. They are to be addressed by building upon the infrastructure which we already have, and not necessarily merely by the allocation of funds. One of the reasons for drop out rates, for example has nothing to do with the allocation of funds. The method to overcome the problem is to enthuse and coordinate the local administration and the local people to be made to understand that sending their child to school is far more important than utilising him/her elsewhere.

The other related aspect of education which is more abstract and less immediately beneficial, but nonetheless very important is our curriculum. There I would single out some degree of value based education, because our curriculum is far too stereotyped. Our curriculum is far too pedantic and predictable in many ways. In many cases it is outdated. It needs to be reinvented, revised and, in a sense, repackaged. Prior to Independence, the President at that time, S. Radhakrishnan, was the head of the education sub-committee of the National Planning Committee and Nehru himself chaired it. Subsequently, they appointed D.S. Kothari as the head of the first Education Commission. All three of them deliberated on the issue of education and they said that the cultivation of the rational and the scientific temper without value based education paradigms is akin to creating rudderless ships. We have to therefore, consider that without leaving out the secular morals, we must somehow inject into our curriculum a sense of India, a sense of the values and philosophy of India. Even our moral science classes were already degrading in the years when I was in school, and now I am told they are taken more as jokes than as real academic sessions. We need to reinvent and rewrite that curriculum. A very remarkable philosophical thinker, Acharya Mahapragya, has put it very nicely. He said that our system gives excessive and first priority to memory and then reluctantly and slowly second to intellect and he said not at all to the third, and most important, intuition. So we have to have the right proportions of memory, intellect and intuition re-injected into our educational system.

The second on my wish list would necessarily have to be the issue of corruption. And as far as corruption is concerned you cannot talk of an India of my dreams unless you cannot talk of good governance. It would sound like a self defeating irony unless you did something about corruption. Even today in the transparency index with all its faults we come somewhere in the 90s in the international transparency index. I think the important thing is to talk less about it and start doing more. The important thing is to think small, to reduce our rules and regulations and to enforce just a few basic ones. During my years in Cambridge we had a contingent of Singaporeans whom Lecon used to send to England and I had many long discussions with them. It is true that Singapore is not a transplantable or an easily applicable example in a country the size and diversity of India. But there are some lessons we could learn from a country, which in the 50s and the 60s was certainly far more corrupt than even India is today and transformed itself in less than five years. It achieved this by implementing a few basic rules and making sure that those basic rules apply. You have to make examples in a few cases and you have to then rely on the fact that the culture will change. The culture of corruption changes very fast once they find that there is a regulatory mechanism in place which means business.

A third area, not surprisingly, is the area of judicial reforms. I say this not only because I am a lawyer, but also because you cannot dream of a country which truly takes its place amongst the comity of nations without transforming its legal system from the one which India has now. Now, in the legal and judicial system there is a very interesting paradox. India, according to me, has a judicial system which is second to none in terms of doctrines, dynamism in the development of law, jurisprudence and truly a fiercely independent judiciary. Yet, one despairs and laments the problems in the judicial system. The main problem is arrears. Just to make the point and not to berate India and not to belittle the advantages, and we have many, I must quote Nani Palkiwala. Many years ago he said, "May I now turn to the situation in India which has the second largest number of lawyers in the world. While it is true and justice should be blind, in our country it is also lame. It barely manages to hobble along. The law may or may not be an ass but in India it is certainly a snail. It moves so slowly that it might be considered too slow in a community of snails. A law suit once started in India is the nearest thing to eternal life ever seen on this earth. Some said that litigation in India is a form of fairly harmless entertainment. If so, it seems to be a very expensive way of keeping the citizen amused. If litigation were to be included in the next Olympics, India would be quite certain of winning at least one gold medal."

The amazing and the tragic part of it is that there is not much which is required to transform it. Despite the so-called staggering figures, it is reasonably easy to do it. It is just that we need to decide on a few issues. We need to implement them consistently without changing for a reasonable period of minimum time which may be three to five years. The approach has to be holistic. It has to be diverse and multi-pronged. There are not just one or two issues that have to be tackled. It has to be accompanied by certain attitudinal changes. Let me give you a few examples. A few months ago we started night courts in only two states. In less than 45 days, those courts have disposed off 16,000 cases. A night court deals with cases which have been languishing. What is the biggest cause of arrears? The irony is that our judges actually dispose off more cases in one day or one week than judges of other countries at comparable positions dispose off in one year. So it is not that they do not work very hard or they do not dispose off a large number of cases. The problem is that for a country the size of India we have a very low judge to population ratio. In 1986-87 it was 10, i.e. 10 judges for a million of the population. It has now agonisingly crawled up from 10 to 13 and the Supreme Court has recently mandated in 2002, for the second time, by judicial order that this figure should be brought up to a minimum of 50. There are countries, which have higher figures, i.e. 50 judges per million of population. But we are still at 13 after about

25 years. At this figure of 13 for this large country we have less than 650 or 700 odd high court judges. A very interesting study said that from 1950 onwards, at no single point of time have all those 650 high court judgeships been filled. At any point of time you will find about 150 odd high court judgeships vacant.

We have a population of over 1 billion. We have a litigating public, which I am sure is a fairly large portion of that population. There are a total of 14,412 judgeships out of which roughly 25 to 30 per cent judgeships are vacant. At the moment the figure is 2,546. We have this strange phenomenon in which we have by law enhanced the strength of some high courts. Originally, say a high court had a sanction strength of x, it was made x + y. The problem is that for many years we have not been able to even fulfill the original strength of x. These are very simple administrative problems. I wrote almost 15 years ago that there should be a rule saying that almost one month before a vacancy of a judgeship, the successor should be notified. As I said, though, a multi-pronged approach should solve the problem. In the planned expenditure prior to the Eighth Plan, astonishingly, the judiciary did not form a part of the planned expenditure at all! From the Ninth Plan the planned expenditure for the judiciary became .071 per cent of the total planned expenditure. And in the Tenth Plan, after much prodding, it became the princely figure of .078 per cent, which is an increase not worth mentioning. As an example, Chhattisgarh's budget of the year 2006-07 is an expenditure budget of 56 to 57,000 crore. The budget for the judiciary is 22 crore, thus .4 per cent. Now if you have a figure of 2.53 crore cases supposedly pending in the lower courts, it is to do with the lack of judges and the lack of infrastructure available to deal with it. It also has to do with the fact that many of these figures are really academic or notional because some of these figures are there on the files merely because they have not been tracked and traced. There is an employee thrown out of employment, let us say in 1975. He filed a suit. The man's term is over, he has been annulated, or he has died. But the suit remains. It is still lingering because there is absolutely no way of tracking this. So if a simple tracking exercise is done, the 2.53 crore figure pending in the 500 odd districts of this country would look much smaller in reality than it is. As I said there are so many other issues by themselves that judicial reform could be the subject of a separate lecture. I would be extremely delighted to be involved in such a lecture because the subject is of great importance and is certainly very high on my wish list of dreams for India. Like education, judicial reform will also have a multi-sectoral impact.

Lastly, although there are many other wishes on my list, I think electoral reforms would qualify in my short wish list of four. Again, it is something which is at the very heart of the Indian liberal democratic system. It is also something which is not that difficult or that insuperable to do provided you have a reasonable degree of will power. This will power can be bifurcated because we need not do all the more difficult tasks immediately. We can do the simpler ones first. Take, for example, the adjudication of election petitions. The term of any elected person is normally five years. Subsequently, after the coalition era, it has become three to four years but is still supposed to be five years normally. There is a statutory provision that you must decide an election petition in six months. This was because if you decide within five years, then the person whose election you are attacking has completed his term and enjoyed the fruits of his office. There are very few election petitions, because the election petitions must be tried and must go to trial which, needless to say, takes a lot of time. As I mentioned before, that is an area which has to be altered and reformed. One solution could be having a special fast track court only for election matters separate from the normal judiciary.

All this will happen only when the political parties involved get together and put their heads together and themselves pass the laws. This will not happen unless the law is changed by one simple two-line amendment providing and empowering the Election Commission to recognise or not to recognise a party according to: (a) the periodicity and the regularity of its intra party elections and (b) according to the filing of a certain requisite format of returns. I think this will fix a lot of the ills and a lot of things we lament today in our political system such as regionalism, caste and a whole host of other divisive issues. We have to candidly recognise that these problems are also a product of the multiplicity of parties. There are over 55 parties in this country. There are only 6 national recognised parties. So, 55 parties necessarily make for divisive politics. It is not something you can legislate away. It is ultimately these very parties which will be involved somewhere or the other in creating a mechanism by which fewer parties can play at least at the national scene.

Personally I do not accept and agree with the topic of state funding of election, which is frequently talked about. I do not think state funding of elections is such a great idea. These views are not in my capacity on behalf of any political party. My own view is that state funding of elections is more a slogan than a substantial beneficial activity. It needs a different kind of political, electoral and democratic set up for its benefits to come down. The situation might well become where state largess and state subsidies are doled out in addition to an already corrupt system. And that is a real danger, but there are so many other issues as well. I think the issue of a simple middle path as far as the disqualification of candidates for criminalisation of politics is concerned, is a valid entry in the dream for India. I think that the requirement of a conviction before a person is disqualified is meaningless, as a conviction is the nearest to eternity which you have on this earth. Therefore, to say that you cannot be touched till you are convicted one way or the other or acquitted as the case may be is an unreal prescription for India. I have had the privilege now of seeing all the three aspects, the judicial as a lawyer, the legislative as a Member of Parliament and the executive as the national spokesperson of the party. Therefore, as Aristotle said, virtue lies in the middle, you have to find the golden mean somewhere.

I am reminded of the definition of the word diplomat. I picked up the devil's dictionary, which I do occasionally when I am going to speak somewhere. One of them said that the diplomats are those who can be disarming when their country is not and in another one, it is described as the patriotic art of lying for one's country. I think those times have also changed. Diplomacy today is an exciting field. Most importantly, it is now a much wider field. It is a much more all-inclusive and all-encompassing field than it used to be a few decades ago. You have huge paradigms, cultural diplomacy, economic diplomacy, a holistic paradigm which makes, I think, life and the world of diplomats much more exciting and interesting. All I can say is that we must continue to dream. We must dream even beyond the capacity and the limits which we are expected to achieve in the near future. But we must always also temper these dreams with a certain amount of realism and work incrementally towards achieving them.

© Evanston Photographic Studio

DIPAK C. JAIN

A distinguished teacher and scholar, Dipak C. Jain has been Dean of the Kellogg School of Management since July 2001. He received his Bachelor's degree in Mathematics and Statistics in 1976 and his Master's degree in Mathematical Statistics in 1978 from Gauhati University in India. He earned his Ph.D. in Marketing at the University of Texas, Dallas. Dr. Jain is the Sandy and Morton Goldman Professor in Entrepreneurial Studies and has been a member of the Marketing Department at the Kellogg School since 1987. He is a prolific scholar who has brought his expertise to a variety of companies as a consultant, including American Express, Microsoft and IBM. He also serves as a Member of the Board of Directors of Hartmarx Corporation, John Deere and Company, Northern Trust Corporation and Reliance Industries.

7 Branding India in a Global Context

DIPAK C. JAIN

I will be talking about Branding India, but before I explain that I would like my remarks on the theme Branding India to be at three levels—India and branding India, Indian and branding Indian, and Indianness and branding Indianness. I would like to speak on the move from Indian to Indianness first, because we should be clear about what are we really good at, and what message we would like to give to this globalised world in terms of what makes India, Indian and Indianness special. Because when we use the word brand or branding in marketing, it means a promise that we make to our target customers. The classical definition of branding is what promise you are making to your target customers or why should they buy your product or service over others. However, I have a different definition of branding. Brand is not the promise that you make but brand is the delivery of the promise that you make. It does not cost you anything to make a grand promise, but delivering the promise is not that easy and it would cost you a lot, because that is where the impressions are formed.

I started work on branding nations six years ago when the then Thai Prime Minister, Dr. Thaksin, asked me to be his advisor on foreign affairs, and the first project I did was advising his government's project called Brand Thailand. He appointed three advisors—you would be surprised to know that of the three advisors two were Indians: Mr. Narayana Murthy was the advisor on technical affairs, while I was the foreign affairs advisor, and the third one was a professor of genetics from Washington. We were advising the Thai government on how they could create a research lab in Thailand by combining the knowledge from biotechnology and genetics and incorporate that into Brand Thailand.

After this I began thinking about how do we go about branding nations. Because people generally think about branding a product or service, but to me the same applies to branding a nation or a city or a region as well. So, that is how I got interested in branding nations.

At a recent talk, somebody asked me why the world's outsourcing operations are moving to India even though there are many nations with a good number of English-speaking populations like the Philippines. Still why are the off-shoring jobs moving only to India? What is it that makes India so special for this job? I told him that there is something that makes India special and that special something is the commitment of Indian parents for their children's education. Our parents would go hungry but make sure that their children have the best possible education. And so long as this drive is going to be with us, nobody in the whole world can touch us. And I really believe that this is something very unique about us—our dedication to education is what makes us special.

I was born and raised in a small, little known town called Tezpur in Assam. During the 1962 Indo-Chinese war, Tezpur was attacked and that was the first year of my schooling. I still remember the teacher telling us that our town was under Chinese attack and that we had to vacate the town by the same evening. We were forced to leave our hometown and head towards Delhi. At that time it took us 10 days to reach Delhi, and then we moved to Rohtak in Haryana. But being raised in Assam and having studied in a small school there, I could have never believed that the journey of life would take me so far and so soon. I still remember the difficulties my parents went through in raising us, and I always think about our role in the world or how can I make a difference to the world. So, though my topic today is branding India in the global context, the real topic I would be discussing here will be "From Success to Significance" or rather the journey from success to significance. Because many of us are successful but only a few of us are able to make or rather get a chance to make a significant difference to the world we live in. And to me, to make a significant difference, mere success is not enough.

Last year there was a large function in Chicago and the Jordanian queen was visiting the city. Chicago is also where the aircraft manufacturer Boeing is headquartered and the chief executive of Boeing was hosting a reception for the Jordanian queen and I was also invited. As I was attending the function along with my wife, a person walked up to me and said "a lot of people in Chicago have been telling me for long that I have to meet the Dean of the Kellogg's School, but I never managed to find time. And today I see you here." I was taken aback as I did not know who that person was. So, I had to ask him his name and he said, "I am Tom Pritzker"—the owner of the global hotel chain Hyatt. Then he asked whether I am an Indian and I answered yes. He responded saying he had been to India many a time. Surprised, I asked him which is the city that he visited first and when. To my utter surprise he said Tezpur was the first city he visited in India. He explained: "I am a firm believer of the Dalai Lama. And the only place to get into Arunachal Pradesh, where the Dalai Lama stayed at that time was through Tezpur." The next day I got a call from his wife Morgan for dinner, because he was so surprised to find that a person from such an ordinary place like Tezpur could be the Dean of the Kellogg's Business School, and he is yet to get over it.

Coming back to the topic, I would like to speak about some challenges that we academics are observing worldwide today. We all need to be first aware of these challenges and prepare ourselves or at least prepare our mindset for these challenges so that we can understand them and work for the betterment. The first challenge is what I call the nanosecond culture. By nanosecond culture I mean that things are changing very rapidly in today's world. Change is inevitable and we all need to learn how to embrace change and work with it. In fact, the only thing that is constant is change. We all have to learn how to embrace change, which means today we should not focus on predictions any longer, but anticipation. Anything you are going to predict is going to be wrong because predictions are based on past experiences and conditions. But things are changing so rapidly that we need to change our mindset from predictions to anticipation. We need to anticipate what are the major trends that are going to happen in the next 5 years, in the next 10 years, in the next 15 and in the next 20 years, and anticipate those trends and prepare ourselves for the changes proactively rather than reacting to them. In fact, we do not get a chance to react today, so be proactive, and not reactive. There is a Greek saying which says we cannot get into the same river twice though the river is the same, the water flow keeps changing continuously. Today we can never say that we tried this effort in the past but it did not work, so we are not going to try it again. Because the past is not the present and the present is not going to be the future and if we let the past control the present, there is not going to be any future at all. So we need to be futuristic in anticipating the trends and proactively dealing with them.

Now, I would like to share with you some trends pertaining to our country and for which we need to really anticipate and proactively see how we deal with them in branding India along with those trends.

The first concept I would like to elucidate here is the word called hyper-competition. Normally, when we think of competition we think of competition within our boundaries. For many years, I was on the board of United Airlines. I would always tell the airline CEO that in the future our competition is not going to be British Airways, Lufthansa or American Airlines, but our actual competition is going to be video conferencing. Because competition is not to the product but to the activities that the product lets you perform. One of the biggest accounts of United Airlines in Chicago is the telecom major Motorola. Senior Motorola executives would travel from Chicago to Beijing or Shanghai at least six times a month because China is a very big market for Motorola. My point to the United Airlines CEO was that once video conferencing becomes accessible and affordable, a Motorola executive who used to make six trips to Beijing earlier would make his first trip to set up his team and to get to know each other. Once he knows the chemistry of his team out there in Beijing, he could simply reduce his six trips to three—the first to set up the team, the second for a mid-term review and the third for a final annual stock taking. So, the person who used to pay $11,000 per trip to Beijing in the business class is going to now pay $33,000 less to United Airlines, and that is just from one person. So, airlines should identify who their actual competitors are going to be in the future and work accordingly.

We generally think about competition from a product-centric perspective, but competition is customer-centric. Which means, what are the other substitutes customers have in mind, and that is how we have to think. Therefore, for a country like India, we have to think what are the substitutes for companies like AT&T and others like Boeing if they have to invest here. And that is why I will briefly touch upon, what you have been regularly doing for some time now, how India can maintain its competitive advantage relative to China. I think China is over-exposed. In fact, to my mind, what India should ideally do is to think about countries like Viet Nam. These are the really emerging economies. There are many such countries as those in Eastern Europe and a few erstwhile Soviet Republics, which are fast-emerging economies. We, at Kellogg's, have been working in areas like Ukraine, Georgia, Latvia, Estonia and the like. In fact, my area of interest is Eastern Europe. You have lots of good talent there. People in Poland, Hungary, the Czech Republic, Ukraine, Latvia, Georgia and the like have so many good people but have no facilities as others have in the world. Our efforts are in getting these people to the US, and help them attain good education and become the future ray of hope. Therefore, competition for a country has to be along the dimensions to what the country can offer to its various stakeholders.

The way to brand a country is along five dimensions: a place to live, a place to work, a place to invest, a place to visit and the fifth one is you do not need to come here to know us. A lot of Americans who have never been to India go to Indian restaurants, lots of American academics who have never experienced or visited India work with Indian students and Indian academics but their interaction with them helps them form an image of India. So, when we think of branding a country it has five sets of customers: people who come here to live, people who come here to work, people who come here to visit, people who come here to invest, and people who have never been to India, but have been consumers of Indian products. So, we need to think about from which dimension we should start with.

The second point I want to highlight—which I think everyone is going to experience in the times to come—is the changing customer demographics. We live in a bipolar world today. Let me explain what I mean by bipolar world. Look at countries like the US, Europe and Japan, and countries like India, China and South America. What is the difference? It came to me while flying to Chicago from Singapore many years back. It was a 15-hour non-stop flight. I asked the airhostess for a newspaper. And she gave me a copy of the *International Herald Tribune*. While reading it I chanced upon an article titled "The Changing Customer Demographics." The article said as of today there are over 20,000 people in Japan who are over 100 years old. The article also mentioned about a Japanese woman who celebrated her 116th birthday the other day. The article quoted her as saying that she has been enjoying the social security cover for the past 56 years. The article went on to add that if the life span of the Japanese continued like this, by 2025, the Japanese government would have to shell out 43 trillion yen in social security cover alone! This is the cost a country pays for its retirees. This was September 14, 2003 and a year later on September 15, 2004, and I was on another flight from St. Louis to Chicago and the flight got delayed and I found the *US Today*. To my utmost surprise, I found the continuation of the same article that I had read exactly a year ago. The article said, by that day, Japan was home to 23,086 people who are above 100 years. What I am trying to tell you here is that when we look at countries like the US, Europe and Japan, the fastest growing demographic segment in these countries is in the age bracket of 65-plus.

Today, we are in a state of healthy ageing. You can mark my words. The population of Italy today is 50 million, but by 2015, it would be down to 15 million, because the fertility rate in Italy is 1.2 and for a population to remain stable it has to be at least 2.2. So Europe has a serious problem with its shrinking population as its population is de-growing and for Japan, it is ageing, as the Japanese are living longer today. But look at our country. Our population is 1.1 billion, our median age is 24 and that means there are 550 million people who are 24 years or younger in our country. And if you take the median age to 34 years, then we have 770 million people who are 35 years or younger. This means that the fastest growing population segment here is 35 years or younger. The fastest growing segment for all other major countries is 65-plus. This is what I call the bipolarisation of the global consumer dynamics. Where is future consumerism going to come from? The answer is simple: India. China has the same population structure in terms of its 1.3 billion population, but in 1978

China liberalised its economy and in 1980 it imposed a one-child norm. And now the various provincial governments in China are facing the consequences. Why? Because today in China, in a family of three, two are getting old and one is young, whereas in India, in a family of five, two are getting old and three are young. That is why we say China will grow old before it gets rich and India will get rich before it gets old.

From where are all the economic activities going to come from? Again the answer is India. We would become the largest supplier of the global workforce. In fact, I am writing a book on this and I am actually thinking about titling the book as "The Browning of the Global Workforce", because it is India that is going to be the global supplier of workforce sometime soon. Thanks to our education system, our values, which I call the *Sanskar*. It is not the country, it is not brand India that is important but its 1.1 billion people that are important. But brand India is also our cultural values, it is the Indianness in us, a culture of caring, culture of working under tough conditions that is what Indianness is all about. And this is what I call our *Sanskar*. Look at the Americans, they just cannot live with any sort of uncertainty. They are not used to dealing with uncertainties. But we Indians grow up under a lot of tough conditions. This has been a hallmark for all of us. Uncertainties do come, for the world is never certain. It is such feelings that make us very different.

In Central America—I travel a lot in Latin American regions, especially in the Honduras, Nicaragua, Salvador, Costa Rica and Guatemala—60 per cent of the population is 35 or even less, for a lot of the older people got killed in the Sandanista movement. I was an advisor to the Vice-President of Salvador and she asked me to undertake a study to brand Salvador. I told her I have only one advice for your country: since you have a very young population, keep them engaged, because if you do not keep them engaged you will have two industries emerging—kidnapping and drug trafficking. She was taken aback by my response, yet she asked what would be my advice for her. I said the country should form strategic alliances with the TCS and the Infosys and the Wipros of India. She asked me what I meant by that? I said look at what India has done in the past 10 years. Call centres involved in BPO and KPO works for the Western corporations. Go to TCS, Infosys and Wipro and ask them to set up operations in Guatemala. But Indian call centres serve only the English-speaking population. Look at the American population. The 100 million people who were added to the American population from the 200 million Americans in the recent years, as many as 42.7 per cent were the Hispanics and 37.6 per cent were the Asians, while the growth of the white population was just 1.6 per cent during the period. So, I told her that the American population is fast becoming ethnic and the American corporations would need the same ethnic hardware to serve these ethnic populations. So, Indian tech majors can bring the hardware to Guatemala and Guatemala could provide the software in terms of its young people who can speak the Hispanic language to these companies. Then they could handle the accounts of Nokia or Dell or any other company that outsourced its work. I told her this is how she should think about her country—just like a company would do before an acquisition or merger. Then I took this idea to Central America and I met the Indian Ambassador to Panama. I told the envoy this and pointed out to her that the American President Bush has signed the CAFTA—the Central American Free Trade Agreement. Today we have political backlash in the US against jobs going to India, but nobody would protest if it goes to Central America because that would be in the interest of the Americans. I added that if you have created this free trade agreement, then work with it. For instance, you have so many advantages—your proximity to the US: all the flights from Miami to Central America are 3-3.5 hours only—this makes sure that you have no jetlag as you could work in real time with the Americans. Another important enabler is the beautiful climate—Salvador has 343 days of bright sunshine, while Chicago has the rest of the days of sunshine in a year. The point I am making here is this: you will see the same ideas that companies develop before forming alliances with others, and that countries also must think along the same dimensions to form alliances. This is a major mindset shift. Though she was pleased like punch and sent her entire cabinet for a three-hour discussion with me, unfortunately, nothing happened on that suggestion.

I was giving a talk in Mexico City last year and after the talk, a Vice-Chancellor of a small Mexican university told me that there are 65 Indians who have enrolled in his university that year. Surprised, I asked him, did you ask them why they are there. He immediately replied: because they want to learn the Spanish language with the Mexican accent and then return to India and set up call centres to serve these Spanish speaking customers! This is what actual entrepreneurship means. That, people who already know the language are sitting pretty and our 65 students are away learning a foreign language in order to start a business. Educated people speak English and they do not ask too many questions. But less educated people who ask a lot of questions are the ones who do not speak English. And this is where the whole debate of the language comes in. Therefore, customer demographic changes are something which we would increasingly be seen in the times to come.

My final point is that we would see a severe shortage of good people throughout the world. It is not easy to find good people. Searching for talent is a tough job today. Ask the CEOs around the world, and you would hear this overwhelmingly—that it is not easy to find people who are capable and trustworthy.

The brand of an individual is his credibility. For all of us Indians, if we have to be credible in this context, we need to make sure that we can deliver our promise and if we were to brand India then it has to be credible and trustworthy and branded along those global dimensions. Because we never get a second chance to make the first impression. In short, we badly need to change our *ho-jayega* approach (somehow it will happen). First and foremost, we should know how to get things done; that is to say that we should learn to respect time and stop procrastinating things.

While doing my Ph.D. in applied mathematics from the Guwahati University—though I run a business school, my educational background is completely Maths—I had a very useful insight. The insight was that Maths was going nowhere. So, my advisor suggested to me to move to marketing and management education. That is how I entered the world of management. He also suggested that I go to the Kellogg's School as that is the best place to learn management, adding the best way to learn something is to teach, because as a teacher you should always anticipate what questions your students will ask and that forces you into the culture of always thinking and digging deeper. I asked him why should the best management school hire a worst person to teach? He said something very meaningful—have some aspirations in life; it never hurts to apply. He added, you have done very well in your education, so I will write a letter to the Kellogg's recommending you. I applied and I got the job. And that is how I have become a marketing teacher.

About style of doing things: humility matters, because humility is the essence of learning. I am a simple person and I have no egos and thus learnt the new subject from no background. I learnt a lot from the previous Dean of Kellogg's. He was the Dean for 26 years and built up this world famous institution from nothing. A lot of people asked me why should a reputed university appoint me to this high profile job? I told them because nobody else wanted this job and especially nobody wanted the job that Jacobs was doing. It was a very challenging job, and was more challenging to follow a legend. I was appointed as the Dean in July 2001 and my first day as the Dean was on September 11 the same year. On the first day, I was supposed to address 635 students. As we were welcoming the students that morning, our Corporate Affairs President came and told me that we have to stop the function as there has been a terrorist attack on the World Trade Centre in New York. Think of it, you begin a great task and you end up thus on the very first day.

If the first day was very tough, the following days and years were also not better. Year 2002 was very tough for us as in December of that year, Enron applied for bankruptcy and entire B-schools came under severe criticism. People began to ask a lot of critical questions about B-schools—that whether the B-schools are teaching the right things; are B-school students being taught enough corporate governance and corporate ethics or are they being taught how to become greedy and unethical. There was a concept that

B-schools were teaching their students how to make money and not how to learn.

March 2003 saw the beginning of the second Gulf war, following which the US president massively reduced the number of H1 visas from 1.95 lakh to just about 60,000. So, there was a massive decline in the number of students who could come to the US and study; and how it hurt us was that most of these students come not only to learn but to work for some years in the US and experience how American corporations work. This was no longer possible because of the visa curbs. And 2004 was the year of the tsunami.

I go to Bangkok every year to teach. The tsunami struck when my family and I were in Phuket. While over 1.65 lakh people lost their lives, no animals died in the devastating tsunami. Why? This strange fact was a big learning for me. In fact, the tsunami gave one of the biggest insights to me. Because animals know the changes in the earth much faster than human beings—animals have their feet on the ground and on the morning of the tsunami, they felt the changes in the earth and they ran to safety. But we human beings get used to sitting on our leather chairs and live in comfort, away from the natural realities. While animals live on the earth and on the day of the tsunami, they knew that the earth they were living thus far has changed, hence they ran up to the mountains. In fact, a tsunami survivor told me that on the night of the devastation, his elephant broke its chain and ran to safety because the elephant could sense the changes in the earth as it has its feet on the ground, while the humans who lost their lives were not so.

After the tsunami, in early January I came back to my school and told my students that I have learnt an important lesson of my life at the tsunami, and the lesson is that, in the time of crisis, the people who make the right decisions are those who have their feet on the ground or the people who are in touch with the ground reality.

The problem we see in our quest for talent is, and this is a problem sometimes I see in our country too, that our loyalty for the people we work for has diminished. My father worked for decades with an organisation and that was considered to be part of social respect. But today, the new MBAs think that if they do not switch jobs in 15 companies they are not successful. Our loyalty to our people has decreased dramatically. Today our MBAs work for the pay packet and not for the organisation or the people. This is not good for any country in the long-run. Whatever I am today is due to my loyalty to Kellogg's. It is not that I did not have other offers, I had offers from many prestigious schools like MIT, Stanford, etc. But I decided to stay with Kellogs. Recently the president of MIT called me and offered the top job to me. In the history of MIT it has never happened that a non-MIT faculty has even been called in for an interview. But he told me that we do not want a beauty contest and if you say yes, we will just meet you and offer you the job. I thanked the MIT President for the good gesture and told him that I am very happy at Kellogg's. I am happy because Kellogg's gave me a job when nobody wanted me. It invested in me so much that if at all I serve them for 30 years, my gratitude and loyalty to it would not be over. Whatever I am today is because of Kellogg's.

We have to teach our students to rethink about their loyalty, and the caring attitude. I am on the board of Reliance and I am often asked about what is the difference between being on the board of Reliance and the companies like United Airlines or John Deere? I tell them that what I like about Reliance is the loyalty of the people at Reliance to Mukesh Ambani. People spend time up to 1 am working in the office. I have noticed one more thing. At the board meeting, Mukesh always addresses the directors as uncles—most of the board members, barring Prof. Misra and me, were appointed by Dhirubhai. This respect we have for our elders is a unique quality that we have gained from our families, our culture and our teachers. So we should not give up or forget these stages which made us reach where we are today. Also, difficulties should teach us to remember our past. Difficulties come in our way to make us better and not bitter. So we need to learn about frictions—if life is all smooth, then we will not learn anything new and we will always slip. Frictions and difficulties are to be taken as moments to pause and reflect and also to renew our thinking and then go forward. We should help our new talent to build our future while maintaining these good traits. But sometimes, I think we are also going to become like the rest of the world. We need to preserve our heritage and our culture to move forward.

Given these global challenges, let us see what drives brand reputation or how brands can face the challenges arising out of globalisation. When we discuss about a brand, the first thing that we should talk about is its growth. A brand is like a plant, we have to nurture it to grow. A brand is not like a diamond. A diamond does not grow, it remains as it is. Brand has to have life in it. So, the first and the foremost part of a brand is growth and the second is innovation. You as a brand owner have to always come up with something new. India today contributes a lot to the whole world thanks to Sam Pitroda. As the head of the Knowledge Commission Sam Pitroda has worked out a system of developing how knowledge process outsourcing or business process outsourcing can be done—India has already shown the whole world how one can outsource jobs for which you do not have the knowledge or the capabilities to handle them. This has enabled us to adopt what I call a modular approach to business—just like there was a modular approach to flexible manufacturing that the Japanese have taught us in running a business.

The third part of a brand is leadership. We all know that leaders make all the difference. I really believe that if we look at the brand reputation of India, we can develop the brand India from all the three sides—

growth, innovation and leadership. Let us touch upon how countries can do this.

The first type of growth is organic growth which comes from R&D as R&D drives organic growth. Today, India has become a centre for many global pharma companies to conduct their clinical trials and R&D. We see today Reliance investing a lot into life sciences. They are coming up in bio-fuels too. We have already seen how Brazil has developed a whole new idea of developing ethanol from corn and other bio-materials as a substitute for fossil fuels. Similarly, we should think about one or two areas where we can really make India grow. The other area we should think about is inorganic growth which is what we call mergers and acquisitions or what I earlier said about Central America. I do not know what is the structure for mergers and acquisitions in the country but in the US, companies focus on growth with as much as 52 per cent growth coming in from the inorganic route, 42 per cent coming in from the organic route and the remaining 6 per cent coming in from a combination of the two. So, we should think about what kind of alliances we can sew up to drive growth.

I feel when it comes to inorganic growth we are the best in the world, because we are naturally inclined towards it. Look at our practice of arranged marriages—I particularly am a candidate of arranged marriage—it is nothing but a merger and acquisition activity. In an M&A, you go and do due diligence on the target company and the same is done in an arranged marriage too—you go and see the families and get to know each other. In fact an Indian marriage is between two families and not between two individuals. If we have perfected the art of arranged marriages so well, why cannot we replicate the same in our business relations too?

The point I am trying to make here is that inorganic growth is in our blood, it is part of our DNA. So we need to think about how we can grow our country with right partnerships. We cannot grow in isolation for long. We need to find out the right alliances to grow faster and to sustain it for long.

I am currently working on a project on Turkey—the current Turkish Foreign Minister Alibaba Jaan was a student of mine. Last month, he came to see me. The Thai Finance Minister also was my student—he did his doctorate in marketing under me. Since I have a number of my students and friends in governments across the world, I have been telling my colleagues and students that it is high time that B-schools stopped serving the American and other corporations and moved into advising governments and start thinking about social and public policies.

We should think about research problems in the social and public domains and advise governments on the same. For instance, an important issue coming up is the retirement policy. We Indians also have to rethink about our retirement policy and retirement age, otherwise the cost on the working population in maintaining the non-working population would be so high. Unless something is done on these fronts, governments the world over would have a tough time managing this huge non-working population—those in the 0-15 and 65-plus age bracket—from the incomes of the working population—those in the 15-64 age-bracket.

How do we look at the immigration policies? Western Europe, which is already ageing, will have to rework its immigration policy sooner than later. Where would growth come to these nations unless they have working population in right numbers? So, working on retirement policies, immigration policies and looking at retirement benefits, working on social security policies are the areas that B-schools should look at to find out answers. Because management does not mean managing corporates alone, it also means managing governments and advicing on public services and policies.

We are a unique country where an economics professor is the Prime Minister. We do not know when this would happen again, but my personal feeling is that this is the beginning. I am very bullish about our young generation. The way we have been doing all over the world is tremendously good and this would be the beginning of a transformation for our country in terms of growth.

I again would like to touch upon innovation, and I feel that this also is an area where India can make a difference. Normally, when we think of innovation we think of products—Apple's iPod and iPhones. These are very expensive innovations. Very few countries in the world have the economic resources to put in billions of dollars to develop these products. Rather than product innovation, the next step is process innovation, which means getting the same product in a different way. For instance, at the American airports, you need not stand in the line to get the boarding pass, but you have kiosks where you can swipe your mileage card and get the boarding pass. In fact, I told American Airlines to be innovative and stop selling tickets and start selling miles. In fact this should be their new innovation—selling miles in the place of tickets. So, in the beginning of the year you buy miles, say for a million, and every time you fly, the mileage points would be deducted. If so, where is the need for selling tickets? The same card can have every thing; it is like a debit card. With tickets there can be problems like cancellations or rescheduling of the date of journey. But if you look at it carefully, it is a function of flying miles or the distance—which is mostly a function of pricing or rather distance of pricing.

My point is that developing countries would have better luck in developing process innovations, rather than product innovation. When it comes to us Indians, we can be very creative in doing things. BPO is a perfect example of process innovation.

The third point I want to discuss is the concept called business model innovation which again is more suited for developing and emerging countries. Let me explain it with an example. Everyone has seen the success of Google as a search engine—in fact this is the best example of business process innovation when it comes to online search business. Google is not the first search engine. There was Yahoo, MSN, and Netscape before Google, as search engines. But what was the innovation that Google brought in? The major difference between Yahoo and Google is that for Yahoo, the customer is the person who does the search, while for Google the customer is not the person doing the search, but the person who is being searched. In doing so, Google takes the information and tells its advertisers that X number of people are searching you, say from India, and asks them whether they would like to reach out to these people. But for Yahoo this is not the model. For Yahoo, the information was and still is what are the people doing, but for Google it is what people are looking out for, because the customer for Google is the advertiser, the persons doing the search are not giving any revenue to Google. So, we need to rethink about how we redefine our business. Developing and emerging countries should think about business and business process innovation rather than product innovation as the latter is too expensive for them today. They can get into product innovations once they have the economic stability. But till then their minds should focus on the process innovation.

Then comes the question of leadership. I truly believe that the only real source of differentiation in the world is people. Business is all about people. Because of this, I earlier used the word talent. In marketing, there are four Ps—product, price, promotion and place. You can differentiate your brand through your product, through your pricing, through promotion or brand communication and you can differentiate through the placement or distribution channel of the product. But I do not think anyone of these is not surmountable. Anyone can match your product, your pricing, your promotion or advertising and the distribution model. But the true differentiation in the future is going to be the people.

The person who is working for you is not working for anyone else. So, your differentiation lies in the manner in which you focus on your people. In fact this is your real differentiating factor from competition. Therefore, every organisation should ask: are my people my biggest advantage? My message to those marketers, who say marketing is all about focussing on the customer, is to better change their approach and instead direct it first onto their employees. Because marketing begins at home—if your employees are happy, they would then serve your customers better, if customers are served better they would come back to you again and again, and if they keep coming back to you then your sales will increase and the result is increase in your profits, and if your company is profitable, your shareholders will be happy. Therefore, we need to focus on our people. And leadership to me is letting the people working with you to blossom under your guidance. That is why today people are talking about humility. If leadership is exercised by instilling fear in one's junior, then we will not get the best out of our people. So, an organisation should make sure that its leadership is filled with people, with personalities that help people grow or blossom.

There is a book called *From Good to Great*. It talks about the leadership of successful businesses. And India's advantage is that the qualities that are cited in the book are already available here for the past five millennia. The author has put all of them in a book and it has become a best-seller. But the problem with us is that we do not believe in our own good things. *Ghar ki murgi dal barabar* (chicken cooked at home is equated with lentils) is our typical attitude. But today, we know these are the things that make people successful the world over. People around the world are talking about us and adopting our yoga and meditation methods. But we do not acknowledge them. Actually these are the real brands of India.

Recently, I had the opportunity to meet Dr. Deepak Chopra. He and I teach a course called the "Soul of Leadership" at the Kellogg's for three days. The entire course is on leadership based on our *Vedas* and the *Upanishads*. Let me tell you, at the end of the course most of these students walk away with tears in their eyes because they realise that there is so much richness and goodness available, but unknown to them so far to make some difference to their lives as well as to those around them.

I have two more things to tell you before I conclude. The first is: where are the opportunities available for us? If we anticipate the trends, the first emerging trend of opportunities for us is customer well-being. If people are going to live longer, then wellness becomes important and wellness depends on two things—consumer health care and wealth care. Not only that you want to live a healthy life but you also need financial security to do so, and you just cannot rely on the government to give you all these. We should teach our people better financial management, better investment options and this should become a part of our education irrespective of the discipline. Financial savvyness is very important in every American's plan and I think this is something we also should adopt.

The second point is the whole area of customer engagement or something generally called customer inclusiveness. Dr. Sam Pitroda recently talked about keeping people engaged. I think in this area, India can focus more on media and entertainment sectors. The Disneys and others are opening their studios in our country, because we have the talent and we also have the resources. When you want an animated movie, you do not need to take it from Hollywood, our Bangalore engineers can do a better job. So, media and entertainment sector is something that India needs to pay more attention in the times to come, especially to keep the huge youth population engaged.

And the third point is customer hospitality. "Incredible India" is a good campaign. Tourism should be there, but my sense is that we should focus more on medical or health tourism. India should be a health destination and the brand of India should not be cure but prevention. When you come here and attend a *shivir* (camp), you get rejuvenated and when you undergo yoga, meditation and ayurvedic treatments, you feel relaxed and get energy. And you would not come here next time to see the cities but to get rejuvenated again. So the brand of India should be prevention and not cure as we may not have the latest medical equipments and facilities for complicated treatment as they are too expensive, but we have the people who can serve with the Indianness in it, and that is the part of our hospitality.

Yes, our Indianness is hospitality. In the US there are a set of restaurants catering to a new set of customers called Romeos. And who are the Romeos? Romeos are the retired old men eating out. Because when the older people go out to eat, they are not going out for food, but to get respect, and they spend hours at a place that is nice to them, where they are respected and cared for. I had the opportunity to have lunch with Dr. Bill Freedman, a few months before he passed away. He took me to a restaurant in San Francisco and when we entered, the owner of the restaurant welcomed Freedman and said he has special fish that day and asked whether he could prepare the same for him and his guest? And we had food and sat there for two-and-a-half hours. There was no rush there. But the same restaurant does not entertain the Silicon Valley techies coming in there nor do they want it to be as they have only 37 seconds for lunch. What these techies do is that they order lunch on emails. Then they come down to just collect the packet. They high-touch and high-tech in the same place, be efficient and effectives in the same place. My point is that we need to think creatively and innovatively to succeed in any domain.

Therefore, my final point is that every product has a brand in it—if it is FedEx, it is known for reliability, in the case of Nike it says "Just do it". What is Just do it? It means be the athlete in you. Star Alliance would talk about global access—you can travel anywhere on Star Alliance.

India has so far been known for its talent of outsourcing, while China is known for its cost-effectiveness. However, both India and China have to rethink about what their brands would really stand for. I have to tell you that cost is no longer an advantage for India. Look at the way salaries have gone up here, I find that some salaries here are higher than what their counterparts in the US are paid. The new MBAs are paid much higher here than their American counterparts. So our advantage on the cost front is almost over.

To me, our real advantage would be our Indianness—who we are, how we take care of people, etc. Therefore, rather than focussing on tangibles like talent outsourcing, we do really need to focus on the intangibles. What I mean by this is that, as I said in the beginning, our journey is about not just being successful but moving from success to significance. If we Indians take our life span, the first 25 years are spent as *Bhramacharya* the period of learning and studying, the second phase is success, the third phase is the move from success to significance—having achieved everything in life, now how do you make a difference, and the fourth phase is sacrifice, the phase of life in the upwards of 75. But when you are studying you are already looking at the next stage of success and when you are successful, you start thinking about making a difference.

My students often tell me that as the world is so big, how can an individual make a difference to such a large world. I tell them, to the world you may be a person, but to a person you can be the world; and if each one of us can make a world for the other person, imagine how much different this world would have been. And I want to tell you the difference that person who invited me to do a Ph.D. in Dallas made to my life. It was that opportunity that made me what I am today and I am confident that I can make a difference to the world. Similarly, all of us have something in us to make a difference to the world. We should not allow fewer resources to act as a constraint for not doing something to make a little difference.

Recently I did a project for the Mayor of Chicago. It was an effort to brand the city of Chicago. As part of this, the Mayor invited me to address the businessmen from Chicago and the rest of the US. During my address one guy asked me how could I compare Chicago with the Silicon Valley. I said I did not say that Chicago is like the Silicon Valley, but this city has one of the best infrastructures for business in the world and is also well located. He persisted that Chicago is bloody cold and therefore how can I promote it as a city for entrepreneurship. I too persisted saying, yes, since I am the Dean of Kellogg's I can control what is happening in my school, but I have no control over the weather in the city of Chicago. But I did not want to leave my presentation in a depressing note, at the same time I was confused as to how to conclude on a positive note. Hence I told him, in life you should believe in the principle of a refrigerator—what is kept inside the refrigerator will remain safe for a long time. Well after that he did not dare ask any more questions. The same cold weather can be a plus point, when it comes to Chicago.

India still has a very important challenge ahead, because as I said earlier, brand is not a product but an experience. Yesterday, on the way to Delhi, it took me an hour and a half to move from one side of the airport to the other which had me missing the next flight to New Delhi. It just tells us that infrastructure follows growth and not growth follows infrastructure. So, we need to really think about what are the challenges lying ahead of us. I believe in what someone wrote in the past: "if you want to build a ship do not expect your men to run up to the forest and gather the woods, saw them and then build the ship, instead teach them the desire for the seas." And this is what I tell my students too. Life is about desires and aspirations—so long as we keep those dreams alive in our young generations, we as a nation have a great future. I always tell people that my success is due to being an Indian and the Indianness in me. We should never apologise to anyone for being an Indian or for that matter for our colour or the way we speak. What we have inside us is our differentiation.

> *Jhole mein rakhi huyi cheez se jhole ki keemath kabhi zyaada nahin honi chahiye, nahin to aap bhi jhola ho jayenge.*
>
> (The bag in which you place a product should not cost more than the product itself or you will be reduced to a mere bag (will loose everything).

So we need to think about what we have inside and it is that which makes us special.

As the world is fast becoming one place, we have a great responsibility to shape this world so that collectively all of us make this world a better place to live in.

SHASHI THAROOR

Shashi Tharoor is Chairman of Dubai-based Afras Ventures; a prize-winning author of ten books, both fiction and non-fiction; and a widely-published critic, commentator and columnist. In 2007 he concluded a nearly 29-year career with the United Nations, including working for refugees in South-East Asia at the peak of the "boat people" crisis, handling peace-keeping operations in the former Yugoslavia, and culminating as the Under-Secretary-General for Communications and Public Information. In 2006, he was India's candidate to succeed Kofi Annan as UN Secretary-General, and emerged a strong second out of seven contenders. Dr. Tharoor earned his Ph.D. at the Fletcher School of Law and Diplomacy at the age of 22, and was named by the World Economic Forum in Davos in 1998 as a "Global Leader of Tomorrow." He has been awarded the Pravasi Bharatiya Samman—India's highest honour for overseas Indians.

8 Realising India's Soft Power Potential for Shaping it's Future

Shashi Tharoor

At the midnight of 15th August 1947 Independent India was born, when our Prime Minister Pandit Jawaharlal Nehru proclaimed to the whole world—words that certainly all the professionals and probationers here have learnt by heart—"The Tryst with Destiny"—"a moment comes, which comes rarely in history when we step out from the old to the new, when an age ends, and when the soul of a nation, long suppressed finds utterance." With those words he launched India on a remarkable experiment in governance; remarkable in some ways, because it was happening all around the country. "India", Winston Churchill had remarked, "is merely a geographical expression, and is not a united country." And Churchill was very right about India. But it is true that no other country in the world embraces the extraordinary mixture of ethnic groups, the profusion of mutually incomprehensible languages, the varieties of topography and climates, the diversity of religious and cultural practices, and the range of levels of economic development as India does.

India is more than the sum total of its contradictions. If one is asked to speak about the India of his dreams, how can one approach this land of both snow-peaks and tropical jungles, 23 major languages recognised in the Constitution as the official languages with 22,000 distinct dialects, including some spoken by more people than say, Danish or Norwegian, inhabited in the seventh year of the twenty-first century by over a billion people of every ethnic extraction known to humanity. How does one come to terms with a country where even after 60 years of Independence over 40 per cent of its population is illiterate, but it has the world's second largest pool of trained scientists and engineers. A country whose teeming cities overflow, while two out of three Indians still scratch a living from the soil. What is it like dreaming about a country that is rife with despair, but which nonetheless moved a Mughal emperor to claim that if on earth there is a paradise, it is this, it is this, it is this!

How does one engage a culture that elevated non-violence onto an effective moral principle, but its freedom was born in blood and its Independence still soaks in it? How does it explain a land where just seven years ago, some peasant organisations and suspicious government officials attempted to close down KFC presuming it to be a threat to the nation? It is a country where a former Prime Minister, who passed away recently, bitterly complained about the booming sale of Pepsi and Coke even as villagers do not have clean drinking water. And yet, the same country invents more sophisticated software for American computer manufacturers than any other country in the world. How can one talk about one's dreams for a country with an ageless civilisation that is the birthplace of four major religions? A nation that has a dozen different traditions of classical dance, 85 political parties represented in Parliament, and 300 ways of cooking the potato!

Now, the short answer is that it cannot be done, at least not to everyone's satisfaction. Any truism about India can immediately be contradicted by another truism about India. Anything can be said about India but the opposite is also true.

Now, our country's national motto, which I am sure everybody has learnt, emblazoned on governmental crest is *Satyamev Jayate*—Truth alone triumphs. But the question remains however, whose truth? It is a question to which there are at least a billion answers, that is if the last census has not counted on us again. That is so to answer, but I realise there is no answer at all. So, another answer to all these questions has to be sought.

And this may lie in simple insights. The singular thing about India that one likes to say is that you can only speak about it in the plural. There is this hackneyed phrase "many Indias". Many of you are familiar with the American motto "out of many, one". India really has to say "out of many, many" because everything exists in countless variants. There is no single standard, no fixed stereotypes, no one way of doing things; our pluralism is acknowledged in a way in which we organise and arrange our own affairs. Here all the faiths, all the ideologies survive and contend for place in the sun.

Do not forget that at the time when most developing countries opted for authoritarian model of government to promote nation-building and to direct development, India chose to be a multi-party democracy. Despite many stresses and strains, including the 20 months of Emergency that the autocratic Indira Gandhi slapped in the mid-70s, a multi-party democracy prevailing upon a corrupt and inefficient bureaucracy and political masters nonetheless India remains flourishing.

The one image that India gives to any foreigner is that of a maddening, chaotic, inefficient and seemingly non-purposeful nation that muddles its way through the first decade to the twenty-first century. Another image is that perhaps India is not just a country, it is an adventure, one in which all avenues are open and everything is possible. A British historian, E.P. Thompson wrote that India is perhaps the most important country for the future of the world. All the convergent influences of the world, wrote Thompson, run through this society. There is not a thought that has been thought in the West or in the East that is not active in some Indian mind. I am glad that it is a Brit and not an Indian who said that the Indian mind must have been shaped by some remarkably diverse forces. Ancient Hindu traditions, myths, scriptures, the impact of Islam and Christianity and of course the two centuries of British colonial rule, all left a mark on this country. The result is unique and many observers are astonished by the marvellous way in which India has been surviving all this while as a plural state. But India could hardly have survived as anything else. Pluralism is a reality that emerges from the very nature of our country. It is a choice that is made inevitable by our geography and reaffirmed by our history.

I think that the first challenge about India is that we cannot generalise. The fact that Foreign Service trainees from outside should be told about a little generalisation that can safely be made about India, and that nothing can be taken for granted about our country, not even its name. The name India comes from the river Indus, which now flows through Pakistan. That of course can be explained by what is today's Pakistan, was a part of India until the country was hacked off by the departing British in 1947. Yet each explanation brings another anomaly. Pakistan was created as a homeland for India's Muslims but the fact is that there are more Muslims in India than in Pakistan now.

My focus here is on four of the more important debates facing the world at the end of that point of the twentieth century, because I feel that India is still on the cusp of these debates. Summarising briefly, my book *India from Midnight to the Millennium*, which was published on the 50th anniversary of our Independence probes the following issues: the bread-*versus*-freedom question, can democracy literally deliver the goods in a country of poverty and scarcity, is inherent inefficiency impeding its rapid growth, is political instability and makeshift coalitions a luxury that a developing country cannot afford? As today's youths concentrate on earning their bread, should they consider political freedom a dispensable distraction? Then comes the centralism-*versus*-federalism debate. For a country of India's size and diversity, does it need to be run by a strong central government, able to transcend the vociferous tendencies of languages, caste and culture or is a government that centralises the least is the best? Does every question being asked in Dharwar have to be answered in Delhi?

Then there is the pluralism-*versus*-fundamentalism debate. The secularist establishment in our Constitution is now being attacked by some of the political elements. Is that essential in a pluralist society like ours or should India, like so many other developing countries and indeed like all our neighbours, find refuge by asserting the majority religious identities?

And fourthly the Coke and the colonisation debate; globalisation *versus* the saffron lands. Should India, where economic self-sufficiency has been a mantra for more than four decades, open itself up to the global economy? Can Western goods thrust the alien influences on us and disrupt our society? Should we raise our barriers to shield our youth from the seduction of MTV or McDonalds? Or for that matter, since the East India Company came to trade but stayed on to rule, were our nationalist leaders right in suspecting every foreigner with a briefcase as a symbol of a new imperial age? As you know we did spend nearly four-and-a-half decades suffering economic nationalism. Our earlier leaders felt that you could not have political independence without economic independence, and self-sufficiency, and is globalisation an answer to that is a crucial debate we have to undertake.

And there is a fifth debate that I did not discuss in the book out of deference to the restraint demanded by the UN, my then employer. And that is what one might call the economics-of-gun-*versus*-the-butter debate. The case for defence spending against spending on development as we enter the twenty-first century. Amidst new threats of terrorism and renewed talks of nuclear confrontation, there is an ideological battle looming between the advocates of military security, freedom from attack and conquest and those of human security, freedom from hunger and hopelessness. It is difficult to deny, but without adequate defence, a country cannot develop freely according to its own likes, but it is also equally impossible to deny that without adequate development, there would not be a country worth defending. But these are not merely academic debates; they are now being enacted on national and world stage and the choices we make will determine the kind of Indian nation that we can truly dream about in the new century. And since the century has begun with Indians accounting for the sixth of the world's population, these choices are bound to resonate throughout the globe.

But I do not want to dwell further on all of these debates. Instead I would like to focus on one cautious aspect of the theme of this speech, the India of my dreams, of dreaming of India's potential and that is I think the nature of India I dream about. And what that could mean for India's place in the world in the twenty-first century. Because after all, after that famous midnight that I have spoken about 60 years ago, the British empire came to an end at a time when the carnage of partition and sectarian violence that accompanied it, showed up a great challenge facing the nation even after the six decades that have followed.

Many observers have seen this country acutely conscious of the divide that region, religion and caste could make. One can well ask what does make India a country. Well to answer that I would like to take an Italian example.

Amidst the popular ferment that made an Italian state an Italian nation, out of a mosaic of principalities and identities of the eighteenth and the nineteenth centuries, one Italian nationalist by the name of Masimo, once wrote memorably that we have created Italy but what we need to do is to create Italians. I quote this because what is striking is that no Indian nationalist would have ever written that. Be it Gandhi or Nehru, they would have never written of creating Indians or India because they believed in the existence of India and Indians for millennia before their nationalist movement gave a twentieth century political expression to tens of millions of Indians. So Nehru could speak of that quote I gave you for being an Asian, for reassertion of being what always existed but long suppressed.

Nonetheless, the India that was born on 15th August 1947 was in a real sense a very new creation, a nation that made fellow countrymen of the Ladakhis and the Lakshadweepians. It divided a Punjabi from a Punjabi for the first time. For the first time, it asked a Keralite peasant to feel allegiance to a Kashmiri Pandit ruling in Delhi. Though, Nehru may not have written about the challenge of creating Indians, but creating India was what the national movement led by him did in fact.

Let me illustrate what does this mean with a simple story. When we celebrated our forty-ninth Independence Day eleven years ago, the then Prime Minister H.D. Deve Gowda stood on the ramparts of the Red Fort and gave the traditional address to the nation in Hindi, which was always called our national language. Now, each of the Prime Ministers before Gowda has always done exactly the same forty-eight times earlier. But what was special about this is the fact that Gowda who hails from Karnataka, spoke to all the Indians in a language of which he knows not a word of. Tradition and political expediency of the time required a speech in Hindi and he gave one. But the words had been written out to him in his native Kannada script which of course made no sense. While what is astonishing is that such an episode is almost incomprehensible anywhere else, but it represents the oddities that made India, the India of today. Because only in India could a man who does not understand what is called the national language could rule the country. Or for that matter, ours is a national language that is not understood by more than half of the population of the country. And only in India this particular solution could have been found to enable the Prime Minister to address the nation in the national language which he does not know.

I have seen this solution earlier when my fellow Keralite, singer K.J. Yesudas, who sang his way to the top of the Bollywood film music charts in the 1980s, singing Hindi songs, showed me his songbook. All the lyrics had been written out for him in the Malayalam script. But to see this practice elevated to the Prime Ministerial level was a startling affirmation of our pluralism.

Then you see we are all minorities here. You take for example a typical Indian stepping out of the train, a Hindi-speaking, a Hindu male from our great Gangetic plain state of Uttar Pradesh. Stepping off the train he might cherish the illusion that he belongs to the majority community, to use a phrase which is today much favoured by the less-industrious of our journalists. But he does not. Yes, as a Hindu he belongs to a faith adhered by more than 80 per cent of our population. But a majority does not speak Hindi or hail from UP. You would be forgiven to think otherwise when you visit there. And if you were visiting my home state of Kerala you would discover that the majority there is not even male.

Worse, this archetypical, UP Hindu has only to mingle with the multi-lingual, multi-coloured crowd and here I am not talking about the colours of their clothes but of their skins, thronging the country's major railway stations to realise how much of a minority he really is. Even his Hinduism is no guarantee of his majority, because, his caste automatically places him into a minority. If he is a Brahmin then 90 per cent of his fellow countrymen are not. If he is a Backward Class then 85 per cent are not, and so on.

Or take our language. The Constitution recognises 23 languages. Our rupee note has 15 different scripts spelling out the denomination of the currency. There are in fact, 35 regional languages spoken by more than a million people each. And these are languages, and not dialects, as they have their own script, grammatical structures and cultural assumptions. Each of the native speakers of these languages is in a linguistic minority, for none enjoys the majority status in our country.

I think a part of the popularity of Bollywood, something which Surendra Kumar and I have a shared interest in, is due to the fact that Hindi is undisputedly not always very well spoken by half of the population of our country. But in no sense it is the language of the whole country because its elocution, its gender rule and its script are unfamiliar to most Indians in the South or in the Northeast. Then ethnicity further complicates any notion of a majority community. Because most of the time an Indian name immediately reveals where he is from, or what his mother tongue is. When we introduce ourselves, we advertise our origins. Despite some intermarriage of the elite levels in the leading cities, Indians largely remain identifiable — the Punjabis can be easily distinguished from a Bengali.

Now the difference this reflects is often more than the elements of commonality. The Karnataka Brahmin for example shares his Hindu faith with a Bihari Khurmi, but they share little identity in terms of their appearance, dress code, customs, taste or language. But at the same time, a Tamil Hindu would feel he has far more in common with a Tamil Christian or a Tamil Muslim than to say a Haryanvi Jat with whom he formally shares a religion. Why do I harp on these differences—only to make the point that the idea of India, albeit the Indian nationalism that I am trying to dream about with you today, is a rare Alamo today. It is a rare Alamo altogether.

In fact, this reminds me of an Italian story about an argument between an American and French diplomat outside the Security Council on a particular problem. The American said you know how we can solve this, we can do this and that and this and that to solve the problem. And the French diplomat said yes, yes, yes and that would work in practice but will it work in theory? The point is that Indian nationalism works in practice—it is not based on theory, it is not based on any of the classic theories of what makes a nation state. Our nationalism is not based on the languages that I explained, since they are 23 or 35 depending on whether you follow the Constitution or the aflo-linguist. It is not based on different geography because in as much the Sub-continent has a natural geography framed by the mountains and the sea, which was all hacked by the Partition. It is not based on a philosophy. I explained how the combination and diversity of the racial tribes constitutes India.

Indians also ethnically have more in common with foreigners may be more than with each other. An Indian Punjabi or an Indian Bengali has ethnically more in common with a Pakistani or a Bangladeshi respectively than a Poonawala or a Bangalorean. And of course it is not based on religion, because they are home to every faith known to mankind with the possible exception of Shintoism and Hellenismos. But our Hinduism is a faith without a national organisation, no established church or a proper hierarchy, no Hindu pope, no Hindu Sunday, no single sacred book, no compulsory rites and uniform modes of belief and worship. So it is a faith that exemplifies as much our diversity as does our common cultural heritage. In fact, our nationalism is a nationalism of an idea; an idea emerging from an ancient civilisation united by a shared history, ruled by a pluralist democracy.

This land imposes no narrow conformities on its citizens. The point about being an Indian is that you can be many things under one thing. You can be a good Muslim, a good Keralite and a good Indian all at once. During my days at the UN handling the disaster in the former Yugoslavia, I learned the notion of the narcissism of minor differences when people with the same ethnic heritage and language and so on heightened the differences between themselves to attack each other. In India we celebrate the commonality of major differences. So the famous phrase on its head, India is a place of belonging rather than of blood. Therefore, my dream of India is indeed of this one land embracing many. Besides, India as a nation that makes no difference of caste, creed, colour, culture, cuisine, convictions, costumes and customs and still rallies around the common consensus. The consensus, of course, is a democratic consensus on the super principle that our democracy does not really need to agree all the time. So long as you agree on the ground rule of how you will disagree, there is consensus. All these years, India has survived all the stresses and the strains that have besieged us for 60 years. In fact, that had led so many learned political scientists in the 50s and the 60s to predict India's imminent disintegration. But precisely India has maintained her consensus on how to manage without consensus.

But my generation grew up where often nationhood meant this clichéd slogan of unity in diversity; we were brought up to take pluralism for granted. And to reject the bigger tree, the communalism as we call it, has brought to shake the country, when the British left. In rejecting a place for Pakistan, Indian nationalism also had to reject the very idea that religion should be a determination of nationhood. We never fell into the trap of agreeing that since the Partition has established a separate state for Muslims what remained as India was a state for the Hindus. That was explicitly rejected by Gandhi, Nehru and the Indian leaders of the time and thereafter. Because, to accept the idea of India, you had to reject the idea that divided the country. And that is what after, all the secularism of our dreams really means. Western dictionaries define secularism as an absence of religion. Indian secularism always means a profusion of religions, none of which is privileged by the state, because you cannot have irreligiousness in a country like India, where even viable atheist parties like the Communists or the southern DMK have found is as unpopular amongst their voters.

In Calcutta during the Durga Pooja, the Hindu Christmas of Calcutta, the Communist Party's youth wings would compete with each other to put up the most lavish pavilions for the goddess Durga. That is Indian atheism. So, the fact is that secularism has to mean multi-religiousness in India. And in the Calcutta neighbourhood where I lived during my high school days, you could literally hear the wails of the Muslim priest calling the Muslim faithful for prayer, blending with the tinkling of the bells accompanying the chanting of the *mantras* of the Shiva temple, the crackling loudspeakers outside the Sikh gurudwara reciting the verses from *Guru Granthsahib*, and the St Paul's Cathedral just around the corner. That is India. And so for the first decade after Independence in particular, the political culture of the country reflected this dream of India in its true sense. And to think that the population in those days was 82 per cent Hindus and the country had been partitioned as a result of a demand for a separate Muslim homeland.

Three of our eleven Presidents were Muslims. Several governors, cabinet ministers, chief ministers, ambassadors, generals, Supreme Court judges are Muslims. But why stick to that? During the Indo-Pak war in 1971, our Air Force in the Northern sector was commanded by a Muslim officer, Air Marshall Latif. The Army commander was a Parsi, Field Marshall Sam Manekshaw, and the general officer commanding the forces that marched into Bangladesh in the Eastern command was a Sikh, General Arora; and the major general who piloted the helicopter into Dhaka to negotiate the terms of surrender of the Pakistani forces in what later became Bangladesh, was the Jewish Major General Jacob. That is India. That is the India of my dreams.

The onus is of course on all of us, as the clock is ticking and we all know that we all are Egyptian mummies, pressed for time. So let me move on to one more point that Surendra Kumar particularly wanted me to address. And that of course is the place of India among the comity of nations in the time to come, for this India that we have been dreaming about together in the twenty-first century. Because I think that when we hear increasingly not just from outside as they say, of India's prospects of being a world leader or the even the next super power, I have to admit that I become a bit nervous, because the notion of world leadership is a curiously archaic one anyway. The very phrase is revealing of the Kipling ballads and James Bondian adventure. Because what makes a country a world leader. Is it population, because for that, India is on course to top the charts—we are going to overtake China as the world's most populous country by 2034. In military strength, India is already the world's fourth largest army. In nuclear capacity, India's status has been made clear despite not having been formally recognised and now with the Indo-US nuclear agreement on the anvil, that will be taken care of too.

When it comes to economic development we know that India is making extraordinary strides in recent years. It is already the world's fourth largest country in PPP terms and it continues to climb up the ladder, though many of our people still continue to live in deep poverty. As many as 260 million are living below the poverty line even after six decades of Independence. So, what is the Indian place in the world all about? Is it any of these things; is it a combination of some of them; or is it something different altogether and something very difficult to define? So, may I call the power of example. In answering this question we need to examine India's strength and where they lie as we move in the twenty-first century.

Many of the conventional analysis of India's stature in the world rely on all too familiar indices that I have mentioned like the GDP growth rate, military strength and all of that. But, why do not we turn our attention briefly to something quite different. Not the economy, not the military strength but the quality of India that emerges from the India of my dreams that I have described to you. What one might call India's soft power. The notion of soft power is quite new in international discourse; the term was coined by Harvard's Joseph Nye, who explained the power as the ability to alter the behaviour of others to get them to do what you want. And there are three ways to do that—there is coercion, there is sticks and carrots, and there is attraction which is soft power. If you can attract others you can economise on the sticks and the carrots. So, Nye said that the world politics which is traditionally seen in terms of military power where the largest army is likely to win, then even in the past that was not enough because after all the US lost in Viet Nam, the Soviet Union was defeated in Afghanistan.

And the world's only super power is discovering in Iraq today that one thing that you cannot do with a nation is to sit on it. So what are the alternatives? Enter soft power—the power emerging from a country's culture, its political values, its non-military role in the world, to the extent it is seen as attractive by others. Because in today's information era, as Nye had argued, and I am going to quote him, there are three types of countries which are likely to acquire soft power, and I am going to think about India, though I am sure he had America in mind when he wrote this, "those with dominant culture and ideals are closer to prevailing global norms, which now emphasise liberalism, pluralism and autonomy. Those with the most accessed multi-channels of communication and that's more influence about issues that are framed, and those whose credibility is enhanced by their domestic and international performance." And this seems to me where India fares rather well today. China has started establishing Confucius Institutes to promote Chinese culture internationally. But, soft power does not rest merely on the governmental actions; even the US knows that, because Hollywood and MTV have done far more to promote the idea of America as a desirable and admirable society, from the governmental efforts of the Voice of America or Human Rights Commission. In India's case, we now have to seriously acknowledge the aspects and products of the Indian society that have begun to enhance our intangible standing across the globe. Bollywood for example, we have mentioned. And as an aside I have to say, my own favourite story of Bollywood is of the two goats sitting on the garbage bin who are chewing on the discarded cans of celluloid. And the first goat says you know that this film is not bad, and the second goat says the book was better. Bollywood has done a great duty to enhance the image of India by bringing its brand of glitzy entertainment not just to Indians here, or to the diaspora, as well as also to others outside this group. An Indian friend who was serving in Damascus a few years back told me in those days the only posters and photographs that were as large as that of the then President seen in Damascus were of Amitabh Bachchan.

In fact, Indian art, Indian classical music, have all had the same effect. The work of Indian fashion designers is adorning the world's beauties today. Indian cuisine is spreading around the globe because after all, as the French have known for longer than us, the way to a foreigners' heart is through their palates. What is striking is that in England today, Indian curry houses employ more people than the iron, steel, coal and the ship industry combined. So, the empire can strike back. And yet as we know there are a lot of Indians who fear that globalisation and economic liberalisation would bring with itself some sort of cultural imperialism and that Baywatch and burgers would replace Bharatnatyam and *Bhelpuri*.

I would argue strongly that India's recent experience with globalisation demonstratively can bring Coca-Cola without the country becoming coca-colonised. And what is more is that our own products are themselves going out as part of globalisation. Indians would not become any less Indians, if in Gandhi's famous metaphor, we open the doors and the windows of our country, and let foreign winds blow to our house. Our popular culture has stood resilient enough to absorb all these, competing successfully with MTV and McDonald's. It is more than that, because a Bhangra beat is infused into a Western pop record today, or a Hollywood star comes and practices Yoga here. Or when Indian women sweep the Miss Universe or Miss World contests, or when *The Monsoon Wedding* woos the people, or when *Lagaan* claims an Oscar nomination; when Indian writers win the Bookers or the Pulitzer prizes, then you can see that the soft power of India is enhanced.

Ask yourself how many Chinese novelists, a typical literate British or American reader can name? Can many non-Western countries even claim a presence in the Occidental mind considering what India has today. We see that the Americans speak of our IITs with the same reverence with which they used to accord the MITs and the Caltech, or Indian engineers and software developers are taken as synonymous with mathematical and technical excellence. Then of course India's respect and standing gains a million fold. I had an amazing experience running into a fellow on a trip to Amsterdam—an Indian who had done probably History (Honours), told me that he was approached by a Caucasian facing problems with his computer, asking him whether he was an Indian, and could he help him with his laptop? The old character of Indians used to be of snake charmers and *sadhus*, now it is of software geeks and computer gurus. So, what does all this mean?

I think it means that what is extraordinarily interesting is that in the information age to succeed, to have an influence in the world, you have to be a land of better story, and India is that. Without being typically conscious of it, we are a land of the better story today. And this is not about propaganda, probably it will not work. It is directed from above, not least by our government. But its impact on intangible, can be huge. I met an Afghan foreign service trainee here. Let me say that one of my favourite examples for this indeed comes from Afghanistan because we all know how important

Afghanistan is for India's national security. We do not have any military missions there. What is India's biggest asset in Afghanistan? I would argue that do not try to call an Afghan at 8.30 in evening. Why, because that is when an Indian television soap opera *Kyunki Saas bhi kabhi bahu thi*, dubbed into Dari, is telecast on Tolo TV. And I am told no one wishes to miss it. It has something like a 90 per cent audience penetration rate. It is the most popular television show in Afghan history. It has been directly responsible for the spike in sale of generator sets, and leads to absence from religious functions which clash with the broadcast time. In fact, this thorough capture of the public imagination in Afghanistan is striking, that in a deeply conservative Islamic society, it is an Indian television show that often provides the entertainment for half an hour. And even in a measurable increase in crime at 8.30 pm, because watchmen are sneaking a look at the television rather than minding the store. In fact, a Reuters despatch that I read recently and this is Reuters, a British news agency and not a PTI report, recounted how robbers in Mazar-e-Sharif stripped the vehicle off its wheels, windshield wipers, mirrors, during the broadcast time and then wrote on the car, in an allusion to the show's heroine, "'*Tulsi Zindabad*."

That is our power, and India does not need to thank the government for this exercise. Instead Indians too can simply say *Tulsi Zindabad*. Of course, government policies can also play a role and I know that India has done a great deal to look at last year's European calendar to show India in Davos, India in Hanover trade fair, India in Frankfurt book fair, the festival of India in Brussels. So, all kudos to the government, our hardworking foreign-service officers and our cultural council relationship officers for doing all this. But I would argue that soft power is not just what we can deliberately and consciously exhibit and put on display. It is rather how others see who we are, whether or not they are trying to show it to the world.

To take a totally different example, I was travelling as a UN official, and not as an Indian in the Gulf countries in May 2004, and none of my senior interlocutors in three different countries could stop talking about the extraordinary scenes they had just witnessed. After the largest democratic exercise in the world, the election of 2004, in which a Roman Catholic political leader of Italian background, a woman makes way for a Sikh to be sworn in as the Prime Minister by a Muslim, in a country of 81 per cent Hindus.

This is what India stands for in the world. And living in the US as I was in the world's oldest democracy which after 220 years has not yet managed to elect a President or a Vice-President who is anything but a male, white and Christian, this seems to be a rather startling lesson that the relatively young democracy of India could offer the world. So, it is not just material accomplishments that enhance India's place in the world. Even more important are the values and principles that the Indian society stands for. After all

Gandhi won us Independence through the use of soft power before the phrase was even coined. Because non-violence and *satyagraha* were the classic uses of soft power in those days. But I do want to stress that there is no ground for complacency in the India that we are dreaming of. Because we have a lot of internal problems that we need to solve, our society is going to be projected as one we are admiring. We still have a lot more to ensure that our people are healthy, well-fed and secure—secure not just on jehadi terrorism, but from the daily terror of poverty, hunger and ill health.

Of course, we can take satisfaction from our success in carrying out three kinds of revolution in feeding our people—the green revolution for food grains, the white revolution in milk production and the latest to some degree is the blue revolution in fisheries. But, the benefits of these revolutions still have not reached a third of our population who are still living in horrendous conditions. And we have to do that otherwise we cannot really say that the India of our dreams has been accomplished.

I have written in some of my books the very problems that our country faces—the poor quality of much of our political leadership, the rampant corruption, criminalisation of our politics. And yet we know that corruption is being tackled by an activist judiciary, and by energetic investigative agencies. Those are the sorts of example that our institutions are able to give. The rule of law, therefore, remains a vital Indian strength.

The non-governmental agencies are out there defending the human rights, promoting environmentalism and fighting injustice. The press is free, lively, irreverent, disdainful of sacred cows. On my frequent visits, I find that India is nothing like the unchanging land of the western cliché. There is extraordinary degree of change and I would not spell it out. I would argue that we have gone through in last 15 years a thorough change in economics, in social relations and in politics. That in almost any other society would have constituted a revolution. And yet in India all three have taken place and yet this has been absorbed in the transformation of the Indian society, because of the democracy that we have talked about, and because of the idea of India that I have dreamt about with you. An idea which safeguards the common space available to each identity. An India that remains safe to diversity.

India is not a melting pot. What it is, is a *thali*, and if you have not got one, the dishes do not run into each other, they have distinct taste. But they combine with each other on your palate to give you a satisfying meal. *Thali* is the metaphor for what India is all about. And this precious pluralism is to me the greatest civilisational asset that India has in today's world. The Indian dream must be a dream that can be dreamt in Gujarati or Tamil, be dreamt by a Muslim or a Parsi, dreamt by a Brahmin or a Bodo, on a *charpai* or a luxury king bed. It is our founding fathers that wrote a Constitution for their dreams. Today we have given passports to their ideals. Any narrow definition of Indianness than the one that I gave to you, not just only punishes it, it would be an insult to Indian nationhood. This is my quarrel with the so-called *Hindutva* brigade, because an India that denies itself to any Indian would no longer be India that Gandhi and Nehru fought to free. It would no longer be the India that the rest of the world would look up to with admiration. To me, the India of my dreams is the one that is open to contentions of ideas and interests within it, unafraid of the prowess or the products of the outside world, wedded to the democratic pluralism that is our greatest strength and is determined to liberate and fulfil the creative energies of the people. Such an India is one whose sixtieth birthday this year was well worth celebrating.

"India conquered and dominated China culturally for 20 centuries without ever having to send a single soldier across her border!"

— Hu Shih,

Former Ambassador of China to USA

SUNIL BHARTI MITTAL

Sunil Bharti Mittal is the founder, Chairman and Managing Director of Bharti Group and runs India's largest GSM-based mobile phone service. He can be called as originator of cellular phone revolution in India. He has been honoured with several awards. Mr. Mittal was chosen as one of the top entrepreneurs in the world for the year 2000 and amongst "Stars of Asia" by Business Week. He also received IT-Man of the Year Award 2002 from Dataquest and CEO of the Year 2002 Award from World HRD Congress.

9

India of My Dreams

Spectacular Future Beckons India

SUNIL BHARTI MITTAL

I am going to share with you a little bit about the journey of Bharti, interspersed with the realities on the ground that I have seen. This will cover the process of economic reform that started in 1992 and the huge struggles that an entrepreneur faces in building and shaping his own dreams as the nation's overall dreams shape-up. For the young diplomats who are going to be serving this nation in different capacities, I think it is a very important moment in India's history that we are entering. We are entering a phase of hyper growth, which will see India as the third largest economy in real terms in 2040 and by 2050 we may well be the number two economy in real terms in the world. And that is truly a daunting thought for all of us as Indians. But the fact is that we seem to be heading towards the real picture and why I say this, I will reveal in my story.

Let me start at the outset. I started in 1976, at the very young age of 18 with Rs. 20,000 as a capital which, in those days, was about US $ 1000. I grew up in Ludhiana, which is up North in the State of Punjab. It is an industrial town and almost everybody has a small enterprise of his own. Therefore, it was natural to get inspired by my friends, business families and get into business. I must also confess that I was not a great student so getting a decent job was not an option. So one had to start working as an entrepreneur and that is what I started doing. In my early days, about two to three years were spent in doing what almost everybody does in Ludhiana, manufacturing bicycle parts. In Ludhiana, you either made bicycles or made parts of bicycles. Those few people, who were not into bicycles, were into hosiery products, by either making yarn or sweaters. I chose to make bicycle parts as it needed small capital. There was a friend of mine from college who was willing to become a partner. We pooled the little capital we had and started the journey of manufacturing bicycle parts. My first customers were Hero Cycles and Avon Cycles. Brij Mohan Munjal, the grand old stalwart of Indian industry for Ludhiana, was my first customer. In that sense he was also my mentor and I truly learnt how to develop businesses at his feet.

In two to three years time, I was very clear that if I had to make a significant impact in my business, I had to do something dramatically different. I also saw that Ludhiana was not the place to do anything different and therefore I had to leave and look at new opportunities that were emerging, in a nascent way in the Indian economy. I took the contrarians view. Almost everybody was becoming an exporter from India, which was desperate for Foreign Exchange. Exporters were being awarded and hailed. But given my limited resources I decided I would rather import small or large products from large foreign companies and sell them in India. This was a tall order given the huge restrictions India had on foreign exchange and, more importantly, in terms of import restrictions. It was almost impossible to import anything into India. But in a period of three years from 1979 to 1982, I dabbled in a number of imports—plastic, zip fasteners, metals, copper—basically whatever I could lay my hands on in an opportunistic basis. I did this just to keep me going from one day to the next, to tide me over from one month to the next. During this period of my life I lived mostly in Bombay as that was the place of trade. Bombay was also the place where one imported everything and I learnt my skills of international trade from there.

In October 1982, I was in Japan and I was struck by a wonderful product called portable generators which were being used in Japan and western countries as an outdoor accessory for running either ice-cream vans or little stalls on the roadside. I saw in this product an opportunity for power-starved India, a product which will come straight into Indian homes and light up a few bulbs and fans. Having grown up in a city which was starved for power almost all year round, and having seen other parts of India I thought that if I could bring this product into India, it would be a great success. I spoke to the Suzuki Motor Company, which was not known to India at that point of time. The Suzuki Maruti joint venture had not happened yet. With my knowledge of import policy, I imported India's first portable generator which became a huge rolling success. For three continuous years I became Suzuki's largest importer anywhere in the world. I opened up offices in Mumbai, Calcutta, Delhi and a representative distributor in Chennai. This business started taking me forward in my international trade and in my education in distribution. But this was also the time when India was deeply mired in the socialistic fabric. It was during this time that Mrs. Gandhi was in power, and our Soviet bear hug was in full play. Almost everything was being done in a uni-direction that was in the erstwhile Soviet Union's interests. Most of the exports, products, quality measures were directed towards that. In return we were getting a lot of armaments and other forms of aid from the Soviet Union.

But I was very clear that as we were living in times of great regulation and great restrictions, one had to, as an entrepreneur, be prepared to move on to the next thing if something struck you. And sure enough like lightening, I had a ban of import on my portable generators. One fine evening, there was no business to fall back upon. As per the regulations whatever generators were in the pipeline were the only ones that could have gone to the customs. One had to go out and look for something else. We were still small, but we were making some impression in the market place. In 1984, I saw a push button telephone in a trade fair in Taiwan. On seeing it, I thought to myself that this was a product which has never been tried in India. Until that time, we had about four or five hundred thousand rotary phones, a far cry from the 7 million phones that we connect every month now. The nation had less than half a million phones and they were all rotary phones. I thought to myself that this will be one product which will be of great value and great success. I brought the first push button telephone into India in 1984, and sure enough, it became a huge success. It was launched with great fanfare and most of the people who had either small PABXs in businesses or additional phones at home started picking up push button phones. That, incidentally, was also my connection with tele-communication and my romance with it started thereafter. Between 1984 and 1992, we started manufacturing cordless phones and answering machines and started importing and distributing fax machines. We became a company which was known for telecom products in the market place. We were making an impact, our company was becoming visible and our brand, at that time Beetel, was becoming dominant.

But just to give you a context, the company in 1992 was all of 25 crores in sales, a reasonable amount at the time but even in those days 25 crores was not that much. Something had to be done if we had to move on the charts and that is what we did in 1992, when India offered for the first time a chance to the private sector to move into telecom services. That was a big deal. At that time, Dr. Manmohan Singh was the Finance Minister and Shri Narasimha Rao was the Prime Minister. They had no choice but to start opening up some segments of the society and the industry in a dramatic manner and that, to my mind, was a big opportunity for all the entrepreneur communities in the country. Some companies, like

Zee Telefilms were born at that time. They started getting into broadcasting. Some private airlines, air-taxi services and then finally airlines like Jet Airways came through. IT companies like Infosys, Satyam, Wipro and TCS were getting a firm footing, and the telecom area was also developing. As a rank outsider, as a company which had 25 crores in sales, I moved in and put in my bid, in competition with 30 other bidders. Finally, after a very arduous difficult process, eight companies were selected. We got Delhi. This was tested in the High Court and Supreme Court. A lot of people were juggled around. I was in Bombay and was moved to Delhi.

In 1995, we launched India's first mobile phone, right here in Delhi. We were still a modest, small sized company. Not many people gave us a chance to succeed. I was continuously told that telecom services are deep pocket businesses and surely our pockets were not deep enough. But we had learnt the model of doing business with large foreign companies. It is an art I had learnt at that point of time and I can tell you, managing foreign companies, foreign relationships and joint ventures is nothing short of deft diplomacy. It requires a great deal of diplomacy to get the foreign companies to buy into a vision of a very small company for a very large dream that we had in India. But we were clearly successful and company after company tied-up with us. In fact, I had the pleasure of dealing with at least 20-25 top notch world companies, which includes British Telecom, Vivendi, Casio, Suzuki Motor Company, AT&T, Singtel and Vodafone. Axa was my partner in insurance and they manage over a trillion dollars in assets. Wal-Mart is the world's largest company in the world. El Rothschild, the traditional banking family is now our partners in the agricultural projects. So, one thing which we did very well was to tie up with many companies who, along with the resources, had the skill we needed. Today this is very easy. If I raise my hands, almost everybody wants to tie-up with Bharti. But back in 1992, when we had to sit across the table of large foreign companies, selling a company which did not exist in the telephone directories, it was a tough job.

I must share with you one example because all of you are going to be in situations where you are going to be coming up from weak positions to negotiate very difficult, bilateral, multilateral agreements. In 1992, the Government decided to open up services in telecom and only those companies could bid which had partners of large value. They had to have a certain kind of experience. They also had to have experience with GSM, a technology which was just coming into the world. This meant there were only a dozen companies and each one of them was between 15 to 50 billion dollars in size. We were 5 million dollars in size. We had to go and make an impression on one company in the world which would give us their name and some share equity of the company for making a bid. That was the qualifying point for us. There was no option whether to have it or not. It was the only way we could have moved forward. We, through the French Embassy, approached a company in France. After having failed in two or three other places, we finally landed in France. It was a difficult country for a young entrepreneur. Compagnie Generale des Eaux, some of you would have known the old French company, one of the largest companies in France. They also have a company called SFR which is the largest and widest company today. I went with my representation to him, and in about two hours, could make an impression on him. He turned back and told me to come on Monday and we would sign a MoU and move forward. I was very clear in my mind that almost every other Indian company was roaming around in the international market looking for tie-ups. I pressed him to sign the MoU that very evening. His view was that they were a large company and that the matter needed to go through their legal department. There was no way he could do it that day. He said it could be signed on Monday. But I requested him to loan me his secretary for half an hour and said that I would produce the documents for him. If he liked it, we would sign, if he did not, I would wait till Monday. He gladly loaned me his secretary for half an hour and I produced the documents which he approved and signed.

On Monday morning, a very large Indian firm called upon them through a very strong recommendation from a higher up in the French system. But he told them that they had already signed with another Indian company. The large industrial house asked who this other Indian company was. When he said Bharti, their response was Bharti who? This was when, the Vice Chairman of the company started to panic. He called me saying that he believed he may have made a mistake, and that he needed to revisit. He sent a small team of two people. They came here, landed in the French Embassy and checked about us. The French Embassy had no clue. They tried to look for us in the telephone directory but we did not exist there. They came and visited us and saw our small operations. By that evening they reported back to say that they had made a serious mistake and that they should pull the plug because we were too small a company. Our life depended on it because I could see how far this business could take us. Michel Villaneau, the Vice President of the company, and I spoke for hours on the phone and I told him that he had seen something in me when he signed the MoU with me. I told him to stay with his instincts, to stay on course. All I could promise him during this period of bidding was that we would not ask them to spend any money. Thankfully, he did stay with us, and the rest is history.

We created India's first mobile phone and now we have created India's largest telecom company which is growing at 80-90 per cent a year. I personally believe, this really is the power of a dream, because it not only charges you, it motivates, inspires and charges those around you. We were a bunch of small managers, who did not have experience behind us but we had the will to go and do something. And bit by bit, we kept on moving up the value chain and created a company which became fairly big. But five years back, we faced our biggest challenge when Reliance moved in and through BSNL the Government of India decided to move into mobile telephony. The Government opened up this sector for significant competition, which was probably rightfully their job. They had to create more competition. Many people asked when we will close down. The question was never if we would close down, because a lot of companies were closing down one after the other. On the contrary, we said this was a great opportunity for us. We knew this business; we had done it for many years. We believed that we would see lot of companies closing down and would get the opportunity to acquire them. And that is precisely what happened. We picked up six mobile companies in the country to create an all India base. That, in turn, gave us the necessary momentum to move forward. So, there was clearly an opportunity in the change the Government brought in its regulations. We fought those battles, and emerged on the other side. In fact I would say that Bharti is a real battle hardened machine which has come through the great turbulence of regulatory curbs and very intense competition.

I personally believe that in India now, there is an opportunity for every entrepreneur to realise their dreams because the government today has become an enabler rather than a hurdle in the process of meeting and fulfilling these aspirations. There was a time, when I had to wait for one and a half year to get a license to manufacture telephones in this country. This was way back in 1984-85 when you could not manufacture telephones without a government license. Now things are totally different, you can do anything that you want. You do not actually have to even file any papers, when you start production or start manufacturing. There are only a handful of services or areas of production which are in the critical lists where government approval is needed. Otherwise, the whole field is open to do anything. And there are several reasons why I believe that this entrepreneurial spirit will get further fuel and momentum.

India is today a country of consumers. Our population is 1.15 billion, growing at 62,000 people every day, and it is going to be continuously asking for more products and services. There are 630 million people in the working age. This will grow to 830 million by 2016. In 10 years, India will have 830 million people in the working age. There are 320 million people in the age group of 6-16 today. In 10 years time, they will be between the age group of 16-26. This truly makes India a power house of consumers. I believe if the Government does a great job of providing the right environment, India will grow continuously at 10 per cent year after year. And that will realise what has been mentioned in the Goldman Sachs report that we will be the third and then the second largest economy in the world. But even if there are hurdles of coalition politics, or some hiccups from time to time, even if we were to grow at 8 per cent a year, over the next 30 years it will still make us number three and then number two in the world. This is the power or the dividend of demographics that we are going to have in our country. Therefore, I believe, that whichever way we look at it, this nation is poised to become one of the largest economies. And today, as we know, the economy drives politics and it also drives diplomacy. It will therefore, be in India's advantage to move forward. When we go on the world stage, the power that we will yield will be enormous.

I had the privilege of co-chairing the World Economic Forum in Davos this year. I opened the Plenary Session with the German Chancellor Merkel and closed it with Tony Blair, the Prime Minister of UK. And I can tell you that in every session, including those two sessions in which China also participated, India was always present in their words and speeches and their minds. In fact, the theme of the Davos Economic Forum this year was "Shifting Power Equation", and this to my mind is nothing but the shifting of the power into the hands of countries like India. Clearly, countries like India and China were the theme, but I could sense very clearly that China was looked on as a threat by the global players. India was on the other hard seen in a positive way, as a power which will develop in the future. All the leaders were willing to cast their lot with India more strongly than any other country, including China. This to my mind is a remarkable shift. The western world on the other hand is ageing very fast. To my mind, some of the western countries, including the US, Germany and many others are today in a denial mode. They are not facing the facts. In 20 years, I guarantee you that every second hand that will work in those countries, either off-shore or on-shore, will be an Indian—plumbers, nurses, doctors and people who are in the profession which can be run off-shore like accountants and lawyers will be from here. So, as the world ages and as India's youth becomes even more productive, this transfer of power will start kicking in a big way. This offers enormous opportunities to all of us as Indians in the form of career opportunities, because we will be handling a much bigger part in the market place.

Are there challenges? Of course there are challenges. Out of 320 million people that are in the age group of 6-16, 250 to 260 million will never go to school. Some of them, if they go to school, will drop out in the first year itself. So, in 10 years, these young boys and girls of 16 and 26 will either be great human assets to serve not only India but also the world, or they will be potential criminals and terrorists. This is a challenge that India is facing today. Some of you must have noticed that in the budget which came out in February last year, there was a remarkable shift, to which industry has cried foul in some ways. There has been a remarkable shift in directing resources, both monetary and human, into rural areas, into development of skills and education. If we do not bring in this shift, in the next 10 or 12 years we will be sitting on a big potential disaster. This country cannot afford to do that because if we can convert this talent into productive assets, then nothing can stop us. And that, to my mind, is the biggest challenge that this country faces.

Not all of them need to go to school necessarily. They may need to go to primary school. We should start a process whereby there has got to be pride in being a plumber, an electrician, a technician, a driver or a chef. These professions are respected all over the world. But in India, we have traditionally said, my son must become a doctor or he must be an IFS or IAS officer. These are noble professions and important professions. But one must create only as much capacity as one can absorb. We cannot have 320 million diplomats. Neither can we have 320 million doctors. The masses have to learn a lot of vocational skills which will be beneficial for society not only in India but overseas as well. Therefore, I think, all of the industry chambers such as FICCI and CII have to work along with the Government towards providing vocational skills to the masses.

My biggest objection is the allocation of resources. An education cess will have to be created, but along with that, education in the rural areas must be visible. This is where a public-private partnership, a buzz word which has started over the last few years, is essential. Three days back I was at the Delhi International Airport. I spent half a day looking at the plans just out of the sheer interest because I was bidding for the Delhi Project. I did not win it, GMR has won it. They wanted my feedback on what they were planning and I can tell you what I can see. In four to five years time, India will have one of the finest airports anywhere in the world. It is fantastic. There is a plan for four runways which would cater to the 100 million passengers. It will be one of the rarest of the rarest airports in the world. It will happen only because the private sector has got involved. The airport which we have today belongs to the 1930-1940s. Even if the government had the will and the money, we would have probably made the next airport as something out of the 1960s. Many of you must have seen some of the new airports which have come up such as in Jaipur and Ahmedabad. These are in the 1960s mould and have been made just two or three years back. A public-private partnership is absolutely essential in several areas and that is where my fight with the government will remain, to make the process of spending accountable. Our present Prime Minister himself fully recognises the benefits of this approach and one will see more and more public-private partnership developing as one goes along.

I will touch upon a few more reasons why I believe that the dream for India that I have is very strong. India has huge tracts of arable land. In fact, India has the largest amount of irrigated land anywhere in the world. It has the second largest amount of valuable land anywhere in the world. Yet, it participates in less than 1 per cent of the global food trade. India produces 145 million tonnes of fruits and vegetables, of which about 40-45 million never reaches anywhere, it rots. There is a great deal of opportunity that lies here. Equally, there are also big challenges that are to be faced. I believe that we can turn our rural hinterland into food factories and start making mini Hollands out of our rural areas. I would personally believe that those 250-260 million people, that may become potentially a danger for the country, will all be employed and will fully get into the mainstream of the Indian economy. That to my mind will deliver the biggest inclusive growth possible in this country. For a job like this, all we need is a shovel and a spade and a will to work on the farmland. The good news is that this government is aware of this potential. We have plentiful sunshine, we have over 600 million people in the rural area willing and able to work and there is a whole world including the domestic market waiting for India to start pumping in fresh and processed food. A large amount of attention needs to be given to this area. I am very hopeful, but before that happens, a large amount of logistics has to be put into place. Our country does not have cold chambers, cold trucks, cold storage facilities, coolers, in the farmland and perishable centres at the airports. More importantly, very little of what is produced is processed. There is a great deal of opportunity here. The government is encouraging both domestic and foreign players to come and participate in this.

The other point I would like to stress upon is our great culture—our culture of peace. We do not aspire to be a threat to the world in any form. And this message always needs to be carried by both our own diplomats and the foreign diplomats back to their respective places. A strong India, guarantees a lot of things that are required in the world today. And that is why I say that when India wants nuclear energy for its needs, it should be given gladly. The good news is that some breakthroughs have been made. But foreign powers need to be more liberal in their views towards India. India has established its credentials in being a nation which will follow nothing but the peaceful process in anything that it does. We will need this energy. If we do not get this nuclear energy, we will start burning coal in India. We have got tremendous deposits of coal. We will burn them, we have no choice. We have to move this nation forward. Every western country has done that in the past. Today, we are being asked to do carbon capturing and sequestration. We would gladly do it, because India has and will never adopt the policy of an eye for an eye. We are willing to skip the burning of the dirty coal and the creation of emissions in the sky but we need the right technology. We need the right support. This can only happen through the nuclear route. Either this, or we need tens of billions of dollars to convert our emissions from the coal back into the ground through carbon capturing and sequestration. I think the latter option is a little far-fetched because the world may not be able to give us 100-200 billion dollars immediately for it.

Therefore, the message is clear: support India in its nuclear dreams. One-sixth of the world lives here. It deserves your attention. We will deliver the promise that India has always upheld—of peace, support, and of balancing the negative forces around the globe. We are blessed that we are at a time in India, when a lot of things are moving in the right direction. Ten, fifteen years back if I was invited to speak, I would have not been able to say this with much confidence. But truly, we are blessed to be living in these times. These times will always be remembered by our children and grand children as a time of profound change and transformation. To my mind, these next 10-20 years will determine how fast India will achieve the Goldman Sachs prediction of being the second largest economy in the world.

"India was the mother of our race and Sanskrit the mother of Europe's languages. She was the mother of our philosophy, mother through the Arabs, of much of our mathematics, mother through Buddha, of the ideals embodied in Christianity, mother through village communities of self-government and democracy. Mother India is in many ways the mother of us all."

— Will Durant

SHEILA DIKSHIT

Sheila Dikshit is the Chief Minister of National Capital Territory of Delhi since 1998. She was Member of Parliament from 1984 to 1989, and has been Minister of State for Parliamentary Affairs and Minister of State in the Prime Minister's Office. She was also the Chairperson of the Implementation Committee for Commemoration of Forty Years of India's Independence and the Jawaharlal Nehru Centenary. She is also the Secretary of the Indira Gandhi Memorial Trust. Her government has focused on reforms in various sectors, and worked for involvement of people in decision-making by introducing the concept of *Bhagidari* (partnership) with Resident Welfare Associations. Ms. Dikshit has been especially interested in the promotion of handicrafts, rural artisans, and folk theatre. She has also been an active champion of secularism and democracy.

10 *Bhagidari* for Building a Better India

Sheila Dikshit

We are now dreaming a new dream. This century, we are dreaming something very different from what we dreamt or what we thought of dreaming when we were young. I think we had very limited dreams then. All that we could dream of was having a good home and a comfortable job. Job opportunities were what the government could offer, which were IFS, IAS, IPS, and so on. The corporate sector was mostly tea gardens, or maybe ITC or Tata or one or two other such companies. Women rarely ever dreamt of anything more than perhaps becoming a teacher or a nurse or sometimes a doctor.

One of my dreams was to become a member of the Foreign Service or the IAS. However, I took an easy way out and I married an IAS officer, enjoying it all without the responsibility. Then I took the plunge into politics. But I had never dreamt of politics. I had dreamt of Nehru and Mahatma Gandhi and other such national figures. I thought they were the most outstanding human beings of their era and perhaps the century. This was all as far as politics and I went. But lo and behold, or call it the quirks of nature or destiny, I found myself in politics, something that I never really admired. However, I am here now, without a choice.

People like you and me have the great fortune of being able to really transform a lot of dreams into reality. India is booming economically but is this boom equitable? It is doing extremely well in the manufacturing sector but is there food security? Are people getting enough to eat or is it the case that some people are getting too much and some are getting too little? Is the civil service able to deliver and meet the aspirations of people? All these are daily irritants which arise in everybody's minds and we wonder what we are supposed to do about them. It is irritating to have prices constantly rising, but what we forget is that our pay packages have also gone up.

I remember that when my husband joined the service, we had a princely income of Rs. 390 per month and I think we lived exactly the way we live today, with two servants and a car. So money has changed its very parameters and definition. I recall that at that time our generation used to think that if we had just Rs. 100 more, we could really be living very lavishly. Today, I find people earning in thousands, in fact, in hundreds of thousands. I was reading the other day that the earning mark is almost a crore a year for young people who are coming out of their training and management institutes! This is one dream that has been realised. India now has the kind of incomes that we could not even have dreamt of four, three or even two decades ago. But has more money brought us greater happiness or greater satisfaction? Has it brought a bigger smile on our face? I find that many millionaires look grumpier than a poor man.

I would like to share with you what I read in a book some months ago. The book, by a psychologist, said that as a baby you smile about 300 times a day and as you grow up you smile barely 30 times in a day. Does it cost anybody to smile? I wonder why we lose our smile. Little things irritate us. Lots of money irritates us. If we have lakhs, we worry about turning lakhs into crores. If crores, then into 100 crore. I wonder, though, if Ratan Tata can eat more than you or I can, or the man who works for you and me.

It makes us very proud to think that India has more millionaires than Japan. But is there equitable distribution of wealth? What about quality of life? Is nutrition better? There are many more cars than there were earlier but has everybody got a car? We have a metro, but has it stopped the use of cars? Is our culture changing or is it the culture of rudeness which makes us impatient with others, make us want to push our way through? Is education more in-depth or is education flipping through the television set and getting information which we forget the very next minute because there is so much of it coming at us? Do we analyse this information, rather, do we have the time to analyse this information? What is it that we are imbibing? Why cannot we eradicate corruption? Are we, after a point, becoming a catalyst for change and is it change that we want to see? I think these are issues which we really ought to look at.

Above all, I think we need to concentrate on equitable distribution. Equitable distribution can only be achieved if the right kind of information is made available to the right kind of target groups. I know many people who go to ration shops and are told by the ration shop keeper, "I am so sorry, *aap chale jao* (Please go), ration came yesterday, it has already finished." It has not finished. What he did overnight was sell it to a mill-owner who took that ration at a cheaper rate and will sell it at a much more expensive rate. Why cannot we have vigilance squads, officers or government administrators who are more sensitive towards all these ideas? Bad governance is becoming an impediment to our growth and democratic functioning.

The Right to Information Act has made our country one of the few in the world which gives their people this right. But people do not know how to utilise it. And, I must say, with all due respect to the officers that there are those who always have smart answers to why you cannot get this information, why this is so and why that is not so. If a nation does not have a sensitive leadership or a sensitive administrative system, I doubt it can have a sensitive society. If you really want a city of dreams, with dams, enough power, roads, buses, schools, buildings, water supply and clean streets and more, how do we achieve it?

It is not enough just to be able to dream. We need accountability. About 30 years ago I was associated with a garment exporting association. India was at that time just starting the garment export industry. We were told all the time to emulate Korea, Thailand, Singapore, etc. So we sent a study team and prepared a report for the Ministry of Commerce. We also sent some people to see how the forms could be made easier from those used by the Controller of Imports and Exports. This went on for three or four months. At the end of it all, both the ministries agreed to simplify the forms. To my utter shock, where we used to fill in 70 forms, this wonderful committee came out with 25! That was their simplification. After that I am petrified every time somebody says, lets simplify things because I know simplification will mean an addition to what you have to already do.

Why are the various procedures so complex? It is because we do not trust each other. Those who sit on this side of the office desk do not trust the citizen. The citizen does not trust the man behind the desk because he feels he has become an officer and therefore his only objective in life is to try and make a fast buck. Therefore, it starts with mistrust. Now these are the areas which are of great concerns to our civilisation, our way of thinking, and the India of our dreams.

We have tried some experiments with governance in Delhi. One of them is the *Bhagidari* Movement—governance through partnership. It is aimed at strengthening democracy and involving the citizens in education, health, garden maintenance, etc. It also ensures that they are a continuous part of the government and not just a vote giver or a vote catcher. The other experiment that we have tried is *Streeshakti*. It involves women's empowerment through health and self-help groups. We find that many women want access to some training which can enable them to earn Rs. 1,000 to 3,000 a month from home. Health, I am afraid, is not as good as it ought to be. We are trying hard through *Bhagidari* and *Streeshakti* to ensure that women who are anaemic or children who are anaemic do not remain so.

Unfortunately, along with the advantages of democracy, there are also disadvantages. It empowers individuals but it is also a very slow process. People compare us to China, which I do not think is fair. We have to compare ourselves with ourselves. We have a culture and a history. We have a long tradition of democratic governance which is what I think we need to strengthen within ourselves and make a model for the whole world to follow.

India is wonderful and I am very proud to be an Indian. I think nowhere else in the world is there the kind of variety and vibrancy of life that we have here. The manner in which we merge into each other's communities and religious groups, like colours merging into one another, I think, is the envy of the world. We celebrate Id, Diwali, Christmas, New Year followed by the national holiday, our Republic Day. We have the tradition of a sister tying a thread around her brother's wrist—a symbolic gesture, which I think no other civilisation has. These are the good things of our lives. Development in the economic sense of the word is not, I would say, a prerequisite for happiness. You will probably find much more happiness, many more smiles in the villages of India, which are deprived of all the comforts that you and I in the city have. Think about this as you dream of a better India.

"The future beckons to us. Whither do we go and what shall be our endeavour? To bring freedom and opportunity to the common man, to the peasants and workers of India; to build up a prosperous, democratic, and progressive nation; and to create social, economic, and political institutions which will ensure justice and fullness of life to every man and woman."

— Jawaharlal Nehru

SAM PITRODA

Sam Pitroda, born in Orissa, is an inventor, entrepreneur and policy maker. Currently, Chairman of India's National Knowledge Commission, he is widely considered to have been responsible for India's telecom revolution. He is also the Chairman and CEO of World-Tel Limited, an International Telecommunication Union (ITU) initiative. He holds many key technology patents, has been involved in several startups, and lectures extensively around the world on management, governance and the implications of communications and information technology. Dr. Pitroda is the founder and CEO of C-SAM Inc., which has developed a suite of patented mobile transaction technology called OneWallet. He has served as an advisor to the United Nations. In 1992, his biography, "Sam Pitroda: A Biography" was published, and became a bestseller on The Economic Times list for five weeks. He has lived mainly in Chicago, Illinois since 1964.

11 Knowledge for a More Just, Equitable and Inclusive Society

SAM PITRODA

Knowledge for a more just, equitable and inclusive society indeed is a very complex subject and not easy to grasp, understand and find answers for. I will like to share with you some of my views on how I see this challenge.

The world we live in today respects material prosperity because success apparently is connected with lots of material prosperity. Therefore, a model of prosperity that we have created in our mind is that of migration—moving from rural areas to urban areas or to foreign shores to earn money and thus attaining the respect that we aspire for. The other path is that we remain in the villages, do a little bit of service, be happy with what we are doing and not struggle to be part of the global picture. But somehow this is not a very desirable thing to do.

When we think of knowledge, we have to think about it at two extremes: knowledge for what, and knowledge for whom. Today at the Knowledge Commission we are unfortunately looking at knowledge perhaps from the view point of the top of the pyramid, which perhaps does not constitute more than 30-40 per cent of our population.

We know that in our country there are a great deal of disparities, discriminations and diversities. We have very rich as well as very poor people, urbanised population along with utterly rural population, highly educated people but also 400 million illiterates. It is these disparities that are mounting in our country and for which we are all searching for solutions. Sometimes I feel that we are not doing enough to counter these issues but at least it is the topic of discussion at all the social forums. Get together four good friends and the immediate topic of discussion will be poverty, disparity, rural development and the desire to do something for these issues.

At the National Knowledge Commission, set up by the Prime Minister two years ago, there are seven of us focused on looking at knowledge institutions and infrastructure needed for the twenty-first century. We have been told time and again that the country has severe skill shortages. If we are to sustain our nine per cent growth rate, we will need the right kind of people with adequate skills and good network infrastructure to further fuel our economy. On the other side of the coin is the fact that the economy is not necessarily the whole picture, and I am beginning to realise more and more that ecology is also equally important. But not many people pay attention to this fact. So, let us first go through the Knowledge Commission and then try to address the other issues and hopefully try to link them with the basic question of how do we use knowledge for bringing about a more just, equitable and inclusive society.

We seven people at the Knowledge Commission meet once in every two to three months for a couple of days—we meet regularly on the 14th and 15th—and focus on five key areas of knowledge. First being access. Access is the most critical part of creating an inclusive society. It includes languages, literacy, translations, libraries, networks, portals, reservations and affirmative action programmes. These eight areas essentially focus on improving access to knowledge. If you cannot read or write, it is difficult in this age to access a large amount of knowledge. However, this does not mean that you are not knowledgeable. But in the technological world of today, unless we have access we will not be able to build upon knowledge not just for the few but for the large number of people.

The second area relates to education—primary education, secondary education, distance learning, vocational education and higher education. The third area focuses on creation of knowledge—Who creates knowledge? How is knowledge created? And essentially focussing on science and technology, patents, trademarks, copy rights, innovations, entrepreneurship, etc. The fourth area is application of knowledge which mainly deals with agriculture, health and small and medium-scale industries. And finally, the role of knowledge in the field of governance which in today's world is related to e-governance and providing access to government through modern technologies and tools to public services.

In totality we have around 30 to 40 topics that we look at and we have constituted working groups consisting of prominent experts on each of the major topics, for we are not qualified enough to understand each and every issue and give advice on everything. For instance there is the question of teachers' education.

How do we get more of our kids to learn maths and science? How do we get more PhDs out of Indian systems? These are very complex but very fundamental issues. So we have working groups on such issues and the members go out and meet the experts and also talk to the public and have discussions and come back to us with a white paper. We then discuss it and debate the same and then summarise it into normally three pages and submit the same to the Prime Minister. Yes, we do not write long reports, because there are hundreds of other long reports pending with the government on all of these subjects and we do not want to wait for years to come out with long reports. So far we have submitted 12-13 reports to the government like language, translations, libraries, networks, portals, higher education, vocational education, e-governance, and innovation amongst others.

Presently we are working on five other areas like legal education, medical education, management education, intellectual property and health and IT. The report on these with our recommendations are under progress and we would be submitting the same to the Prime Minister in the next fortnight. In addition, the Commission is also working on a series of 8 to 10 other relevant areas. In all of these, the key really is to address three fundamental issues, which I personally believe are very critical for the country at this stage to achieve a more just, equitable and inclusive society.

The first is the issue of disparity which relates directly to the inclusive society; the second being demography. Everyone knows that we are a nation of 1.1 billion out of which 555 million are below the age group of 25 years. What do we do with this massive number of young people? What kind of a world do we want to create for them? How do we create jobs for them? What do we train them in? If this young population is going to be the workforce for the world as well as for our country in the future, what kind of tools and techniques do they need to acquire growing up? And the final area of concern is development. Lots of things are happening in the country today. We are building roads but not fast enough; we are building schools but not fast enough. So everything in our developmental activities has to be expedited. We need to improve our efficiency, our productivity, and reduce the costs. In our society of a billion people, unless we have the right cost-structure, it is really difficult to achieve scale.

I spent 42 years in the telecom industry. When I started off in 1965, the cost per line of a telephone connection from instrument to wire to switching to fibre to network was $1000 a line and it remained at $1000 per line until almost 1990. For the same cost you had so many features—call forwarding, various ring tones, etc, until the wireless technology came in. Even the wireless telephony was very expensive in the beginning. It was meant for the urban elite. But soon the costs began to tumble from $1000 to $200 a line to $100 and now it is just $50 a line. We are now adding 10 million lines a month. It is all about affordability. Ten to fifteen years back when I was working in Africa, I went to Malawi to work on telecom infrastructure. I met with all the telecom ministers of the COMESA countries, and even then the cost was very high and no one would have imagined that Africa would have 150 million telephone lines within the next 10 years.

So, whenever we talk of inclusiveness or access, cost and affordability become the key factors. Even in knowledge, if the cost of delivering the right kind of educational services is not proper and low, the access would be limited and it will remain for the people at the top of the pyramid.

With this background on the Knowledge Commission, I would make an attempt to compare the two models of development that we have witnessed during the Freedom struggle. One was the Gandhian model of development which talked about focussing on villages and self-reliance and reaching out to people with a message of friendship and trust. The Gandhian model of development stressed on rural development as the key to our development, where we reach out to the people, learn from them, respect their viewpoints and not impose our model of development on them. And Gandhi decided to "walk his talk" and he began to reach out to them and understand them as they were.

The second model was the one which Nehru focussed on, rightfully so for a country that was just getting out of colonisation. We needed steel plants, industries and talent to build bridges and dams, so the Nehru model focussed on IITs, IIMs, steel projects, and so on. Thus becoming the symbol of our development and in the process, after Gandhi died, we essentially lost the focus on the rural model of development. As a result, what we have seen now is the clear focus on economic prosperity. When you watch television, you see continuous bombarding of messages related to economic prosperity and we accepted that this is what progress is all about. As a result, all our knowledge is diverted to fuel economic prosperity as opposed to improving the quality of life.

We recognise that an agricultural economy needs land, a manufacturing economy needs machines and a knowledge economy needs minds. If we can take the real knowledge to the poorest of the poor or those at the bottom of the pyramid, we can really transform their lives. In my own life, the biggest factor to transform myself and my family has been education. I was born in a tribal area in Orissa where there was no school, so I left for Gujarat to study and that in turn empowered me to do many things. However, when we look at knowledge for an inclusive society, we essentially look at people who really do not need land to prosper. Nor do they need machines to prosper. I realise that we do not have answers on connecting the pyramid that we have in the Knowledge Commission, namely, access, concepts, creation, application and services to the bottom of the society or the pyramid.

What do all of these mean to the people of the villages? Does it matter to them to get a Ph.D. in maths? On the one hand, if we provide them access we are also providing them the migration path to development. On the other hand is the entire informal sector. What do we do for this informal sector? Do we give them formal education? Do we impose on them our rules which are meant for the formal structures in the system? Or do we accept the need for a new model of development where people do not need certificates or degrees, but they need skills to perform their jobs and do them properly.

Many experiments are being conducted in India and some of them have not been able to scale. One of my friends is running a college for doctors where you do not have certificate or exams. But you get trained, you make your livelihood, you move on and you are happy. Is this inclusive? Is this the model we should multiply? I am not very clear about it. But what I am clear is that we need to pay much more attention to the bottom of the pyramid than we ever did in the past. And I am hopeful of this happening mainly because of good communication facilities. I remember when I started working in a telecom company here in the early 1980s, the general message was that the telecom is for the rich and the urban elites. People in the rural areas do not need telecom. But we learnt from the STD-PCO experiment that telecom empowers the people and transforms their lives. It has helped many to reach out. The other side of the equation is that telecom also brings about openness, accessibility, connectivity, networking, democratisation, and decentralisation. The Gandhian philosophy also preaches openness, accessibility, connectivity, networking, etc. All these messages ultimately are geared towards creating a self-sustaining community.

When we look at knowledge, we should look at knowledge in different segments—knowledge for economy, for governance, for the urban and the middle class, knowledge for a large number of people at the bottom of the pyramid, so that they are able to rise without barriers—social or economical.

As a society, we need to provide enough flexibility to our children so that they can attain the best education possible. These are some of the issues we are trying to understand. In the Eleventh Five Year Plan, we are increasing our budget for education to $60 billion which is close to six per cent of the GDP, a four-time increase compared to the Tenth Plan. Does this mean inclusiveness? It surely does mean commitment towards better education, expansion of education and education for a larger number of people. There are lots and lots of challenges when it comes to knowledge and we really do not understand why it is so. There are issues on intellectual property, globalisation, and teachers training. The question I have been trying to look at was how our universities would look like in 2050. Today, we automatically assume that we get a graduate degree in four years. I do not know who came up with this idea. But we all accepted it. When we think about education, we automatically think about teachers, textbooks, exams, grades and certificates. Many of these things do not make sense anymore as the learning paradigm has changed.

I think, many of the structures we created in the past need to be broken and a whole new model of learning has to be evolved. Perhaps we do not even need to go to colleges if we are knowledgeable enough. But this requires bold initiatives and experimentation on the part of the government and institutions. We are not willing to do that. Today when we are telling somebody that we are building a university, the first thing that comes to our mind is 100 acres of land. Is that the model university that we want to build? I think the future university structure is going to be very different. Today with the kind of knowledge we have in the form of the Internet, wireless, search engines, we can do anything without learning through formal education. I have a six-year-old niece in America. She told me that she did a whitepaper on the first female doctor of America. I thought she could not even read at six. So I started probing her. She said all the doctors whom she met were males. So she tried to find out if there are any female doctors. She started searching on the Internet and found the name of the first female doctor and studied about her. Then she did a whitepaper on that female doctor! But if you put that six-year-old in a school, the teacher would say that "I will organise you, I will discipline you, there will be exams and I will decide whether you are qualified or not."

I think this is something we should keep in mind when we look at the issues of, equitability and inclusiveness. These ideas have different meanings today. If we provide access, it would probably mean inclusiveness. With the technology of today, if you want to do something, you can get it done. You do not need government subsidies or support, but you need guts. This is where the technological interventions have been critical. I can go on and on. But I will conclude by saying that we do not have the answers on knowledge for a more just, equitable and inclusive society. All we know is that we need it. Old models have not delivered it and new models need to be explored. What will work or what will not work, only time will tell us. But these are very exciting times to experiment. I am a firm believer in the power of communication technology. I think communication technology will change India in this knowledge era. We had the communication revolution and now we keep talking about communication as the key driver for development. I think we will have another revolution. Maybe it will take 20 years when we will say "yes, knowledge is indeed accessible to everybody and has empowered everybody to create their own destinies in this great country."

"India 2015 will be a nation of capable and empowered men and women, well-fed and gainfully employed, modern and rational, and actively engaged with the world. That is my dream for India."

— Manmohan Singh

LALU PRASAD

Lalu Prasad is currently the Minister of Railways in the ruling United Progressive Alliance (UPA) government and the President of the Rashtriya Janta Dal. Earlier, he served as the Chief Minister of Bihar from 1990-1997. He is known for his charismatic leadership and mass appeal. He was a student leader and was inspired by the renowned freedom fighter and popular leader Jai Prakash Narayan. He was elected as a Member of Parliament at the age of 29, becoming one of the youngest members of the Parliament. He has made significant contributions in improving the functioning and efficiency of the Indian Railways, turning it into a profit making enterprise. This has earned him laurels world wide. Well-known schools of management including Harvard and Wharton have been organising lectures and interactions with Lalu Prasad for their students and faculty.

12 Historic Turn-around of the Indian Railways

LALU PRASAD

Indian Railways is indeed the lifeline of India. Progress of a country is not possible until we touch the basic aspects in the field of infrastructure. Railways being one of these aspects, it cannot be ignored. Our network runs about 11,000 trains daily and the coverage is about 63,000 kilometres long.

Today, there is an increased interest in the Indian Railways. What has happened suddenly that the Indian Railways has been able to earn a surplus of rupees 20,000 crore? There are the same trains, same rails, same staff, same locomotives, same compartments, same stations etc., but what miracle has happened during the last few years that it has become profitable. Just before the advent of this government, Indian Railways was on the brink of virtual bankruptcy. A Committee was constituted under the chairmanship of the renowned economist Shri Rakesh Mohan. Raghuramanji was also associated with it. The committee in its findings, made a forecast about the Indian Railways for the coming 25 years. It found that Indian Railways is mired in deep trouble and there is no ray of hope for recovery. One of the recommendations of the committee was that fare should be increased by 30 per cent in every budget. Emphasis should be given on privatisation; manpower should be reduced, etc. Anywhere in the world, if a government organisation starts running into losses, it is suggested that it should be handed over to the private sector. We have proved this myth wrong.

Soon after the UPA government was formed, we took the restructuring of Indian Railways as a challenge. Prime Minister Manmohan Singh announced from the ramparts of Lal Quila that if India has to move ahead, it should focus on building infrastructure. The railways cannot be ignored. We have to make Indian Railways the number one organisation in the world which at present is at number three. When I took charge, I reviewed the situation. I was amazed to note how a mammoth organisation like the railways can run into losses. It has a vast network and it is world's largest employer with 14 lakh employees. If a businessman purchases and runs a bus, he purchases another bus the very next year from the earnings of the first bus, and he purchases third bus next year and so on. Then why is Indian Railways running into losses?

There was apprehension among all the officers and staff members that trimming of the railways was inevitable. Some posts had already been abolished. There was a long debate. I studied the recommendations of the Dr. Rakesh Mohan Committee.

My focus was on the common man because Indian Railways has some social obligations also. I felt that if we went on increasing the fare without giving attention to business and if there was inefficiency and rampant corruption, it would be impossible for the Indian Railways to progress. After taking charge, I had a meeting with members of the Board and other officers. I categorically told them that Indian Railways would not be privatised. I am dead against reckless privatisation. But private participation will be invited in certain areas such as container services, building of world class stations and new dedicated lines. There are other areas also which I will take up later.

The proposal for increasing fare was put before me. I did not agree to increasing fare because I felt Indian Railways is a Jersey cow. The more you serve it, the more it may be milked. If you do not milk it, it can catch the disease of inflammation of the udder. Hence, I issued instructions for reducing fare. I reduced fare not only in the air conditioned class but in all classes. Suburban trains which run in Kolkata and Mumbai were running into losses, and yet we reduced the fare. We also took the traders into confidence. We realised that if we go on increasing taxes it may not be in the interest of the railways. Our business would be transferred to the road transporters. Even today, 60 per cent goods are being carried by road transporters. We had to take into confidence the traders and some rebates were also to be offered. We forwarded this message to them with honesty and integrity. We went to the field for inspection and caught the malpractices in loading goods in Kolkata and Muri near Ranchi. Iron ore, coal and other goods were being overloaded for which they were being charged less. I got these goods weighed and consequently punished the erring officials. But Indian Railways has many good and dedicated persons also. Many of them are honest who work like armed forces in the battle field. For example, there is the gang man. Most of his work is manual. He uses minimum machines. Gang men, key men, assistant drivers and drivers work hard and they are punctual too. Their work is full of hazards. Indian railways today run 11 thousand trains for 24 hours. We have reduced the fare keeping in view the common man, the last man in the row. We started preparing the budget keeping in view the common man. Right officers were placed at right places. We tried to build a family and decentralised power at the headquarters. Not only that, we transferred power to the zonal managers who could now spend hundred of crores on civil works. Now they are not required to come to the Railway Board for small things.

As far as turn around is concerned, we effected maximum utilisation of our assets and properties. We are running big trains with 24 compartments and we are expanding the network of the railways. Earlier, loading and unloading of goods train took seven days which we reduced to five. We have a strict monitoring system. Earlier, there was no vision regarding how many electric locomotives, diesel locomotives, compartments, wheels will be required in the coming 25 years. There was no vision regarding the condition and direction of the Indian railways. There was only one option and that was to increase fare. Without disturbing the system, we have achieved what we call in Bhojpuri: *bina harre fitkiri ke maal chokha* (chokha is a kind of vegetable, prepared from potato and tomato mixed with salt, garlic, chilly and some mustard oil).

I have visited some European countries. It was a very good experience. These countries are beautiful and pollution-free. I have visited five countries in a span of 15 days. When I was in Vienna, Austrian trains used to pass near the hotel. We used to see through the window. I saw only two or three passengers getting in and getting out of the train. Everything is very expensive there. Engines are like jet planes. Engines are well computerised. I visited France also. I was very much impressed to see neat and clean stations. There is no pollution; noise of the trains must not enter the villages, otherwise cases would be filed. Here in India, you are free to make noise. As a matter of fact we have now got used to this form of pollution. There is less traffic in foreign countries. Trains are running at losses in spite of subsidy. Our railway is the cheapest in the world. We have brought the operating cost down to 78 per cent.

I would like to point out that there are so many unmanned railway gates in India. Soon we are going to deploy staff there. There are frequent cases of accidents on these unmanned gates. Before I took charge there were so many accidents. However, now the situation has improved a lot. There are a few cases of accidents due to human error which is a different matter altogether. In foreign countries, most of the functions are machine operated and these machines are very expensive. In India, personnel like gang men and key men do their job manually. They inspect one kilometre of line daily with their hammers and other heavy equipments.

We have to make the Indian Railway number one in the world. We are trying hard to achieve this goal. In order to achieve this objective, we are working like one unit, a cohesive force working in a single direction. We run goods trains which are as long as one kilometre. We are also having research done on how to reduce fuel consumption. Some results have already come. Most of the energy of our locomotives is consumed in pulling heavy goods bogies. We are therefore, thinking of making aluminum goods bogies so that we could load maximum goods on them.

Existing rail lines have become saturated. Timely departures and arrivals should be ensured for our goods train. If these trains reach late, there is every possibility of the raw contents getting perished causing huge losses. Demand for new trains is increasing daily. It is simply because train journey is affordable, safe and it runs on time. Now we propose to put our goods trains, which are indeed earning horses of Indians Railways, in loop lines. We are, therefore, going to lay a third line in the country and that is Dedicated Freight Corridor.

In the first stage, we are doing it from Ludhiana in Punjab to Howrah in West Bengal covering all major ports including Haldia. The foundation stone was laid by the honourable Prime Minister in Ludhiana. We are also going to make the Western Corridor. We are in final stages. In this work we are being assisted by Japan. We will also take the help of private participation and invite global tenders. In the first phase, 30,000 crores of rupees will be incurred on this project and we hope to complete this in the next six years. The second phase of the Dedicated Freight Corridor will cover Guwahati, Barauni and Kharagpur. We are going to lay double lines. Dedicated Freight Corridor will facilitate free movement of goods trains and as a result the existing rails will be vacant. If there is vacancy on the existing rails, we will be able to introduce and insert new passenger as well as express trains on them.

People frequently ask me as to what magic I have done with the Indian Railways. I tell them you have seen only the magic, witchcraft is in the offing. People ask what will happen to the Indian Railways when you will not be on the scene. We have made such binding rules and regulations that whosoever steps into my shoes, will have to carry the process forward. Otherwise they will be a target of criticism. History of India will not forgive them.

Indian Railways is indeed a golden bird. People have ruined it. If the Prime Minister of the nation speaks about the turn around of the Indian Railways then he speaks it with firm belief. Children of our country and the world, whether they are from Boston, MIT, and Harvard or from Ahmedabad, know that World Bank used to generally keep away from the Indian Railways. Credibility of the Indian Railways has now grown internationally. American newspapers and other newspapers worldwide published my budget speech.

As a result, we were able to get money at lower interest rates even cheaper than Reliance. Investors now firmly believe that if we invest money in India, we will get good returns. Earlier, this sense of credibility was lacking, and nobody was ready to invest.

We have taken our employees into confidence and awarded a bonus of 65 days to them. Wherever I go, I associate myself with the lower level people, fourth grade people. As a brother, I arrange clothes, shoes, raincoats and hats for them. As a result, they feel that this minister is theirs and one amongst them. All the members of the Railway family work hard, standing shoulder to shoulder, to make Indian Railways the number one railway organisation in the world.

We are working towards building world class stations. A consultant for Delhi has been appointed and we are soon going to appoint a consultant for Patna also. Such stations will be built in Mumbai, Chennai, Nagpur, Rampur, Amritsar and other big cities of India. These stations will have hotels, motels etc. In European countries, I saw underground markets on stations where people can shop also. First, we will make such stations in Delhi to be followed in other big cities.

One most important issue is hygienic food and hygienic stations. Toilet system is very faulty. We have got research done on this issue also. We are going to introduce the system that is used in aeroplanes. This very system exists in European countries also. This will be our biggest achievement. Children standing on platform should at least get clean oxygen. The toilet system is being changed to suit our needs. It should be dry and we are working towards this.

India is primarily a land of farmers. Our economy is based on agriculture and animal husbandry. There are seven thousand stations in India including junctions and this number can increase also. Our farmers purchase costly fertilisers, spend a lot on irrigation, electricity etc and face natural calamities. But there is no market for their products. There is no market for vegetables, pulses, rice and other perishable goods. Suppose, there is bumper production of tomatoes, the crop perishes for want of ready market. Shoes and sandals which we wear on our feet are kept in air conditioned shops in cities like Delhi but the perishable fruits and vegetables etc lay on the footpath. There are seven thousand stations and anyone can participate in this endeavour because we are going to invite global tenders.

Vegetables are costly in Delhi. You simply cannot consume the vegetables which are grown by the side of the Yamuna. These vegetables are coloured before coming to the market. A quarter kilogram vegetable costs Rs. 12 in Delhi but in Patna you pay Rs. 1 for the same. Gulf countries need onions in good quantity. Our onion is of very good quality. When I was in London, I went there with all the spices but did not carry with me the vegetables. I had to buy potatoes and onions. For the first time in my life I saw such onions. Indian onions have a different taste. But there is no marketing in India. That is why we are going to open agricultural outlets at stations.

Indian Railways has a huge surplus land. We will build air conditioned markets on these lands. A farmer can sell his produce there. We will provide container services wherein there will be refrigeration for perishable goods. It will also create jobs for our boys and girls. We will provide land on lease. Our services will help the farmers get right price for their produce and their income will increase. Otherwise goods will perish when there are no consumers in the market. If income of the farmers increases, income of the labourers will increase. If a house is built labourers will get jobs. Artisans will get jobs. By providing agricultural outlets, we will be able not only to distribute perishable goods but we will export also. We are making ports also and by increasing the access of the farmers to the market, we wish to enrich the farmers and thereby boost our economy.

We are now running fully air-conditioned "Garib Raths." Earlier, if a poor fellow was found to be standing in front of the air-conditioned compartments; policemen used to beat him asking him to get away saying that it is not meant for you. He must have been suffering from some kind of inferiority complex. He also must have wished to sit in the air-conditioned comfort. We have reduced the fare of the "Garib Rath." Its fare is 40 per cent less than the fare of three tier AC. A ticket in this train costs Rs. 560 only which is equivalent to three kilograms goat's meats. One can travel one thousand kilometres at this cost. If a labourer is able to travel from this even for a single day, it is a matter of pride for him. It increases his stature in his village. Four such trains were introduced last year and eight this year. We will provide such trains on all routes.

People compare railways with aeroplanes. Aeroplanes cannot give competition to the trains. How many people travel by aeroplanes? We were accused that trains generally run late. We have belied all this accusations. Now, aeroplanes are running late.

We are establishing coach factories, locomotive facilities and electrical goods factories. IRCON and RITES are our two organisations which have undertaken huge projects in India and abroad. RITES have undertaken some work in Myanmar. We have provided them locomotives and coaches also. We are assisting African countries also by providing training to their railway personnel. Financial condition of those two organisations is fairly good and they are enhancing their business not only in India but abroad also.

Wherever you are, honesty, commitment and vision is necessary. Wherever one works, one should work with honesty and integrity. All of us should move ahead. We should be like a big family. And if someone is rich he should share it with the poor.

Man has come empty-handed and he will go empty-handed. Sufi saints have reiterated that money is the root of all evils. Greed is essentially evil. Kabirdasji also advised to stay clear of greed. One Sufi saint used to come to our village when we were children and used to live in a mud house. He used to chant:

Daulat duniya maal khazana duniya mein reh jayega
Mutthi bandhke aaya bande haath pasaare jayega.

(All the treasures and riches of the World will be left behind when one departs from the human abode. One is born with clenched fist but leaves with hands wide open.)

Our mother earth fulfills all our needs but does not cater to our greed. The village in which I was brought up had virtually no amenities. We remained hungry with no shoes and no meals. There was land but no yield. Now the same land is being cultivated and giving good yield. Nature fulfills all our needs. Man is not going to take anything with him. Death is certain and a great leveler. Of course, longevity has increased in this age due to medicines and proper treatment but death is inevitable. This world is like a platform. We should try to do virtuous deeds. Only then we will have peace of mind.

MEGHNAD DESAI

Meghnad Jagdishchandra Desai is an economist, writer and Labour politician. Born in Vadodara, India, he obtained a Master's degree before the age of 20, and a Ph.D. at the age of 22. He did his doctoral studies at Pennsylvania and served as Professor of Economics at the London School of Economics (LSE). In 2005, he retired as Director of the Centre for the Study of Global Governance, which he founded in 1992 at LSE, where he is now Professor Emeritus. He is Chairman of the Trustee's Board for Training for Life, Chairman of the Management Board of City Roads and on the Board of Tribune magazine. He is an Honorary Associate of the National Secular Society. From 1984-1991, he was co-editor of the Journal of Applied Economics. He has been both Chair and President of Islington South and Finsbury Constituency Labour Party in London and was made a life peer as Baron Desai, of St. Clement Danes in the City of Westminster, in April 1991.

13 Emergence of India and China as Major Economic Powers

MEGHNAD DESAI

The world has entered a new phase of capitalism. It is called globalisation, but it is basically a new phase of capitalism. In a sense, this new phase of capitalism, which I call Paleo-Marxism, began in the late 1970s or in the early 80s and it matters little today. But it resumed the march that capitalism had failed before World War I. Before World War I, the world was globalised but it largely consisted of empires, with very few independent nation states existing. However, there was free flow of capital and you could raise money to build a tramway or run companies or even build infrastructure. The Indian Railways was financed by the money raised from the London stock market. There was also a free flow of labour. One-third of the Europeans went to North America, especially to the US in the 19th century; a lot of Indians went to Africa and to the Caribbean, and Southeast Asia; lots of Chinese moved to Australia and to the US West Coast as also South America. All that stopped since World War I. The Bolshevik Revolution took place in 1917. Then the world entered a phase where it was very pessimistic about the prospects of capitalism. Both India and China, by and large, took the view that capitalism was imperialism, and imperialism was hostile to development. Indeed, imperialism was responsible for the colonisation of underdeveloped countries and continents. Therefore, when they became independent their first task was to avoid capitalism or constrain it as far as possible.

When I was a student in the 50s, there was a very powerful book titled the *Political Economy of Growth* by the leading Marxist thinker of the time Paul Baran. Baran said capitalism, as we have known now, would never allow the Third World to grow, and the only way for the Third World to grow was to break away from capitalism and embrace the path of socialism.

As per my views, the Soviet Union was practicing socialism outside capitalism. A lot of the developing countries were also practising socialism, but not the Soviet way but as a half-way house. But that whole promise and the whole picture of capitalism is in a terminal crisis. As Lenin described, it has collapsed completely, and within my lifetime I had to change my views. To me then, ideally capitalism was a busted flush and it would never ever grow. The only way countries would grow was through socialism, state-directed ones.

Luckily in social sciences you do not get experiments, but it happens in empirical sciences, so people can always hold onto any views and follow whichever line they want. But the most remarkable thing about the collapse of the Soviet Union was that it showed how state-controlled systems could not work, whereas we in the 50s thought it was a great miracle, and we urged our leaders to go the Soviet way. And that is the irony, now I feel that none of us ever thought whether the Soviet model would work or not in the long-term.

An interesting part in terms of my topic is that India and China, at some stage or the other, had to see that all the models were not working. And it is a very difficult and extremely painful thing to do—to believe that all that has been taught and believed was wrong. Deng Xiao Peng is really one of the greatest persons of all times. Despite his incredible credentials as a Marxist-Leninist, and having had many ups and downs in his political career, many a rejection and approval, what was so remarkable about him was that he saw way back in 1978, 10 years before the Soviet Union collapsed, that socialism, what it stood for, would not work anymore. He also actually had the intellectual calibre to see that socialism did in fact help China become an economic power. And once he saw that, thanks to the way China is, he did not allow rounds and rounds of debates to come in the way of the change of direction. He took China onto the path of rapid growth. This is a very good example of how one can have capitalism without democracy and how long one can have it and also see how economics changes that too without having democracy in practice. But certainly in terms of economics, this was remarkable as lot of foreign investments have been flowing into China for decades; there is lots of export-led growth and very high level of savings. Basically, he could harness the technological revolution going on in the West for China's growth.

Again, in the Third World, a lot of delusions were in place. They did not use foreign technology, but they depended on their own technology. India had this Third World delusion running so deep that we refused to use computers because it was a Western product. Thank God it is no more the case now, because economics is all about division and better utilisation of labour, and if someone has better technology to improve it, and if you do not have it, then borrow it. No amount of fancy arguments should prevent it. And so, China embarked on this revolutionary path of capitalism and that too with great success. Today it is a real success phenomenon, not for the size of the People's Army but for the marvellous size of its economy. China today is feared not for its large army but for the sheer size of its economy and huge export volumes.

India took its own time. India was a semi-open economy and both a quasi-socialist economy and quasi-market economy. Our leaders were also very much opposed to capitalism. Hence, it took its own time to change. It was indeed the 1991 balance of payments crisis that catapulted her onto the path of change and made her follow a new economic direction. Before that of course, there was some improvement in the 1980s.

But an interesting thing about India is that while China has a foreign exchange of $1.3 trillion and sits happily on it, we have a little over $200 billion and are worried about this! At the time of opening up, the biggest worry was whether India would ever attract foreign capital at all? Fears were running wild that foreigners were going to capture our resources and would enslave us again, that the IMF would take over the control of our economy etc. But the irony is that many of the respected economists, who are good friends of mine, too signed on these petitions. I broke with them in the 90s as they seriously believed that any further serious reforms would harm the country.

In the meantime, for the first time in five centuries—Vasco da Gama came to India in 1498—India and China are considered as serious world economic powers today. It is a historical fact and is a great emergence. Around 1750, India and China had a share of the world GDP matching their share in the world's population. Now their share of the global population is about a third but their share in the GDP is not matching anywhere near, although it is really high. But by 2050, they are expected to get a GDP size that would match their population size. That of course depends on the fact that foreign capital continues to make its way into these economies. But there is no guarantee on that, and I will come to that later.

India and China are however, treading different paths. China is following a much more capital-intensive growth path with high capital-to-output ratio and with very high savings. With its high capital investments, China would become an export-driven market and would have high level of production efficiencies. On the contrary, India is following a Western model of primarily developing a domestic market as it is not having either a high export growth and is not enjoying high saving rates, hence is investing more money for bringing in better capital efficiency. It is also partly because India has not gone into really expensive investments like infrastructure, and when infrastructure comes in, it will cost more money. But in the meantime, India's savings rates are going up and therefore in all probability, India would jump on to a double-digit growth trajectory very soon, and I think India would maintain that double-digit growth rate for the next four to five years, unless something very horrendously goes wrong on the political front.

Now what are consequences of this growth? The consequences of this for India and China are of course that internally they will be able to meet the challenges they are now beset with. Whatever be the numbers, even today both India and China are substantially poor countries in terms of their per capita income. They have not caught up with even medium-sized countries like Singapore or Taiwan in terms of per capita income. India's per capita income is just about $2,000 and it has a long way to go to catch up with the rest of the world. But having these resources will help both these countries to deal with the challenges arising from poverty, deprivation and civil unrest, which is too high in China today. Both these countries are also fast establishing serious symmetries in property rights. It is also likely that to some extent the fast rising GDP growth will provide both these countries with the cushion to meet the challenges and march ahead.

Another important consequence of this rising growth is for the foreign services to choose: how it is going to change the map of the world? Because the map of the world was drawn in 1945 under the governance of the P-5, and China was at that time given the status of a great power, partly because of its large size and partly for the help it offered in the Asia-Pacific war during World War II, and also partially because of Chiang Kai-Sheik's statesmanship and persuasiveness. That apart, China did not actually get any serious status in the economic life of the world. For instance China took a long time to get WTO status.

I am a great fan of the WTO because it is the only global economic governance institution where there are no inequalities and has one vote each for all and no inequality in the voting rights. But from what we have seen from the developed countries, especially the European Union and the United States, it seems that they are fighting a very wrong battle as they did at Doha and the subsequent discussions on the Doha Round. Thankfully they are now beginning to learn that the negotiations on the economic front are going to be much smoother, much more symmetrical and much more equal than they had been through the 20th century. But this learning has not quite gone through. For instance, the way the EU has treated Chinese exports, especially the textile exports is nothing but disgraceful. The fact that the EU and the US have thwarted the Doha Rounds by refusing to cut agricultural subsidies to the necessary levels, and I do not know why the EU is behaving this way, shows that they have not realised that the balance of economic power is changing and changing very fast. While the income levels in India and China are still very low, their rate of growth is such that things are going to change very fast and radically. I think the way Brazil, India and China have cooperated at the WTO talks is an exemplary instance of how the balance of economic power across the world is radically changing. And I fully agree with our Prime Minister in saying that, while everybody talks about economics of globalisation, nobody talks about the politics of globalisation. Obviously being a Paleo-Marxist, I believe that politics is ruled by economics. But the important thing is that the politics of globalisation would require that the world economic institutions reflect the balance of economic power as is present today and that would mean that the rules governing the World Bank and the International Monetary Fund would have to be redrawn. Why do the World Bank and International Monetary Fund have this ludicrous arrangement that while the Americans run the former, the Europeans would run the latter and vice versa? It may have made sense in 1945 but it makes no sense in 2007 at all. It makes no sense, for example, that the governance of financial and trade matters are built on asymmetrical lines. So, one major consequence of the economic arrival of India and China is going to be that international economic diplomacy will have to be redrawn. Over the next few years, it may take 10 years in diplomacy as everything takes a long time in diplomacy, this is going to happen.

Partly what is happening in the world right now is that with a mountainous surplus of foreign exchange that China as well as other countries are holding, is creating over liquidity in the global financial markets that the central banks are not able to reduce. With every country free to borrow from abroad, thanks to the very fungible nature of money and with half of the $1.3 trillion forex that China is sitting on today being in American treasury bonds, very soon we will be getting into a global microeconomic scenario that the World Bank and the IMF are not designed to deal with. Both these institutions were designed to deal with the capitalism of 1945 and in the immediate next decades; and that is past now, though not completely over with.

But again the economic emergence of India and China has made it necessary that we rethink the economic relationships that we have been following so far. Again it is reflected in the way the Americans are dealing with the hardening Chinese renminbi. The Americans still believe that China should float its currency—I too believe that China should go for floating rates but economic nationalism has its own dubious benefits. But whether China floats the renminbi or not is China's business and not that of the US. But if it does not float the renminbi, it is going to have serious economic consequences globally as China's trade surplus is rising very fast and such an outcome will be worrisome for the whole world due to the large size of the Chinese economy.

And I think we have found a clear head-run in devising a global micro-finance economy. Before I wind up, I would like to speak about the political consequences of India's and China's growth which are much more puzzling as to what will happen—because politics lags behind economics in any international relationships. The Indo-US nuclear deal is a good example. It is not in India's interest to have China as an enemy nor is it in the American interest to have China as an enemy, because in foreign relations, there are no permanent enemies and no permanent friends, but only permanent and lasting economic interests. The way foreign relations work is based on the simple principle, never trust anybody, not even your best friend. I think basically the Indo-US deal is like buying insurance.

Given that background, how is India going to emerge politically? One of the most important things about India is that while it is an economic power, it has many political problems in its backyard. It is surrounded by a number of neighbours who are not its friends. I am impressed with the Europeans for their ability to come together and agree to eschew war in future. Germany and France fought wars for more than a century over a barren piece of land but today they have one of the best economic cooperation pacts in place and have even set up large steel plants in joint ventures. Today the European Union is the largest economic and political union in the globe with a clear understanding that they will never fight each other. Though they have many other problems but they will not go to war with neighbours. So, while the Europeans have come together as one forum, being a largely divided region with many countries, South Asia went the other way, from being a united country to a divided region of three countries. But if the Indian Subcontinent were to be united again, what a fantastic economy it would be.

"Because of the dynamism of the (Indian) economy, there is a very optimistic view of the direction of the country."

— Lee Howell

World Economic Forum

KAPIL SIBAL

Kapil Sibal is the Union Minister for Science and Technology and Earth Sciences since June 2006. He was earlier Minister of State (Independent Charge). He joined the Bar in 1972 after his LLM from Harvard Law School, and has served as Additional Solicitor General of India, and President of the Supreme Court Bar Association. Owing to his leadership and guidance, he has been successful in fructifying several initiatives, including enunciation of a National Biotechnology Development Strategy; operationalising a National Spatial Data Infrastructure; initiation of a National Early Warning System for Tsunami and Storm Surges in the Indian Ocean; and strengthening bilateral science and technology cooperation with various countries. He was the first-ever Indian Minister to visit the Indian station at Antarctica as a result of which a third Indian station is being established there. In his personal capacity, he serves on the Board of International AIDS Vaccine Initiative and Bill and Melinda Gates Foundation's India AIDS Initiative.

14

Science and Technology for India's Economic Development and Prosperity

Kapil Sibal

I think the topic before me is a great topic to talk about in the sense that the nature of diplomacy is changing and the world has changed radically since the end of the twentieth century and in the beginning of the new millennium. The kind of challenges that are going to confront us in the new millennium are distinctively and qualitatively different from the challenges that had confronted us in the past and in that sense the nature of diplomacy is also going to be qualitatively different.

Both non-violence and science and technology are exceptionally relevant in today's world as far as science and technology is concerned in the sense that we have seen technology being used for violent purposes in the past many times and it will only increasingly be used for violence in the twenty-first century. Therefore, I think the message of non-violence and the message of Gandhi are exceptionally important in the times to come. The other thing I would like to impress upon is the application of science. When we look at the beauty of the Taj, we actually see the application of science in building this exceptionally beautiful structure many centuries back, and this is applied science and what emerges sometimes from applied science is beauty. So, the challenge in front of us is: how do we carry the message of non-violence forward; how do we use science and technology for the benefit of mankind; how do we apply science and technology to create beautiful results; and what are the problems that are going to confront us in the twenty-first century?

Let me just broadly set out a few major issues that we will have to address in the times to come. We are about 6.2 billion people today, and by 2050 this number will be about 8.9 billion. I would say that out of this 6.2 billion people, more than 5 billion lead very difficult lives. If we talk of India alone, we always talk about the 300 million middle class and never about the 900 millions who are not part of this middle class. And of the 900 million, 500 million live with less than two dollars a day. Similarly, if we talk about Africa or many other parts of the world, there are many more millions, in fact billions of people, who are seeped in poverty and lead very difficult lives.

The biggest problem that is going to emerge as we move along the twenty-first century is how are we going to feed these people? I am not talking about India alone, but how do we feed these large swathe of people elsewhere in the world too. This is going to be one of the biggest challenges that we will have to deal with.

The other major challenge, which is talked about here as well as globally, is the issues relating to climate change. I do not think the global community is really seized of the enormity of the issues arising from the rapid changes in the climate; perhaps there are some leaders who are leading the way, but by and large the man on the street does not really understand the extent of this problem. The problem in very simple terms is going to be the following. If we look at the world and if we look at our atmosphere, that is our atmosphere from seven miles from the surface of the earth, only one-third of these seven miles, is the source of oxygen. Beyond a certain height, there is no oxygen; that is why if you climb up the Mount Everest you have problems in breathing as there is no oxygen up there. So, basically, it is the oxygen at the one-third bottom of the surface of the earth that is the source of sustenance for humanity. And getting rid of all other complicated arguments, if you deplete this source you are in for trouble. The other fact that I want to mention here is that if you increase the levels of carbon dioxide by just one percentage point, the average temperature on the surface of the earth would be the boiling point. That is all there is to climate change. We can talk about the melting in the Glaciers; we can talk about the Northern Hemisphere having much higher temperatures, etc, but in essence the problem is the emission of carbon dioxide and the reduction in the level of oxygen.

Carbon dioxide is emitted through fossil fuels and everybody knows that. There is no way in the world that we can continue to consume these fossil fuels at the pace with which we are consuming them, and if we do the level of carbon dioxide in the atmosphere will keep on increasing and then the temperatures will rise to unacceptable heights on the surface of the earth. The fact of the matter is a very simple argument which people normally do not make: if you look at the source of the fossil fuels, it is really millions and millions of years of foliage and trees embedded in the bowels of the earth. What happens is that as the foliage and trees are further embedded in the bowels of the earth, the oxygen is extracted from the bowels of the earth, because of pressure the material becomes more carbonated. So, after billions of years, this becomes soft carbons, then it becomes hard carbons and finally diamonds. We are trying to consume all what the nature has taken billions of years to create in just 300 years of human history! And that is the real problem—if we consume and deplete all what the nature has taken millions and millions of years to develop, in just 300 years, we are really asking for trouble. But this precisely is what we have done and are still doing.

So, that is the second problem that will confront humanity in the twenty-first century. And this by itself will result in many other problems. Number one, it will increase the incidences of newer, deadly diseases, because the moment you breathe, you increase the levels of temperature and you also increase the chances of more bacteria forming, and with the new bacteria formations, you increase the chances of newer diseases. I call this the new kind of terrorism that we will face increasingly, which is far more dangerous than the kind of terrorism that we are dealing with today. Because the new disease will strike you without notice and you being unaware of it—just as terrorists do—and it decides the place, time and the people for that strike. And you have no solutions to counter this. At least you can counter terrorism of today with many a measure, but you have nothing of that sort when it comes to this new form of terrorism that we will be engulfed with when it happens.

Therefore, the health sector becomes extremely important. We have already seen new strains of diseases coming up. There are newer strains of tuberculosis for which there is no cure already. Similar is the case with malaria, small pox, SARS etc., which can all come back. Thus, the health of the 8.5 billion people is at risk.

This also has impact on food security, because when temperature rises, it impacts food production. They say, for example, that wheat production in the country, though this year it is one million tonnes more than the previous year, by and large, is on the decline. Because what is happening is that due to over exploitation of the soil, salinity has gone up, with multi-cropping, over use of fertilisers following the Green Revolution, our food production by and large is on the decline. However, our population is on the rise. So, we need a new kind of evergreen revolution to meet the growing food demands of these ever-growing people in regard to agriculture. This in itself is a bigger challenge. And all this is the result of global warming.

Having understood this scenario, now how do we meet it? I strongly believe that the only way to counter it is through the proper application of science and technology. There is no other way to meet it. If you look at the growth of civilisation and the paradigm shift that has taken place in the course of civilisational progress, you will find that it is through discoveries, through the intervention of science and technology, whether it is the Wright Brothers who flew for the first time in 1903, or be it the discoveries by Thomas Alva Edison, or the discovery of the dynamite, or the steam engine, or the discoveries by Graham Bells, or the discovery of the penicillin by Alexander Fleming. But, in a sense, the global community, by and large, does not understand the inherent interconnections between economic progress and science and technology. And I think that the future of diplomats and diplomacy is in being able to understand the synergy between the two. The increases in the levels of trade from a hundred or two or three hundred billion dollars is not going to ultimately solve the problems of tomorrow. Trade is a system through which you buy and sell for gaining economic power, but it is not a solution for the basic issues which we will be beset with in the twenty-first century.

Accordingly, politics is ultimately the art of understanding the ecosystem in your country and projecting it to benefit by and large your country. But this again is not going to solve the problems that we as a whole face in the world today and tomorrow. The debate on climate change so far has been a debate between the developed world and the less-developed world, where one country tells the other that you consume more tonnes of per capita coal than we do, and therefore you have to cap that consumption. Debates like these are not going to solve the problem of global warming. For instance, if America consumes 22 tonnes per capita of coal and India consumes just 1.7 tonnes, then the argument is America must reduce its coal consumption. But this is not going to solve the problem.

The solution to this problem will ultimately be found in alternative technologies. The solutions to these problems will be found by discovering new molecules and the new sources of energy. And in this context, the sector that is going to be at the heart of economic development is biotechnology.

People talk about information technology and we are very proud of the fact we have done exceptionally well with information technology. But information technology is a very generic technology. Far more important is biotechnology, because, biotechnology will resolve the issues relating to agriculture, it will resolve the issues relating to health, and it will attempt to resolve our issues relating to environment.

Why agriculture? Because it is only through biotechnology that you will get seeds which are resistant to both biotic and non-biotic stresses. I will give you a small example. We in the global community consume 160 billion tonnes of water more than we replenish on the planet annually. And if we were to convert these 160 billions tonnes of water, it is equivalent to a convoy of trucks that runs 17 times around the circumference of the earth. That is the amount of water that we consume annually more than we replenish across the globe. And if we were to look at the economics of it, to grow one tonne of any agricultural produce, it needs an enormous amount of water. Most of the water is used not for human consumption but for agriculture. Now you must have a solution to produce the same amount of agriculture produce by using much lower amount of water. And this can come only through better application of science and technology. Most of the soil in the Punjab region has already become saline. Therefore, the question is how do we grow crops even in saline soil? Again this can be achieved only through science and technology. We need to raise the levels of farm production by newer scientific and technological interventions, so that we can have more food grown with lesser intake of water and fertilisers and thus serve the increasing needs of the growing populations across the world and that too at far lesser amount of damage to the environment. We need to discover new chemical entities so that we can deal with the new diseases we are beset with already and will be grappling with more in the times to come. And this can happen only through biotechnology.

We have just begun in this context. For the past 20 centuries man has been trying to conquer nature; man has been striving to empower himself so that he can make nature subservient to him. But the fact of the matter is that it is time for us to start working with nature. There is a vast ocean of knowledge which is unknown to us. There is marine biotechnology, for instance. How do fish survive at the bottom of the ocean without sunlight? How do fish survive in the bottom of the ocean without coming out onto the surface of the water? You can imagine the pressure on their bodies at the bottom of the water. Nobody knows it as yet. There are new microbes which we have not even started discovering. Now people have started moving towards the nature and started talking about traditional medicines and *ayurveda* which are written in our scriptures, the homemade solutions for ordinary disease etc. How does that work? Go back to nature. And what is nature? Nature is the interaction of four elements—nitrogen, oxygen, hydrogen and carbon dioxide. Nature is nothing more than that. If you can understand these elements, you would have understood nature, and if you understand nature you start having a better understanding of yourself and if you understand yourself better then you have better solutions to your problems and if you get these solutions from nature, you get the solutions for the problems facing humanity—be it the environment, be it agriculture, be it health or for that matter anything else.

So there has to be a dynamic shift from our traditional way of thinking and looking at the problems we face. We must start thinking globally, for science has no territorial boundaries; scientists are not citizens of any one particular country, they are in a sense global, because science and technology and its solutions have global applications. Because what we are going to be confronted with are global issues.

MANI SHANKAR AIYAR

Mani Shankar Aiyar is the Union Minister of Panchayati Raj, Youth Affairs & Sports, and Development of North-East Region since 2006. He was earlier the Union Cabinet Minister for Petroleum & Natural Gas and Panchayati Raj (Local Self-Government). He has been a columnist with a variety of newspapers and magazines and has published several books. In September 2007, he was conferred the "Outstanding Parliamentarian Award for the year 2006" by the Hon'ble President of India. Mr. Aiyar joined the Indian Foreign Service in 1963 and has served in various capacities in several Missions and was Consul General of India in Karachi. He has studied in Doon School; St. Stephen's College, Delhi; and Cambridge University, UK.

15

India of My Dreams

Empowerment of the Poor

MANI SHANKAR AIYAR

My dream for India today is exactly what my dream for India was when I was your age. I am not at all impressed with our economic reforms. I am not impressed because we have accelerated our growth from 0.72 per cent, which according to the statistician Shiv Subramanyam, was our annual growth rate in the first half of the past century, to 7.2 per cent now. From 0.72 per cent to an average of about 7.2 per cent over the past few years, a 10-fold increase. It effectively means that we achieved in one year what the British took 10 years to achieve. And today on an annual basis we have already reached 9.4 per cent, and it looks almost certain that we are poised to breach the 10-percentage-points-barrier, the mental barrier of growth this year. There is no reason at all for us to imagine that we will not sustain this plus 10 per cent growth over the next several years. But of course, economics is not an accurate science as it is an empirical science. Therefore, the unpredictable can overtake us anytime, as happened in 1997 in East Asia which overtook them all of a sudden—in fact in about a week only—and it took them nearly another decade to overcome from that setback. This kind of event might happen to us too, anytime, but within predictable parameters. I have absolutely no reason to doubt the recent optimism of Finance Minister Chidambaram that our 8-10 per cent growth can automatically eradicate poverty within the next decade or two.

But I am afraid I do not share the Finance Minister's optimism. And why do not I? I go back to the years of the Hindu rate of growth—a very denigratory term that was used by Prof. Raj Krishna as a joke, but which went onto become the mantra of the upwardly mobile middle-class later on, and now a stock cliché with which to talk down whatever we were attempting to achieve in the economic sphere in the first few decades of our Independence, and to contrast this with the campaigns like "India Shining", if you are Bharatiya Janta Party (BJP), "India Poised" if you are a reader of the *Times of India* and "India Rising" if you belong to the Congress Party. The proof of it is that we are already achieving in one year what it took us 10 years to achieve under the British rule, and therefore there is every reason to believe that all these statistical dreams of poverty eradication and so on will be dramatically achieved over the next one decade or two.

But what causes me to have severe reservations against this optimism is that, if indeed this is so, why was Jawaharlal Nehru such an icon in his days and whose popularity was not matched by any successor other than perhaps his own daughter Indira Gandhi? Stated in other words, what is it about the Hindu rate of growth that made people feel that they have been given opportunities which had been denied to them or to their parents under the British rule? I think if only we understand that, we will be able, at least I will be able, to trace the India of my dreams.

First, the Hindu rate of growth. It was five-times bigger than the rate of growth we achieved under the British rule. Suddenly people saw that in their lifetime the country's GDP was growing five-fold in 1 year from what was the growth in the earlier 10 years. So, there was a palpable sense of achievement. As against this, compared to the Hindu rate of growth, we are only doubling it today, that too in the past few years. We achieved in two years what we have achieved in one year. So, while a plus-seven per cent growth is an achievement in itself and a desirable thing in itself, the real impact it is making on the people's mind is approximately only one-third.

Secondly, that modest growth primarily benefited the poor who form the largest majority of this nation. I think this needs explanation, because although it was a lived experience of Satinder Lamba, Girish Dhume and me, it became a bit of history and memory, which the engineers, the doctors, and the scientists in our foreign service today need to be reminded of.

Governance in independent India, which began to appear from 1948, involved first of all the integration of the princely states into the Union, thereby destroying irretrievably the dominant feudal class which had set the image of India till then. What was the global image of India till then? The little *maharajas* and the snakes, because the snakes were as much a living reality as were the *maharajas*. And without a war, without a revolution, without executions in remote places, as happened in Moscow, we succeeded in integrating nearly 600 princely states into the Union, without a shot being fired, barring in two regions—in Jammu and Kashmir, where there was an international intervention, and in Hyderabad, where there was an internal opinion of the richest person in the world at that time, the Nizam of Hyderabad, that he had the right to be independent—a view that was not shared by almost all of his people. Although there was a police action—it was our euphemism of army marching past on the streets of Hyderabad—the integration of the kingdom of Hyderabad was achieved almost practically without a shot being fired.

The second most commendable achievement was land reforms. With land reforms we almost succeeded in abolishing the centuries-old *zamindari* system, where the large landlords, the gun-totting, large moustached *Thakur*, were a social reality. Although it was not entirely successful in some places, and less than entirely successful in some other places, and still persists in some places, the fact of the matter is that the landlord, the *zamindar*, who was conjured into existence by the Permanent Settlement Agreement brought in by Lord Cornvallis in 1793, and who through the whole of the 19th century and through half of the 20th century had been the dominant class in rural India, was forced to become a part of history, officially at least. This again was achieved without a shot being fired, and I think in this case definitely not a single shot being fired at all, but with only some cases being filed in various courts. This was a process by which an entire dominant class was simply put on the backburner. Perhaps a more important step, which benefited the bulk of Indians, was the fact that within land reforms there were tenancy reforms and tenurial reforms, under which the farm labourers got the tenancy rights on the land they till.

After these processes of integrating the princely states, of abolishing the *zamindari* system and of ensuring permanency for tenant farmers, and all the agriculture developments that went with it, the focus was on ensuring massive amount of public investments flowing into the farm sector, mainly to develop many large irrigation projects across the country. We now know that there was a heavy human cost to these irrigation projects, but there was also huge benefit, which is what led the then Prime Minister Jawaharlal Nehru to describe, after dedicating the Hirakud dam to the nation, that these are the modern temples of the country, and thereby invoking Lenin in a sense that Communism equals the free flow of electricity in the Soviet Union. Today a large portion of our electricity comes from these large hydel power projects which also serve as irrigation projects.

Then he brought in the price-support system for farmers. We introduced and still maintain the world's largest and most widespread and most complicated public distribution system. We have actually managed, without a revolution, to strike a balance between remunerative prices for the farmer and reasonably priced food items to consumers through this massive public distribution system.

There was a man called S.K. Dey in the Nehru cabinet, a completely non-political figure whom the Prime Minister got elected from Nagore in Rajasthan. He focussed on village communities and started the system of community development, which was a form of participatory development, but whose long-lasting evil consequences have been deep rooted as it has been blocking community development completely. This led Nehru to set up the Balwant Rai Mehta study group on Panchayati Raj; and retrieving an idea from the Mahatma's thoughts, Nehru proposed through the Mehta study group report, a system of an effective local government model which drew inspiration from the ancient Indian system of local governance, but was oriented towards contemporary social realities, and which worked towards changing the delivered development model into a participatory development model.

In short, everything was focussed on the poorest of the poor. And all these measures were invoking the name of Nehru, who was left out to explain the policies, and to validate the same. So remarkable was this transformation that in our democracy it became as difficult for a rich man to enter Parliament as for a camel to pull through the needle. But today, the Upper House is full of millionaires and billionaires. However, if you look at the composition of not only the 14th Lok Sabha but also of the previous ones, you can find that anybody who is landed, or anybody who is titled as a *maharaja* has difficulty in securing public support for his election to the Lower House. And to effect these changes in a country which was the absolute symbol of feudalism till 1947, was a miracle without precedents. Governance, under the Nehru regime, was primarily aimed at the *aam admi*, the common man, although the expression did not exist at that time. Moreover, the Scheduled Castes and the Scheduled Tribes were told that they had a part of the Indian state in proportion to their numerical composition. This was guaranteed to them by a form of affirmative action, which neither had any parallels anywhere in the world at that time nor did it have a precedent.

Here I am very concerned about the fact that the emancipation of the slaves that Lincoln declared in 1863 was implemented only after 101 years—that the world's most developed and the oldest democracy took so many decades to pass a bill of rights that enabled the Black Americans to enjoy the same privileges as the rest of the Americans since their independence.

And see how astonishing it is in a country, which for the past 5,000 years had institutionalised social discrimination in the name of ensuring social stability, you announce one fine morning that to call anyone as 'untouchable' is a criminal offence! Today how many of you would use the word untouchable in the country? Nobody even imagines using this word today, though sometimes I have to use it when I have to explain to foreigners what the Scheduled Caste means as they would immediately understand who an untouchable is. Because the most popular image of India among foreigners, after the *maharaja* and the snake, was the untouchables, as everyone would understand who an untouchable was—the condition of our tribals was known to Verrier Elvin and hardly known to anyone else. And that is why this ruthless exploitation of our tribal communities all across the breast of mother India occurred and now we are paying the price for it.

But during that time, suddenly the attention was concentrated on the tribal belts. And we had the inspiration and vision of a person like Jawaharlal Nehru who was against modernising the tribals. Nehru wanted the tribals to remain what they are and also did not want them to become the clones of everybody else. Not just that, he also insisted that give them only that development which they want, and not what we believe is right for them, and also ensure that it is given at the pace and time of their choice. Let them have their own identity, was his standard view. And it was the measure of this belief and enlightenment, which you would understand if only you consider what the justification for colonialism is. The French called it civilising the savage. Yes, colonialism is supposed to civilise the savage, and contrast it with us: the minute we became independent we said, please let them be and that we would do whatever we could do to manage them.

Then think again of how much an individual wants this non-economic thing called identity. How precious it is to be. I once looked up the newspapers to find out the big story on the day I was born, and I found that on the day I was born, Mohammad Ali Jinnah was welcomed in Madras by Periaswamy Naicker who welcomed him onto a Dravidakazhagam stage saying Pakistan is entirely justified as this sets the stage for Dravidistan. And it was the desire of the most popular leader in Tamil Nadu to break away from India. In Travancore-Cochin, C.P. Ramaswamy Iyer disgraced my name—he had established diplomatic relations with Pakistan and even sent out his envoy to the Pakistani capital. And I am not talking about one of the Naga tribesmen declaring independence from India, but its coming from Tamil Nadu, one of the heartlands of the country. In Srikakulam in Andhra Pradesh, there broke out a rebellion, funded and helped by Russia as Stalin believed that ours was bourgeois independence and not a genuine independence. Not just that, Nehru sent his sister Vijayalakshmi Pandit to Russia as the envoy but Stalin, citing the above excuse, refused to meet her even once throughout her tenure in Moscow. It is said that when a rebellious Phizo and others told Gandhi that they did not want to be part of India, he told them that if they do not want, they are free to walk out.

The integrity of India was a fantasy as far as those who ruled us for over three hundred years were concerned. All we had to retain as the unity of India was one man's idea of her, which he talks about in his book *The Discovery of India*. The book begins with Nehru's 1937 election campaign and wherever he went he used to hear only one thing, a shrill cry—*Bharat Mata Ki Jai*. Nehru instead of promising *pani, roti, kapada* and roads, would ask them what was that they called *Bharat Mata* and would then prod them to think about an idea of India. And this is a complete negation of the European concept of nationalism and nationhood. And this is the result of the India of today that would not have succeeded had it not been held by the entire 300 million Indians then.

In contrast, the Europeans way back in 1640 decided to stop killing each other in the name of religion, but only to resume it in the name of race, culture, language etc. So a geographical area which is of the same size of India today—that is *Bharat Mata* without her right arm because that has become Bangladesh, and without her left arm because that has become Pakistan—and we still regard this vast country as one amputated country. Contrast this with the Europeans—at the last count there are 43 nations. Because after Hitler invaded Czechoslovakia in 1938 it took them the better part of 60 years to actually secure their liberation from themselves. And finally when they got freed and they were liberated, and asked what they want to do, the Czechs said they cannot stand the Slovaks, and the Slovaks said neither they could the Czechs. So they split that tiny country into two separate republics. And the one country called Yugoslavia till recently, today is nine and when Kosovo comes into existence shortly, it would be ten.

So, the most dangerous thing to happen to India would be following a European concept of nationalism and nationhood. When I was asked as a probationer in Brussels as to what would be my ideal posting as a foreign service probationer, I said, Belgium. Belgium is a country that broke up from its mother country, the Netherlands, on the grounds of religion somewhere in 1835. After that they have been fighting each other—10 million people cannot stand each other; the Valons and the Flemish are fighting each other. This fight is not even immune to the Communist Party of Belgium as they are also divided—there are two Communist parties in that country, the Communist Party of the Valons and Communist Party of Flemish. Today the biggest problem that Belgium faces is the linguistic conflict between the Dutch speakers and the French speakers. One of the major victims of this linguistic conflict is the Indian embassy in Brussels, as when linguistic troubles break out, the French speakers would smash the Flemish signage on the embassy board and when the Flemish see this, they too would smash the French signage.

And is not the same happening in Pakistan, a country set up solely on the basis of religion and then you ask why there has to be a border between Pakistan and Iran, and now between Pakistan and Afghanistan.

After all, Iran and Afghanistan are even more Muslim than Pakistan. To answer that question they would say the Shias and the Sunnis are going to get at each other's throats. Today, the major national issue in Pakistan is whether the Ahmedias are Muslims or not. After my years in Pakistan during my foreign service days, I came to the conclusion that Islam is what unites Pakistan, but Islamisation is dividing it. When I was there, Zia-ul Haq announced the new Islamic laws and the punishment for theft was to chop off the hand of the offender. But the irony is that both the religious factions could not agree on what the actual hand was, and interestingly during my long stay in Pakistan not a single Pakistani thief lost his arm!

Now with these kinds of complications in defining what is nationhood in Europe, because that was the only available model for us at that time, and the only other model being the US—the best example of integrating people of different origins and nationalities, be they Poles, Italians, Finnish, Irish, Chinese or Indians and where the theory of melting pot is in practice and within a generation you become as American as anybody else, you abandon your previous identity and assume a new one—what was the role model of our idea of nationhood?

Nehru defined the idea of nationhood or being an Indian as follows: an Indian is a Kashmiri who eats *wazwan* but cannot stand *sambhar*, an Indian is the one who eats *aviyal* but does not eat *chapattis*, an Indian is the one who wears the *jabela* but does not know how to put on a *veshti*, an Indian is the one who wears the *vesthi* but has never seen a *jabela*, and an Indian is the one who understands what is *dhoti* but has never heard of *vesthi*. An Indian is somebody who cannot understand a word that a UP *Bhaiyya* says and an Indian is the UP *Bhaiyya* who thinks that Tamil is like putting stones into a pot and rattling it, an Indian is somebody who can dance the Bharatanatyam and who thinks that this is the North Indian Kathak, and at other times thinks that Bharatanatyam is not a dance form at all as the only dance is Kathak. So, an Indian is somebody who cannot understand the other Indians—he cannot understand the language of other Indians, who wears what others cannot wear, and who cannot eat what other Indians eat. But he is an Indian because others claim that they are also Indians. Anybody who wishes to be an Indian is an Indian. We do not ask you whether you are a Protestant or a Catholic, Greek Orthodox or a Greek Protestant, vegetarian or non-vegetarian, whether you speak French or German etc.

We are a country that includes everything—in terms of population, we are the largest Hindu country in the world, and the second largest Muslim country, and when it comes to Christianity, Indian Christians can regard the Pope as a Protestant because St. Thomas reached India and established the Syrian Church long before St. Peter reached Rome. Then we are home to a number of oriental religions like Buddhism, Jainism and Sikhism, and of course Hinduism. The fact is that we do not have any particular difficulty in living together. Contrast this with the bloodstained history of Europe which was the only example we had, and consider the leap of imagination that Nehru and his colleagues took to call this land one nation! Yes, the idea of India is a living reality. This is what Nehru gave to the people of this country, that is many entities in every sense—an idea of a living reality. And what a genius of a civilisation is ours!

Coming back to the economic policies. The economic policy of the India of the Nehruvian period was such that in the first six five-year plans, the farm growth was consistently higher than the average growth of the GDP. And my authority for saying that is Dr. M.S. Swaminathan, and I quote him on this. This growth was the fruit of the developmental seeds, sown in the initial decades of Independence, which were going into that segment of the society that was largely involved in farming. It is therefore, not surprising to note that in 1952, these people awarded a huge mandate to Nehru and they only increased it in 1957 and they further affirmed their faith in him in 1962 with an unprecedented mandate. In 1964 when he died, the baton was passed onto his daughter Indira and when she went to the people, there was a major reversal. Having been defeated on the floor of the House, she decided to go for a fresh mandate, because the entire political class came together with a sole objective under a grand alliance—to remove Indira. To this she responded: they want to remove me and I want to remove poverty. And that was it. The next general elections saw her bagging a two-thirds majority which even her father Nehru could not manage. Because the people felt that the country was getting back the ideals of Nehru and Gandhi, and the fact was that the poor were being focused on again.

Has the status of the poor changed for the better? In relative terms, perhaps yes, but in absolute terms, it is much worse today. The recently released Arjun Sengupta report on the unorganised labour gives us a startling revelation. The report says that there are 836 million Indians who live on under Rs. 20 a day. The report goes on to add that there are at least 270 million who live with less than Rs. 12 a day, and at least 200 million go to bed every day on an empty stomach. Now let me put the under-Rs. 20-a-day in perspective. Under the National Rural Employment Guarantee Scheme, the Central government offers Rs. 80 a day to a farm labourer. But there is a condition here: only one member from a family can get this job. And this Rs. 20 per day per head is for a family of four a day, and if the number of the members is five, then it is Rs. 16 per head, and if it is six members, then we can calculate where we are headed to. The Planning Commission, the great advocate of the India Poised and India Rising fame, has decided that poverty is having an income of Rs. 12 per head at an exchange rate of Rs. 40-45 for a dollar; and when for the World Bank it is purchasing power parity. At the current dollar rate we should be having an income of Rs. 40 per day compared to the 836 million having half of that, and 270 million having even less than that at Rs. 12 a day.

What is the consequence of this? The consequence is that India in 2007 is a rising power. Today India is home to the fourth largest number of dollar billionaires in the world—we have just overtaken from Japan this ranking. The combined wealth of all these billionaires places us amongst the economies of global billionaires at the second position. And when it comes to dollar millionaires, there is a huge drop, however—from the fourth rank last year we have dropped to the eighth rank in the last count. And when you drop from that to the *aam admi*, we have as many as 836 million living on less than Rs. 20 a day, 270 millions living on under Rs. 12 a day, and 200 million going to bed with empty stomach each day. So, while our GDP gallops—yesterday 7 per cent, today 8 per cent and tomorrow 9 per cent and day after tomorrow 10 per cent, and it catches up with the Chinese—we have 200 million Indians having nothing to eat and 270 million who live on less than Rs. 12 a day.

And we have really progressed on the human development index—our latest ranking is 127; it was 126 in 2005. The only area where we performed worse than the human development index is football. And worse, we are a curious country, where we are 137th on the football ranking, we had national newspapers like *Hindustan Times* carrying for one full month football as the lead story, everyday.

All this makes me think which is the reality? The reality of today is that one way of really getting rich, or riding the wave of prosperity, is to do nothing. But I really get angry at the fact that just around one lakh Indians play on the stock markets and we get an *Economic Times* headline saying there was 500 points drop in the Sensex and the nation lost a hefty Rs 1.72 lakh crore! Firstly, who owns this obscene amount of money? Or does it actually mean that we had Rs. 1.72 lakh crore money yesterday and today we lost all of it? How does this notional money get translated into the national wealth? More importantly, who owns this huge money from the bourses anyway? You can become that rich doing nothing other than putting your money into the bourses. The next is the bizarrely growing property market. You do nothing but put some money either into the stock markets or into property, then sit back and see them multiply everyday, the returns are mind-boggling. I know the favourite expression of the World Bank mandarins is that economic growth is like a tide that raises the boat altogether.

What is more ironical is the fact that today nobody, absolutely nobody, is saying that the rich are getting richer and the poor are getting poorer. But the truth is that the rich are getting obscenely richer and the poor are getting mindlessly poorer. How are we going to automatically transform the high rate of growth into dealing with the problems of the majority of these people? The higher economic growth is not reaching into the bank accounts of these 836 million people, but is disproportionately going into the pockets of those few rich, and our rich are hugely rich. If you take the richest million-dollar Indians, each one of them would have a higher personal income that is higher than the per capita income of the same number of Luxemburgese, which is the richest country in the world. The first 10 million richest Indians have a larger market share than the same number of Belgians, the first 50 million Indians have higher purchasing power than their British counterparts, and indeed if you take the first 200 million Indians, it is going to rival the purchasing power of a similar number of Americans! And 300 million Indians are able to buy as much as 500 million Europeans can buy. No wonder why India is shining; it is shining for all European and American companies who are looking for markets and they just love this idea of a backward looking country talking exactly their language. And this is what the *Wall Street Journal*, *New York Times*, *LA Times* and the *Washington Post* keep on writing about India.

Of course, there is a huge change, but for some millions, and not for the huge majority—the change is that a movie ticket that used to come for just Rs. 3 or Rs. 2 a few decades back, would cost you Rs. 196 today and one is happy to dole out that. So, there is a huge change for some Indians. And this "some Indians" mean 300-350 million who are obscenely rich, while the rest are told to wait for their boat as the tide is rising slowly. However, I would love to compare our economic development to a train and not to a boat that the World Bank economists want us to believe, because in India we still have all those third, second and first class AC compartments for MPs and ministers. We are moving together at the same time and in the same direction, but not at the same speed relative to each other. And should this not be the objective of our economic policies? Should this not be the India of your and my dreams? This is the question I keep posing to myself incessantly. As a Member of Parliament, it is my duty to be out in the villages. And as the Panchayati Raj Minister, I have visited over 200 villages so far and as the Minister In-charge of the Department for the Development of the Northeastern region, I go to that part of the country, which is growing only at 4 per cent—and I see real poverty in this entire region, while the rest of the country is growing at 10 per cent. And I cannot believe that the India of the *Times of India* is not the India that one sees in this region. I have an empire to report to me on life, actual life—the life of the 836 million poor Indians is no news today, but the Corus buyout by the Tatas is, and so is Ambani buying out a chemical firm abroad.

And I blame this on Karl Marx. It was Marx who said that the superstructure of the society is determined by the nature of the ownership of the means of production. When I was a college student, everything Marx said other than this could appeal to me but this I just could not comprehend—how my preference for Mozart or Beethoven is related to my ownership of the means of economic production. I also wondered how my preference for Dickens or Wordsworth should depend on my relationship with the means of production. But now I begin to understand that the relationship with the means of production determines our mindsets.

Singapore has just announced that Indians are the largest spenders in the island city-state. And we are proud of it. Or should not we be ashamed of it? As many as 836 millions are living on under Rs. 20 a day and we are beating the Norwegians, the Lithuanians and the Luxemburgese and everybody else in buying things from Singapore and elsewhere. We have 40 million Indians who travel outside the country and we have three million genuine foreigners visiting our country annually. *Wah, Wah* liberalisation!

We are surviving because there are millions of Indians who have gone to the Gulf—who live in the most wretched conditions in Dubai, in Abu Dhabi, in Kuwait, in Muscat, in Riyadh, in Jeddah, in Aden and in Saana and eking out a living there. But when it comes to spending this hard-earned money, we would say that we should go on shopping trips to Singapore and burn all that we earned. This is strange. We send our poor to earn our foreign exchange, and then we send out our rich to spend that foreign exchange in exotic shopping malls in Singapore or any other similar cities.

Is this the India of my dreams, rather is there an India of my dreams? Yes, there was an India of my dream and in this regard I would like to explain our greatest achievement so far.

To me, our greatest achievement is our democracy, which no other country in the world has matched so far. This is the unmatchable achievement. If enslavement of the Africans was the beginning of the American democracy, this went on with more speed during the industrialisation of the Western world. Everybody in the US, including Jefferson was the owner of slaves, and this totally coincided with the industrialisation of the entire Western world. Coinciding with this was also the evangelisation. Though on paper all men are equal, some are more equal than others. So in Britain till 1832 no Catholic could vote and it was only in 1887 that voting rights were given to the landless British labourers. And for women, they had to wait till 1927, after 170 long years since the Industrial Revolution, to get the right to vote, and for the American women it happened in 1920, and in France it was as late as 1950. But we plunged into it from the very start of our tryst with destiny and democracy and freedom. Every man and woman who was above 21 (now 18) has been enjoying the right to vote in this country since the birth of democracy here.

We went into our first election with everyone having horrible memories of the heinous act called Partition. Yet they voted in a united, secular India, defying all notions of nationalism which we have inherited from the West.

When it comes to affirmative action, the Americans added these two words to our vocabulary when our democracy was close to 20 years, but by then the concept of affirmative action had become an integral part of our Constitution for our Scheduled Castes and Scheduled Tribes. And we have been building on it since then.

In 1989, the then Prime Minister Rajiv Gandhi publicly said that we may be the world's largest democracy, but we are also the world's least representative democracy. And the result of this realisation was the concept of panchayati raj institutions—of course he could not live to see it fructifying—and today we have 2.5 lakh local self-government bodies, which together have over 3.2 millions engaging themselves in the business of governance, and of this, 33 per cent or 1.2 million of them are women, which is larger than the entire women legislators put together in the world so far. When it comes to villages, this is more than 33 per cent. In some states like Karnataka, the percentage of women in the village level *panchayat* is a staggering 45 per cent, as this state has elected 54 per cent SC women as against the stipulated 33 per cent! And to me, this is affirmative action running wild! The most astonishing thing about this is that the percentage of women elected from Scheduled Tribes is double the limit, at a staggering 65 per cent. And these are the Scheduled Tribes who are the most discriminated segments of our society, which began not yesterday, not day before, but 5,000 years before, who are so liberated today. When we boast of 45 per cent women in village *panchayats* we are not talking about the well-heeled, the upper-caste women but the most down-to-heel, illiterate, the lowest caste and the most oppressed segment of women in our country. Yes, this is affirmative action running wild. And yet, do these one million Indians who are richer than the Luxemburgese of the same numbers, the 10 million Indians who are on par with the Belgians of the same numbers, the 50 million Indians who are richer than their British counterparts and the 200 million Indians who are on par with the similar number of Americans, know that this has happened? I do not think so.

But why should this be a revelation to this class? It is because of Karl Marx, because the ownership of the means of production determines the mindset of change. And this changed a lot, the children of our rich and evolved have their children waiting for an American green card. The children of our foreign service officers are the distinguished citizens of the US already, and so are those of the IAS and IPS fraternity. So are the children of our ministers and MPs, and some of our journalists. And these few millions have already exported two million Indians to the US. And where do the 1.1 billion Indians stand in this sweepstake?

The IT industry, the shining example of the India Shining campaign, has just about five millions employed in it. What about the rest of the Indians? They are still tilling the lands and committing suicides, because our agricultural extension system has collapsed really badly.

Has something gone wrong? I think so. I would like to end my speech on the India of my dreams as the India of yesterday. In this regard I would like to give you a talisman that the Mahatma gave: he said that when you are in doubt, think of the poorest man, and summon him to your mind, and ask yourself whether what you are going to do will benefit that poor man; if yes, then you are on the right track and soon all your doubts will vanish.

But we are now at that stage of national development where each and every policy is directed and cross-checked with summoning the richest man, and asking him whether the steps being taken are beneficial to him, because that is what validates globalisation as is being propounded by the World Bank and WTO, what validates economic development, what validates liberalisation, what validates modernisation, and also because that is what validates the India of tomorrow. But is it not an awesome tragedy?

Go back to the 1930s. We had furious debates between Gandhi, Nehru and Bose who always used to differ on many a matter. But at the end of it, all of them would settle on one score—the liberation of the motherland. But now we say let the rich get richer and let them get fabulously richer. This is the only agreement we have and somehow this rising tide will keep rising on. Is this not pathetic?

The panchayati raj institutions are the answer to this disparity. That is how we can accelerate our growth for the larger common good. The really wonderful thing about such an accelerated growth is not that it leads to more and more billionaires. There is so much tax collection this year that we have the finance minister announcing that Rs. 81,000 crore more would be earmarked for rural welfare. Rs. 81,000 crore is Rs. 81,000 crore more than Nehru could spend. And the icon is still Nehru. Why? Because, the benefits of his modest growth disproportionately reached the poor, while today the benefits of our accelerated growth are disproportionately reaching the rich only. Unfortunately our people are so sensitive that they would not destroy the mansions of the rich, as they believe that while the rich grow at 994 per cent annually, can we grow only at 0.94 per cent. But can they? Yes, because of this Rs. 81,000 crore. According to a famous statement that Rajiv Gandhi made about the huge loss of money, or the mammoth inefficiency of the system to distribute the benefits of the Central aid, that out of every rupee spent, only 15 paise reach the target audience.

Though he had since been misquoted and over quoted on this remark, which was based on a report by a Planning Commission team headed by Ajit Bhattacharjee, Rajiv was misinterpreted as saying that all this money was being grabbed by politicians. What Ajit was trying to say was that because of the systemic malady that we are replete with, each of the schemes have separate departments to monitor them too. Thanks to our present civic administration system—the British were wise enough not to introduce their system in our country, as they knew how bad the system they gave us would work, because fundamentally the British believed that Indians could not be trusted to behave fairly and equitably amongst themselves. Hence, the reason why someone impartial had to be brought in from outside.

We have scores of departments and sub-departments and the litany of commissioners and deputy commissioners, secretaries and joint secretaries, *tehsildars* and deputy *tehsildars* and so on so forth, to handle the same thing. The British also believed that such outsiders, because of the insidious nature of our society, would get polluted sooner than later. So they ensured that every three years, these outsiders/ outside agencies are transferred. So by definition for the administration to be fair, it has to be alien to the society at large. We followed it lock, stock and barrel. At the same time, the British were kind enough to not introduce this system in their land. They were sure that this system could not work properly, and that it was destined to fail. The very army of staff that a senior government official has makes him ineffective. So, we end up hiring an extraordinary expensive system, which is completely hopeless and ineffective.

In one of my visits to villages, one day one little boy came to me saying he wanted to study. When I asked him was he getting the books, and free meals, he said he gets the books for free, and also there is no tuition fee; he also gets free meals. Then he paused for a while and said, but there is no teacher. It is a pathetic tragedy—we have schools without teachers, we have hospitals without doctors, we have clinics without nurses, we have taps without water, we have rations shops with nothing on the shelves. Where are we headed to? Instead of keeping the charge with development to transferable aliens like the civil service fraternity, why cannot it be entrusted with the local people? Here comes in the need for the *panchayati raj*. That is devolution of power in the true sense. Because through the devolution of power we can attain the three Fs—functions, finances and freedom—and that is what *panchayati raj* is all about. And through this devolution of power we secure the three E's—empowerment, entitlement and ensuring opportunities. Under this, empowerment leads to entitlement, which in turn will ensure equal opportunities. This is the

India of my dreams. The proof of this is our gorgeous democracy, which Nehru and his colleagues sowed the seed for and nurtured well. While our democracy has empowered a huge middle-class, and they are the ones who have captured the levers of political power today, and once empowered they ensured that it is their kind who benefit, while the large majority are left out on the fringes. Our people secured the consequences of this empowerment well in advance and the result today is there for everyone to see—the huge, burgeoning middle-class who have secured all the benefits of the empowerment set in motion by Nehru, because empowerment and the economic entitlement put you on the fast track for enrichment. So, today we have millions of Tatas and Birlas and Dalmias who have secured political empowerment through which they also secured economic entitlements. The fantastic result of the political and economic entitlement is an explosion in enrichments.

And the *panchayati raj* is for empowerment of the poor, and it is by empowering them that they can attain economic entitlements and enrichments. Just as the middle-class has risen on the socialist ladder and they kick that ladder away without any compunctions, thereby denigrating everything they had used in the past. So also, a day will come when the poorest of the poor, having secured their political empowerment and economic entitlements, will bring about an explosion of enrichment at the bottom of the ladder, and huddled up at the bottom of that ladder today are 836 million. Make them grow, help them double their incomes, triple it and then take it to ten times, and help them catch up with the rest of the middle-class.

Once that is achieved, who can then stop us? We can then begin to move towards the US and not when we carry the burden of the poor, while we pretend to be rich. I am sure *panchayati raj* is the one way of accelerating that growth and development into an inclusive growth. An inclusive growth is not the tide that raises the boat of progress to all dramatically. An inclusive growth is like a train, which might keep people in different compartments, but carries them all at the same time and at the same speed and reach them together as well. The India that does this is the India of my dreams. Today when I look up to see the India of my dreams, all I see is the India of yesterday and not today. So let us dedicate ourselves to the larger goals that Gandhi had set for us.

MEIRA KUMAR

Meira Kumar is the Union Cabinet Minister for Social Justice and Empowerment since 2004. She earlier served in the Indian Foreign Service from 1973-1985. She was General Secretary, All India Congress Committee; Member, Congress Working Committee; and has served on various Committees of the Parliament since 1986. She has been President and Founder, All India Samta Movement; President, Institute of Blind Girls, and Jagjivan Seva Ashram; Chairperson, Meira Kala Mandir; Vice-Chairperson, Rajendra Bhawan Trust; Member, Senate, Bihar University; Supreme Court Bar Association; Senate, Punjab University; Governing Body, Indian Council of Cultural Relations; Central Advisory Board of Education; and Advisory Council, Delhi Development Authority. Currently, she is Member of the National Commission on Population and National Integration Council.

16 Need for a Just, Equitable and Inclusive Society in the 21st Century

MEIRA KUMAR

The topic "Need for a Just, Equitable and Inclusive Society in the 21st Century" is very close to my heart and it so happens that what is close to my heart is also my responsibility and work area. When I went to South Africa along with President Abdul Kalam in 2004, the South African President was very happy to know that there is a ministry called Ministry for Social Justice and Empowerment in our country. He was very keen to have such a ministry in his government. These are two very fascinating words—social justice and empowerment. Earlier, it was social welfare. There is something very patronising about its connotation. Now there has been a paradigm shift from social welfare to social justice. It is not just social justice, but social justice to empower those who have had no social justice before.

When I was in the 20th century and was awaiting the next, I thought that when the first sun rise will occur on the Eastern horizon, we would have a just, equitable and inclusive society. That is what one thought of. But of course, these were dreams. And we still live by our dreams. Every man and woman of action should have dreams. It is very important to have a dream, in fact big dreams. Dreams motivate us. The bigger our dreams, the more efforts we put in to achieve them.

I would also like to draw your attention to what has been happening in the world over these years. The world over, there has been no justice. We have found in history, discrimination on the grounds of race, colour, culture, religion and so many other factors. Even language has been a cause of discrimination. A handful of those who gained some military strength were able to colonise others. This injustice got perpetuated for a very long time. With colonisation and spread of imperialism, we found that there was inequitable distribution of wealth and resources across the world and the world's wealth got concentrated in just a few countries. The world is still not just. Even today we as a Third World country, most of the time, have to make effort to ensure that we are not left out or elbowed out in the international scenario. We have to demand for a world order which is equitable and ask for an order which is over and above inclusive. But when it does not happen, we experience the agony, humiliation, pain of someone who has been cast aside. This is happening internationally. Every day we have to fight for it. I want to draw your attention to our own country, our own society. Whatever is happening at the international fora is also happening in our own country. Here also a few people have cornered everything, the power, the resources and the right to decide and all other people of the country have been left out for centuries.

I want this debate about the need for just, equitable and inclusive society in the present century to be held all over the world. All the thinking people, intelligentsia, all who know that they have a responsibility towards their country should have a debate over the subject. But they should have an objective debate. Objectivity is very important but very difficult to get. We have so many deep rooted prejudices and vices that it is very difficult to be objective.

Discrimination was and is still prevalent in our country. All through our history we have made efforts to correct it. And we are still in the process of doing so. Our Constitution is very clear on the issue of discrimination. We have legislations and laws to counter it. But one cannot legislate on the attitudes of the people. We can make as many laws but unless we change the mindset of people, we cannot bring about the revolution we want. We cannot achieve the dreams we dreamt of. This attitudinal change is very important. Unless we have a country-wide objective debate on this very relevant subject, how will we change the mindsets?

Then there is the question of gender discrimination. It is understandable when uneducated people, guided by certain superstitions indulge in gender discrimination. But when you find educated people indulging in gender discrimination, what can you do? Recently, many of the newspapers carried reports based on the Census 2001 survey that the ratio of women as compared to men is falling. There are only 933 women per 1,000 men. And what is more alarming, they said, is that in more advanced and affluent states, which have higher literacy rates, the ratio of women as compared to men is much lower. It is low in states like Haryana, Punjab and in South Delhi where the elite of the country live. In Haryana, it is 861 women per 1,000 men. It is alarming. Where are the women disappearing, where are the girls vanishing? When I was a member of the Eighth Lok Sabha, a test was introduced for the first time in the country. This test was done on the foetus to find out if there is any defect and if this defect can be treated before the child is born. But through that test, one could also come to know about the gender of the foetus. These tests suddenly became very popular. I introduced a Private Member Bill to ban it and subsequently, it was banned. Thus by law, the doctors are forbidden from telling the gender of the foetus. That is in law. But what is in practice? You drive down through small towns, rural areas or even the periphery of big cities and metros, you will find small clinics with boards on the top advertising "pay Rs 5,000 and save Rs. 5 lakh later." These clinics are openly indulging in female foeticide.

I am talking about gender discrimination amongst the society as a whole, and especially among those who are supposed to take the society out of the evils. I know instances of students who go abroad to study at Cambridge or Oxford and when they come back they say, "I have such and such degree, so what dowry is being offered for me?" Dowry is the root cause for female foeticide. There is a strict law against dowry. But has it been abolished? As long as this evil of dowry is not uprooted, the girls will continue to vanish. We talk about equality of gender but here the cause is fighting for the existence of women and girls, stopping their elimination. Various acts have been enacted to fight against this discrimination, but if the thinking of those who are to implement them is not changed, how will these acts be effective.

There is discrimination on account of economic grounds also. If a man is poor, no one calls him by his proper name. A Sundar Singh becomes Sundarwa. He may or may not be educated. Most of the great saints in the medieval times who were responsible for bringing in reforms had not gone to schools. None of them went to schools. This is called "bahushrut". The great saint Kabir never went to school but what an impact he had and still has. And this Sundarwa may also be a *bahushrut* but because he is poor, he faces discrimination due to his economic background. However, if through his hard work and labour, he acquires a huge bank balance, then he again becomes Mr. Sundar Singh. Suddenly the entire society will start respecting him. The society is not respecting the man, but the money he has acquired. We need to evaluate this marked deterioration in our thinking where today more importance is being given to money than character. But what if this Sundar Singh is a Scheduled Caste? He may get respect because of his bank balance, but he will continue to be excluded. Reality is that on the face Sundar Singh, the SC, will be accepted but the general mindset will be against him. Wherever there is a direct confrontation of his interests against the rest, he will get excluded. This is discrimination on the grounds of caste.

Let me now discuss about people who go abroad to study in the most prestigious institutions of the world. They study in these institutions for three years. They are supposed to build your character; they are supposed to broaden your horizon and evolve you as a better person. They study there and come back. But their mind-set has not changed and they look for girls in their caste and sub-caste to marry. This is the reality of an Indian. If you scratch an Indian, he is casteist. There is discrimination and injustice on this ground.

Everything has changed over the years. There was a time, 1000 years ago, when we were living in a very different society. A lot of socio-religious churning was taking place in the society. But all this is in the past. Today we are a democratic and secular nation. But the caste system has not changed. Everything has changed with time, but this caste system remains, challenging the very time itself. I was wondering why this caste system has not changed while everything has changed the world over? Then I realised that there is a reason behind it. To my mind, the reason is this: after our basic needs like food, shelter and clothing are met, we look for love and affection, and then we look for respect. It is easy to get love and affection. We get love and affection from our parents, relatives, children and friends. But getting respect is difficult. To attain respect we need inner strength, commitment, qualities like nobleness and uprightness and we need to make many sacrifices. We need to work hard for years on these qualities to gain respect. But, if we have such a system in the society, where we get respect on being born into the so-called higher caste of the society, getting respect becomes very easy. We do not need education and knowledge, neither do we need to make sacrifices to attain respect. The system earns us the respect and therefore we do not want to give up this system.

Government is taking a lot of initiatives to create a just and equitable society where there is no discrimination. We have put in place scholarship schemes and reservation policy. But what we need more is change in mind-sets of the general population. The well placed and well educated should be more sensitive and socially responsible. They have the opportunity and they must make use of it. Why should it come to a point where the government should force them to do so? Some of them are doing it, but not all. What we need is a collective effort. We need people to be more sensitive and more socially responsible towards others. The problem with us is that our tolerance level is very low. We have to work together to raise the tolerance level of our society and our country. To some extent, this will solve the problem.

Any law is as good as those who implement it. Therefore, those who implement these laws also need to change their mindsets. We have the historical opportunity to create a just, equitable and inclusive society. Let us all come together and make use of it.

"I have never seen India so dynamic, vibrant and full of business opportunities."

— Peter Loescher

President and Chief Executive, Siemens

N. GOPALASWAMI

N. Gopalaswami is the Chief Election Commissioner of India since 2006. He has 38 years of distinguished civil service behind him. He held important positions in the Government of Gujarat and the Government of India. He was Managing Director of Gujarat Communications & Electronics Limited and later, Member-Secretary, National Human Rights Commission and Secretary, Department of Culture, Government of India. Mr. Gopalaswami is a Post Graduate in Chemistry from Delhi University.

17

An Alert, Impartial and Effective Election Commission

A Must for Strengthening Democracy

N. Gopalaswami

Let me start by recounting the discussions when our Constitution was drawn up somewhere before 1947 when the Constituent Assembly was in session. One of the important tasks they were concerned with was holding elections in a democratic country. During the debates in the Assembly, the foremost architect of our Constitution, Dr. B.R. Ambedkar, had the following to say when he proposed the provisions for an Election Commission: "Having regarded the exigencies, it would be sufficient if there was permanently in session one officer to be called the Chief Election Commissioner while when the elections come the President may add to the machinery." At the very early stages of the proceedings of the Assembly we had drafted the chapter on Fundamental Rights, and in that they were planning to place the Right to Vote. The question which naturally arose was how the Right to Vote would be exercised and who would supervise the entire operations. It was clearly understood and decided that the superintendence, direction and control of all elections to Parliament and state assemblies should be entrusted to a body outside the executive of the day, which should not have anything to do with the organisation of electoral rolls and the process of conducting the elections. It meant that the body should be totally free from any influence of the government of the day. The house realised that the franchise would be the most fundamental right in a democracy. In order to allow the people to exercise their franchise in a free and fair manner they decided that there should be an Election Commission which would be a permanent body, but which would be outside of the sphere of influence of the government of the day.

India is a more centralised structure, but with the components of federalism. Therefore, the issue was whether the elections to the state assemblies should be held by a separate body or by the same body which would conduct the elections to Parliament. After much debates, there was a consensus that there should be only a single body to conduct elections to both the State legislatures and the Parliament. What were the expectations of the Constituent Assembly with regard to the way the elections be conducted? Dr. R.K. Sidhva, who was a member of the Constituent Assembly, spoke thus: "I do not think there are two opinions either in this house or outside of this house that the elections should be fair, pure, honest and impartial. If that is the view, I am sure it can be achieved only by an impartial agency as was contemplated in this article." Pundit Hridayanath Kunzru said: "We are going for a democracy based on adult franchise. It is necessary, therefore, that every possible step should be taken to ensure the fair working of the electoral machinery. If the electoral machinery is defective or not efficient, or is worked by people whose integrity cannot be depended upon, then democracy would be poisoned at the source." K.M. Munshi, one of our eminent nationalist leaders commented: "Not only that the Election Commission should preserve its independence but also retain its impartiality."

This was the background upon which the Constitution-makers thereafter had Article 324 incorporated into the statute book and which empowers the Election Commission of India. Articles 324 to 329 are devoted to the powers and role of the Election Commission. While Article 324 talks about the superintendence, direction and control of elections vested with the Election Commission, Article 325 deals with avoiding discrimination. It says that no person should claim to be included in a special electoral roll on the ground of religion, race, caste and sex. This means that the electoral roll shall be common to all citizens irrespective of religion, race, caste, sex, etc. Article 326 says that elections to the State assemblies should be based on the adult franchise. This was a very important issue because there was a lot of debate at that time as India in 1947 had literacy as low as 35 per cent. So, the question naturally was whether it should go for adult franchise or the right should be restricted to only the educated. The decision was however, wisely made to give franchise to all adults.

Article 327 talks about the power of Parliament to make provisions with respect to elections to State legislatures. That is, though the polity was federal in nature, the powers of the States were drawn to the Centre for making necessary laws. One of the important provisions in this regard is in Article 329 about the powers of the court to interfere in the electoral matters. This particular provision has a very far-reaching effect. The article stipulates that once the election process is on, no court will ever interfere with the matter. The question could be on whether a nomination was accepted rightly or wrongly, or, whether the decision of the Election Commission is acceptable to the political parties, etc. The entire thing was set at rest by this one Article which said that no court could interfere "during the pendency of elections." So if there is any question, it can be raised only after the elections are over. No interlocutory proceedings can be made during the elections process. This is to ensure that the election process as such is not derailed.

At this juncture, I will give a bird's-eyeview of the elections in our country. We have held 14 elections to Parliament so far, starting with the first one in 1952. The life of the House is five years. There is a constitutional provision which says that the Election Commission is at liberty to conduct an election to a House within six months prior to the date on which the House term expires. This is an interesting provision. If the House term expires, let us say, on 1 July 2007, the Commission is at liberty to hold elections anytime starting from 1 January, 2007. There is also a responsibility cast on the Commission that is under no circumstances, the Commission can ever say that it is not possible for the Commission to conduct an election and complete it before the term of the House expires. Therefore, the provision itself is made in such a way that no excuse can be offered as to not to conduct an election. What we normally do is that we hold the elections in such a way that there is a week or 10 days to spare before the term expires.

In the Constituent Assembly debates, one point that was repeatedly made was that the primary responsibility of the Election Commission was to ensure that every eligible voter is brought on the electoral rolls. Therefore, the Constituent Assembly placed considerable emphasis on the purity of electoral rolls and their preparation to ensure that every voter is included. Unlike in several other countries, the responsibility of preparing the electoral rolls rests with the Election Commission in our country. So in effect, the Commission ensures it by arranging field visits. When this is done, an individual needs to apply in the prescribed statutory form for inclusion. But that provision is suspended when the Commission holds a door-to-door survey to include the voters. After the survey, the roll is published and any individual who feels that his name has been excluded wrongly can apply for inclusion. By the same token, he can object to any name being wrongly entered. The copies of the finally prepared electoral rolls are given to political parties asking them to suggest any modifications or additions. The entire process takes about four months from the start to finish, including preparation of the rolls, publication and inviting suggestions and corrections. Finally the rolls are published for use in the elections the following year. At present, we have electoral rolls for the entire country and it is available centrally in New Delhi. The approximate number on the rolls is 680 million as total number of voters for the total number of parliamentary seats of 543. Each state has varying number of Assembly seats and the total comes to around 4,120 members for all states put together.

When the last elections were held in 2004, electronic voting machines were used at all polling stations in the country and no ballot papers were used. If we look at the history of electronic voting machines, way back in 1977 the then Chief Election Commissioner was quite concerned about the task of printing ballot papers for such a huge number and ensuring that they were printed correctly without duplicate numbers and mistakes. He therefore, set the ball rolling to find out why we cannot use an electronic voting system and do away with the printing of ballot papers. It took the best part of 27 years before the electronic voting machines were accepted across the board throughout the country. It involved various stages like amending the law and evaluation by Parliament by its own committee. There was a technical group which evaluated from the point of view of whether the machines could be manipulated. Thus by 1992, the decks were cleared for the use of electronic voting machines in the country.

But the Commission decided not to rush into making mandatory the use of machines in all the elections. We did it in stages. We started with a few polling stations in one constituency going for machines and then a full constituency. Then one state and finally in 2004, the entire country was covered under electronic voting systems. This machine is a stand-alone machine and the best way to describe the machine is that it is an adding machine. You push one button against the name of a candidate and it registers one vote. When another voter votes, it is one plus one and thus two. All this is done like an adding mechanism. There is no interference from outside. There is a chip in which the software is burnt i.e. inscribed and kept inside the machine and is not available for manipulation. It is not a two-way machine. You cannot make query and go back unlike the operating system-based machines. We have 700,000 polling stations for 680 million voters. Each polling station covers 1,000 voters on an average. And we have one million machines ready for these stations. The failure rate of machines is amazingly as low as 0.5 per cent. Most of the failures are due to the inability of the presiding officers to connect the machines correctly and not because of any technical reason. An incidental information is that the use of these machines saved 8,000 tonnes of paper.

Over the years, the issue of preparation of electoral rolls has received increased attention. As new ways are found to clean up the voters list, there are those also who are interested to see that the rolls are packed with the names of those who they feel would vote for them. It has been a constant struggle on the part of the Commission to ensure that the rolls remained true to the ground reality. Therefore in 1991, the then Chief Election Commissioner decided that each voter should have an identity card which he/she can produce during the time of voting, not only to establish his/her identity, but also this would enable the Commission to scuttle the ability of political parties or individuals to bring in bogus voters. The issue of these cards has been taken up time and again. But I must say that the results have never been totally satisfactory, the reason being that every year on an average 1 to 1.5 per cent of people go out of the rolls on account of deaths. Approximately, 2 per cent of voters come in as new entrants as they cross the age of 18 and become eligible for voting. Similarly, during the past 10 to 12 years huge inter-state and intra-state movement of persons has been observed. Thus, 6 to 8 per cent of the electoral rolls become off-key because of the huge movement of people. This is particularly so in areas which are not developed yet. From the areas dependent on agriculture, the people migrate to other places in search of labour. So, we have an extraordinary problem on our hand. We have a person who moves out, said to be temporarily out for seasonal employment and is expected to come back. But what is the guarantee that he would come back. The dilemma is whether we should continue his name in the electoral roll of the place he originally belonged to or his name be deleted from the list on the ground that he was not found at that place on the date of enumeration. Frankly, we have not been able to find an answer to this problem as yet.

In many places the officers allow the names to continue in the list on the ground that it is just a temporary migration and the person is expected to come back and therefore it will be unfair to remove his name from the rolls. At other places where they have assessed that the person is gone for a longer period, they have removed the names. Now with all the electoral rolls being computerised, we are going to undertake the work of trying to compare the names of the electoral rolls for duplicate names.

But even when I say this, I am not sure whether we will be able to remove duplicate names. It is nearly impossible as the database contains about 680 million names. We are working on a methodology to where we start by restricting it to some areas. The next step we have undertaken is towards identification. We are hoping that one day every citizen will have a single identity card. There is a proposal under consideration for a national citizenship identity card with a unique number which once given remains throughout life. Once this comes up, we will be in a better position to clean up our electoral rolls. Until then we have to live with some of these deficiencies. On the side of the Commission, what we are targeting for the 2009 parliamentary elections is that apart from giving an

I-card to each member, the photo on the card will now be reflected in the electoral rolls. The electoral roll will thus carry not only the details of the person but also the photograph of the person. Therefore, at the polling station the identification can be done without any hassles.

For these 700,000 polling stations, we engage a staff of five million. It is an average of five per one polling station. Some booths with more voters may have larger staff. But all these staff are drawn only during elections and are not permanently employed. This five million staff excludes the police and other central police government personnel we take from the government to conduct the elections peacefully. While the provision in the Constitution initially was that each constituency would be delimited or rearranged on the basis of equal population every 10 years after the Census, for some practical reasons, this was not done in 1981 and after that no changes have been made until now. Now with the new law being passed, fresh delimitation has been taken up. Hopefully, for the 2009 elections to the Parliament, new constituencies would be available. But in the meantime, there have been lots of distortions in existing constituencies. Influx into some areas has ensured that constituency numbers have gone up, elsewhere it has gone down. For instance the Outer Delhi Parliamentary constituency in Delhi with 3.3 million voters is the largest in the country. The same Delhi has the constituency with the least voter population of 350,000. The Chandni Chowk Parliamentary constituency, falling in the inner city area of Delhi, cannot grow as it stagnates with a population of 350,000. But the Outer Delhi constituency where a lot of construction activity has taken place and people have moved in during the past 30 years has grown to 3.3 million. About 11 years back, we had one Assembly constituency namely Modakurichi in Tamil Nadu with 1033 contestants as a record. Otherwise the average number of contestants in a Parliamentary constituency is somewhere around 8.

Based on the winning margins, we have calculated the percentage of votes that the winning candidates have got. Average polling in our parliamentary elections is around 55 per cent. The polling in Assembly elections is little more at 60 or 62 per cent. When there is a local body election, the percentage goes up to 72 to 75. In the current Lok Sabha, we have 325 out of the total 543 members who were elected with less than 50 per cent of votes polled. Because of the polity getting fragmented, with 25 to 30 per cent of votes polled, a candidate can win today.

I will now take you through the methodology that was used to refine the system over the years. Firstly, we have refined the methodology used in preparation of rolls. We now have the provision for electoral rolls being read out in the villages. It is now mandatory that once the electoral rolls are prepared, they should be read among all the villages so that any names if deleted could be corrected. In urban areas, we have attempted to have the electoral rolls read in every ward, though it has not been very successful. But in cities like Bombay and Delhi where there are housing societies, the secretary of the society takes the responsibility to read out the rolls to his society members or the residents in the group of flats. This way the rolls have improved, though the problems by no means had been fully solved. We still have people on the day of elections claiming that they had voted in the previous elections but their name is not in the current roll.

There are some important issues that I would like to highlight *vis-à-vis* the powers of the Election Commission. Unlike in many countries, notably in Britain, where the government of the day will choose when the next election will be held, this provision is not available in our country. The government can resign and the Election Commission has the powers to conduct the elections within six months thereafter. In respect of two recent elections, the powers of the Commission were tested. In 2002 in Gujarat, the government of the day resigned and the Assembly was dissolved and they asked for a poll to be held immediately. This was a few months after the riots in that state. The Commission assessed that the situation was not conducive for elections and it would not hold elections within the time limit as asked by the government. The power of the Commission to hold elections within six months and its power to choose the timing was upheld by the Supreme Court. In the last election held in UP in 2007, there was a slightly different problem. The Commission geared up for the polls within the stipulated time limit, the last day for the expiry of the Assembly was May 13. The Commission had planned in such a way that the results would be announced on May 11. But the government in office at that time suddenly had an idea of dissolving the Assembly in the State and imposing Central rule. This meant that two constitutional authorities—the Election Commission and the government in office—were, in a sense, in conflict. The Commission decided that it will stick to its mandate and hold elections in the stipulated time. Despite the debate going on over the imposing of Central rule, the Commission declared its intention and date for the polls. Thereafter, the whole idea of imposing Central rule was quietly given up by the government in office.

There is one document related to elections that I would like to bring to your notice. In the conduct of elections, it is apprehended that the ruling party has a slightly upper hand. It has the resources, and the government staff which has to work under the Commission is perceived to be more inclined towards the party in power. To overcome such situations, about 25 years back, all political parties came together and prepared a document called the "Model Code of Conduct." The document restrains the government in office more, obviously because it is expected to have more powers to influence the voters. There are certain do's and don'ts which apply to all, but in particular to the party in power. There is a separate set of codes for the party in power. The party in power either in the Centre or in the State shall ensure that no cause is given for complaints that it has used its official position for the purpose of its election campaign, etc. The implementation of this model code of conduct is in the hands of the Election Commission. In the run-up to the elections, any party or candidate in the fray can make a complaint to the Commission that so and so has violated the code and necessary action be taken against him or her. The Commission enquires and passes its final order as to whether the party, the candidate or the group violated the model code of conduct.

I will also like to bring to your notice some of the steps taken in the last few years, especially in the elections in Bihar in 2005 and the elections in West Bengal and Tamil Nadu in 2006 and in UP in 2007. Three major initiatives were taken. Now that the rolls are available in electronic form for easy checking, one issue which we examined was whether there is any discrimination against women. This gets reflected in the rolls too, like inadequate enrolment of women in the electoral rolls. How do we assess this problem and how do we tackle it? Every 10 years, the Census is conducted and state-wise and district-wise information is available about the male-female ratio of a particular district. We applied this ratio to the electoral rolls of that particular district or constituency. And wherever the ratio in the roll and the Census differed, we made special arrangement for the officials to visit such places to assess whether there are deliberate omissions of female voters in the rolls. This was one of the important steps we had taken during the recent UP elections. It did lead to dramatic improvement in many constituencies. But I would say that we could take it to the micro level of examination.

The second step taken relates to absent voters and bogus voting. Under migratory shift, in some cases, the name of the voter continues to be in the original polling station. We realised that this is a potential area for bogus voting. More than the electoral officials, the political parties and candidates are aware about who is available or who is not, in the polling station area. Therefore, if a candidate decides to commit a fraud, he would look for those who are not available in the area but whose name is still in the rolls. Due to our insistence on electoral identity cards, attempt to exploit this section of absent voters for bogus voting could be curbed. Further we made a special list of these voters and it was distributed to the polling stations. We asked the staff there to specially check if anyone out of this list came up for voting and ask for their photograph to make sure that he/she is actually the person he/she claims to be for future check. In the event, we were very successful and the bogus voting was curbed. By and large there was no bogus voting in UP.

There is also another important step we took. We call it vulnerability mapping. In each of the constituencies, there are groups like women, the underprivileged or the weaker sections of society who could be under threat and prevented from casting votes freely. We took special care of this category, listing out vulnerable groups. We assigned special officers to make sure that these groups got a chance to vote. So, these new initiatives will be a certain feature in all the coming elections too.

All in all, the Election Commission of India is striving its best to live up to the expectations with which it was created, namely to hold free and fair elections. Over the years we have constantly innovated and have used technology to aid our quest to keep our nose ahead of the problems and I am proud to say that we have succeeded and have earned a name for the institution as an election authority with the highest credibility.

AZIM PREMJI

Azim Premji is Chairman of Wipro Technologies, one of the largest software companies in India. He is an icon among Indian businessmen and his success story is a source of inspiration to a number of budding entrepreneurs. Today, Wipro Technologies is the largest independent R&D service provider in the world. In 2000, Asiaweek magazine, voted Premji among the 20 most powerful men in the world. In April 2004, the Time magazine, rated him among the 100 most influential people in the world. In 2005, Government of India honoured Azim Premji with Padma Bhushan.

18 India of My Dreams

Making Right Choices

AZIM PREMJI

In terms of my experience, all things are created twice—once in our minds and once in our lives. Dreams come first, and dreams are also very futuristic. While our country has a rich heritage and a glorious history, the time has come for all of us to carry this pride ahead in constructing the future of our country. But just creating a future for our country is not enough. The future has to be translated into action and it has to create results through commitments and those commitments have to be delivered by the people. Unfortunately, commitments are rarely honoured.

What has been done in the past in our country has been summarised by the finance ministry. But I think it is worth repeating. For the first 30 years, the economy was growing at 3.5 per cent. This growth rate has always been a source of criticism. And the population was growing at the rate of 2.5 per cent. This left us with a huge task of uplifting the standard of the living of the people. Thankfully, there was a change in the policy in 1991. Some bold actions and steps were taken by our political leadership and bureaucrats. This was a major landmark, which, I think, led to a major transformation of our economy, and we got results. This could be a good parameter because it does reflect on the standard of living going up. The growth rate of our economy reached a little under 6 per cent between 1995 and 2000 and then it became 7 per cent between 2000 and 2006. Currently, the growth rate is 8.5 and 9 per cent, and the momentum in the economy and entrepreneurship is reasonably good and it is running in a rather disciplined manner.

I think, it is reasonable to assume that, irrespective of any tensions in the politics or political compositions, the growth rate of 8.5 per cent is almost certain. We should however, be thinking in terms of 10 per cent growth as our ambition. Be it 8 per cent or 10 per cent, given the size of our economy, we should be proud of that. Simultaneously, we are finding our share in the global economy in terms of exports. Though it is just 1.3 per cent currently, there has been a significant achievement—we were just 0.6 per cent a few decades back. Our foreign reserves are strong. They are in excess of $250 billion. Given the way they are growing, very soon we will have $300 billion. This is unheard of, because in the past we have been struggling with just 2 to 5 billion dollars.

Apart from the economic growth, our country has other solid pillars. It is one of the largest economies in the world. It has a democracy which works well. There is a high degree of sensitivity with which our political forces vote. They evaluate the performance of the political masters they appoint. We have a very significant skilled manpower and a professional cadre. We have a lot of intellectual power. We are now getting much more global in terms of manufacturing knowledge, a trend especially during the last two or three years. Global companies are looking at us not just for the purpose of knowledge management, but also as an alternative source of scale, quality and stability for their global manufacturing needs. And significant is the way our companies are becoming aggressive in the global markets. We have one of the largest pools of scientists, technicians, engineers and managers in the world today. For example, India will graduate 500,000 engineers this year while the United States will graduate 75,000 engineers and countries like Germany will graduate only 25,000 engineers. As things get more technical, especially products and services, compared to the rest of the world we will have people who with inherent capabilities through academics will be able to perform more in accordance with the environment that is getting technical.

Demographically, we have one of the youngest populations in the world and this will be a huge strategic advantage. Compared to China, our nearest rival, we have a huge advantage. China came down hard on the population growth over the past 20-25 years and now has an aging population.

More importantly, as a country we have been able to manage coalition governments. It is very challenging and difficult, but we have survived coalition governments. Coalition governments have by and large performed well and they have kept the economy running. Our economy has become insensitive to what is happening in political action and has been running independent of what is happening in the political area. This is one of the most significant achievements which will help in sustaining our economy in the long term and will help in realising high standards of living even for the poor people.

Till now I have been discussing the good things. So what are the challenges ahead? We have so many poor and deprived people in our country. The major challenge is the growing disparity between the haves and the have-nots. There is a major rise in the standard of living of the affluent and the rich. The people who have money have become insensitive to the poor. This is the greatest source of worry so far as the disparity between the haves and the have-nots is concerned. One good thing about subtle wealth is that at least it does not get attention and the gap is not that visible. We have to accept the fact that we have to create wealth and distribute it. We cannot distribute wealth which we do not have. But what I would strongly advocate is that people who are creating wealth should have a certain degree of responsibility in spending it. More important, perhaps is the sense of trusteeship in terms of what they represent and what they are expected to do with it.

The second important challenge is creating a sense of pride in every citizen. We have bemoaned ourselves, criticised ourselves and demeaned ourselves for long. As a result of which pride in ourselves and pride in our country has suffered. We are now in a situation where we have much to be proud of. It is important that an average citizen is proud of our country. I feel that there is such a marked sense of pride even in smaller and less successful nations. Why do we, as a country, always be defensive about our nationality and always be so critical about everything we do? This is not good, because eventually we are demeaning ourselves and hurting our own pride. What we require is a significant change in terms of our character, because character determines our destiny. I use the word character in a broad sense, very omnipresent as a complex mix of thoughts, words, feelings and actions that constitute an individual. And the heart of character is the values that guide our lives. In my own experience, one of the key factors that influence people to strive, share and contribute is to have strong values. To believe in something and hold the cause consistently irrespective of the adversaries they encounter. It is to believe in something and go for it with full force. People with great values drive leaders to choose the right path and prompt right actions in difficult times. In the long-run, values enhance the integrity, stability and visibility of the person and the society as well as the nation. They are the success factors—be it an organisation or a country. They make success more worthwhile, enduring and more permanent. Strong values in individuals, society and the nation creates results. If you ask me what has been our biggest bedrock of success, I would say that we practiced certain values so religiously and unfailingly. Values are of no value unless you practice them. We have done so religiously because we consider it as our character and strongest asset.

The third challenge is to maintain the harmonious diversity that is central to our existence as a nation. It is a unique asset and character that we have as a nation. We must never ever abuse this diversity. It is the fundamental constitution of our society that leads to harmony and we cannot risk abusing this very basic character of our country. We are a very diverse people—diverse in our dress, social and food habits, religion and rituals. Yet we are extremely unified when there is a national crisis. As a nation we have always come together whenever the need arises.

The last challenge before us is our large population. Lot of people consider it as a liability. But we can also look at it as an asset—an asset which we can build upon. Given our population growth, we need to create job opportunities of 7-9 million annually. This appears as a huge task. As a case scenario let us look at our software and BPO industry, which I have studied a lot. Today the BPO and software industry employs 2 million people. For every job we create, we create four support jobs. Support jobs in transportation, security, food catering and in inputs that we require for capital assets and materials. So the industry today employs between 9-10 million people. The industry is growing at 30 per cent annually and even with 5 per cent productivity it is adding 2.5 or 3 million jobs. And these are highly professional jobs. We train people extensively after we hire them. We also take people who are experienced. The industry primarily employs people who are from science background or are engineers. But we also employ people from other educational streams. So there is a great diversity of talent which we employ. Typically we train them from 6 weeks to 16 weeks full time before we put them on the jobs. In terms of changing customer requirements, technologies and refreshing their skills, we also give 10-15 days of training a year while they are on the jobs. It is an industry which keeps on upgrading the quality of talent. Similar things are happening in the pharmaceutical industry, biotechnology and auto-engineering sectors which are also major growth centres. A similar trend is also seen in the textile sector. Therefore, the reality of creating jobs to meet the aspirations of the people is feasible today. And it has been proven in terms of what has happened in the past two years.

The other side of job creation is self-employment. Highest intensity of employment in any country is self-employment. We should step further and induct skill-oriented curriculum into our basic education system like Germany has done. This skill training can be in terms of plumbing, automobile mechanics, electric mechanics, or carpenters etc so that more options of self-employment are created. Dozens of professions are opening in our villages because of penetration of wealth. It is happening with high returns in agriculture, particularly in processing and semi-processing. Mass retailing is also a driving factor. We are therefore in a situation where these challenges can be met successfully. But we need to direct it with policy frameworks and initiatives.

How do we tackle these challenges? Obviously, there are no easy answers. There is a need for structural reforms, strong political leadership and consistency and direction. There is also a need to take hard decisions and a need for strong commitment to make it happen. Perhaps, that is the most important need. The fundamental requirement in an emerging country is education, particularly at the grass-roots level. There are lots of initiatives which are taking place in this. True education is about developing not only knowledge but character. It is about unleashing the innate capability and curiosity of the individual. It is also about developing creativity and empathy in the society. It is about taking responsibilities not only for themselves but also for the society at large, becoming a whole human being who is able to cross across mental barriers and think of the larger good. If we have more educated people, many of these challenges can be met very successfully.

Ultimately it is not just dreams that lead us to our goals. It is the choices that we make. If we make right choices, we create a harmonious and prosperous society with character combined with pride and it gives us enormous confidence to continue on this path of success. If not, we miss out on the enormous opportunities staring us in the future.

I would like to conclude with a very well-known poem written by Rabindranath Tagore, which many of you must have read, I have read it repeatedly. It lists provisions for India to succeed.

> Where the mind is without fear and the head is held high;
>
> Where knowledge is free;
>
> Where the world has not been broken up into fragments by narrow domestic walls;
>
> Where words come out from the depth of truth;
>
> Where tireless striving stretches its arms towards perfection;
>
> Where the clear stream of reason has not lost its way into the dreary desert sand of dead habit;
>
> Where the mind is led forward by Thee into ever-widening thought and action;
>
> Into that heaven of freedom, my Father, let my country awake.

"Now things have changed—many Indians educated and working in America are returning to India because India has changed. India is the new land of opportunities."

— Bala V. Balachandran

Padma Shri Awardee, Distinguished Professor,
Kellogg School of Management, Chicago

19 From Communication to Knowledge

Sam Pitroda

The first opportunity I had to work on telecom was unique in many ways in those days because then, not many had thought that telecom will be the driver for development in developing countries. It was generally believed that telecom is for the urban elite, for rich countries, and the poor countries need to wait till they bring their economic level to a point that they can begin to afford telephones.

In my business, we used to plot the number of telephones per hundred people as telephone density against GDP. This was a standard chart which everyone talked about, that if you are rich, you have lot of telephones and if you have lots of telephones, you are bound to be rich. When we looked at this developmental model for India, we decided to change this and concentrated on access. The STD/PCOs are the examples of the access to telecom and do not emphasise the telephone density. I remember talking to Rajiv Gandhi about this in our couple of initial meetings and he instantly said, "Sam this is it, this is what we need to do." Without his support, his political will, his confidence, his trust, I would not have been able to do any of what I did. There was a great chemistry between the man who had power and vision and will, and someone who had the technical ability to at least dream of something different. Time and time again, we have seen that when you have that deadly combination, things get done.

I want to take you from telecom to knowledge not through my personal journey but through a journey that the world is going through. In what does it mean to India, I see things very differently than a lot of other people see and I have a dream on what knowledge would mean to India 20-25 years down the line and I want to share that with you.

When I talked of telecom in 1981 and 1982, every Indian kept telling me, it cannot be done; you do not understand, there are a lot of problems, this does not work, bureaucracy, hurdles, no investments and government and all kinds of things. The key was not to listen, at times be arrogant and rely on your ignorance, that ignorance is going to be a great asset. If you listen to them, you will be convinced and you will not do it. If I am told to do the same thing that I did in telecom, I would not even begin. So, in telecom our aim was access as opposed to density. As a result beneficiaries were rural, under-privileged, as opposed to urban, elite professionals. To do this, we had to develop human resource; indigenous development was the key, as opposed to going out to the French, Germans, Americans and Japanese to buy their products. Against all odds, we decided that we are going to do this on our own. Then the wisdom was not to waste time. Bring the equipment and install it. There were times when there was so much pressure on Rajiv Gandhi from multinationals to close CDOT. But every time I went to him saying that we are not going to do this, he said, "Fine". The key then was to build people–young people who had no idea what digital communication meant–take them raw and build around them lot of capabilities. We trained thousands and thousands of young people in digital communication. Today, these people are all over–they are in Australia, Europe, India, they are building businesses and are running factories. So besides access, building human resource was another key and the third key was indigenous production and indigenous equipment. To me, India's need in terms of small rural exchanges is something which can relate to the Indian environment, heat and dust. All of this was difficult to do because it required a lot of risk taking. Success was not assured, but we kept at it against all the odds in the system–odds from the vested interests who saw commission going down, odds from multinationals, political bosses, bureaucracy. I had believed then, the only thing India has and I still believe in, is talent. We do not have oil, minerals, metal, diamonds. Can we really energise the minds of the young to do the things that need to be done? The telecom journey took about five years, we faced lots of problems and frustrations. Finally it got to a point today, 20 years down the road that we are adding 6 million telephones every month and when I came to India, we had 2 million telephones for about 750 million Indians. We have created huge companies like TCS with market cap of US $ 28 billion, big software companies, telecom companies, 160 billion dollars of foreign exchange reserve and at the end of the day a lot of confidence in the young that we can do it, that we are capable and we can tackle it. Telecom not only gave us confidence but also global visibility. Everywhere you go today, people believe that Indians are talented, good in software. This confidence works both ways–globally we have the visibility we needed and now we are at a point where we need to look into what can we do with the telecom success story.

The telecom revolution that we had started did not take into consideration the internet. We had no idea that there will be something like the internet. We had no idea of the mobility. These two things–web and mobile phones have really transformed the way you think about everything today including education, research, innovation, science and technology, libraries, and everything is about to change. Because internet gives us riches and richness and mobility gives us freedom and flexibility that we never had before. Today, we are adding 2-3 million mobile phones every month. World over we have already 2.3 billion mobile phones and by 2010 we will have 3 billion phones. This year a billion new phones will be added. People change their phones every 12 months. Today's phones are as powerful as computers. I have seen it all–I got into electronics in 1960s, when one small chip used to cost 35 dollars. I remember buying memory chips of 16 bits for 16 dollars, today I can buy perhaps 135 M bytes for the same amount of money. Electronics, especially telecom, IT, software, has changed the way we could do things. So, on the one hand, we have huge gains in telecom, but we have no gains in knowledge. Knowledge doubles every five years but it still takes four years to take a degree from college. We still teach people the same way we were teaching hundreds of years ago. Today when we think of school, we think of dusters, blackboards, chalk, teachers, books and exams. Telecom revolution is going to force us to think differently. If you were to build a university today, how would you build a university? Immediately people think let us create a campus like Cambridge or Harvard—buildings, auditoria, football fields—telecom forces us to think very differently. The other day I was talking to somebody about the role of the teacher. Someone said that we need to retrain our teachers. We perhaps need to train 500 thousand teachers now, today.

Traditionally teachers have been spending 90 per cent of their time in creating content and delivering content. Day in and out, the teacher goes to the class and says the same things over and over again! I had a teacher who used to take great pride that his notes had not changed in 20 years! Telecom will get the teacher out of the business of creating content and delivering lectures. If 90 per cent of the job is taken away from the teacher, what does the teacher do any more? Do you really need the teacher? Do you need this ratio of 10:1? When people take great pride in saying that we have a student ratio of 10:1, I think it is bogus, when we need 500:1. Internet and telecom has connectivity potential for everywhere, lots of videos, graphics, animation, games, instant information, anywhere, anytime, in whatever volume you need, open courseware. For example, MIT has 1800 of their

2000 courses in open courseware; you can download a course being taught by the Nobel Laureates in Physics. Why complicate life and redo that course, there is no way you can do better than them. So there is no need for local physics teacher to try to figure out how to teach this course; take it as it is, may be modify it a little bit to suit local conditions. This huge database of great courses in the world, best of the best is the content that you want to use. To deliver, you need broadband connectivity. Classroom could be like Barista, a local *chaiwala's* shop; you really do not need old paradigms of schools, teachers and all that.

Today, in spite of all these tools, even in a country like US, the gains in the knowledge industry are little. Tuitions have gone up. With all the broadband connectivity and all that, it still takes four years to obtain a degree. What have we gained? Why have all this technology and capabilities been there? We have done some studies and we can prove that if you use the right kind of IT technologies and telecom, we can learn the same material in half the time. What it means to reduce the time to learn is that we can reduce the cost to learn, we can reduce human resource to learn. But we need new methodologies. When I look at moving from telecom to knowledge, I first look at what are the gains from telecom. Access, bandwidth, content, flexibility and mobility–if we are given all of this today, how would knowledge look like tomorrow? So, let us look at knowledge.

Prime Minister Manmohan Singh decided to set up a Knowledge Commission just over a year ago; the idea was to look into five areas of knowledge—access to knowledge, knowledge concepts, knowledge creation, knowledge applications and knowledge services. Let's take access. To improve access to knowledge you need literacy, languages, translations, libraries, networks, portals, reservations and affirmative programmes. To improve concepts, you need to re-engineer primary education, secondary education, distance learning, vocational education, university education and all of the professional education like health. I can give you an example I went to Stanford University and found that they have a special team of 27-28 people working for the past seven years on computer simulation of cadaver, rather than a dead body. When you learn, whatever you learn, you do it on computers; when you put an injection on to somebody in the virtual world, it gives you the same touch and feel of the real world. So much is going on about how to use these techniques. We are not using any of that. In some of our medical colleges we find that the teachers do not show up, in that environment how do we use technology?

In concepts the issues are still access, quality and quantity. Not more than 7-8 per cent of our children go to colleges, we need that number to be about 15-20 per cent. How do you double the number of colleges and universities? We do not have the money for it. So how do you do it with new technology? For creation of knowledge, science and technology, patents, copyrights, trademarks, applications in agriculture, health, traditional medicine and traditional knowledge and finally e-governance–how is telecom helping to improve governance? Today in e-governance, we are taking age old processes that the British *Raj* left behind and we are computerising them. We have our recommendations in which we say we need to re-engineer processes before computerisation. A lot of these recommendations are already on the web, on the Knowledge Commission website. So when you look into telecom gains in the past decade, you find that there are so many hidden treasures that can really transform knowledge.

India has 550 million young in the age below 25, how are we going to educate them, with what tools, with what kind of training and how can we expedite the process of training? What do they learn and is it relevant? What it means is that we need to overhaul the system completely.

Nothing we do today, according to me, is worth preserving or overdoing it to make a point. But if you start with that mindset, you realise that we need to do so much to improve knowledge. A couple of days ago when I was talking to some reporters, somebody asked me where is the money? Is it all a pipe dream, how do you find money to do all these things? Because in India, people take great pride in identifying a problem, no talent is required in that. I told them, do you realise that we have a telecom company called BSNL, and I have a colleague here with me who has worked in BSNL. This company is owned by the government with a market cap of 70 billion dollars, perhaps it is one of the largest telecom companies of the world, comes in the first 10 companies. Should the government own telecom companies now? Can we sell that in the market and put every bit of money in education? If we had 70 billion dollars to put in education, what cannot we do? We need guts to take decisions like that. That is what you do when you say we want to go from telecom to knowledge. We need to recognise that link. On the one hand, we have no money to set up colleges, on the other, we are holding 70 billion dollars in asset in telecom. But as soon as you say things like this, people react. What do you mean, how can you sell this public jewel in the market? You need to change the mind set, you need to think out of the box. You need to really think the unthinkable. Until then, you never get the difference, because then as soon as you try to do something new, you identify five problems. This cannot be done, that cannot be done–which means continue the way you continue to do.

I was talking to Nandan Nilekani once and he said, "Sam in spite of the fact that we are graduating so many software people, if I want to hire good software people, I need to interview 10,000 to hire a hundred or whatever the number is." Why? Because, a lot of our graduates are not usable. It is about a lot more than just the degree, it is about the ability to communicate, to write, to integrate with people, learn to work as a team. All modern work requires team work. All innovations are multi-disciplinary. So if I am an engineer and I do not know economics, I will never understand business. If I cannot understand the business model, I can never scale it. Things have changed so much that the traditional way of educating people has no meaning. When I see that connection between telecom and knowledge, I get excited about the opportunities. But I also worry that others do not see it. They think this guy is crazy, he has no clue–and I know that they have no clue. But how do you fight this battle? It takes so much time to explain, because a lot of these things come from your guts, they do not come from your brain. For some of this, I have no explanation, but I know that this is the way to do it. Why, because, I have spent 42 years doing the same things differently.

The problem we have today or the challenge we have today is the mind-set. How do you get these people to think differently? How do we break old ties with knowledge systems, how do we create new libraries? One of the recommendations we have made to the PM, which is going to be accepted, is to create a network of 5000 nodes for one gigabyte, fibre network to 5000 locations in universities and libraries, health facilities, science and technology laboratories and agriculture research. We have some work going on where we are connecting with two gigabytes. We are saying gigabytes, 5000 not 57 or 67. And when do we do it? In the next six months, not in six years. How do we do it? We already have the capacity to do it if we make up our minds. These are the kind of bold initiatives we will have to take to transform the education system. Some people say, but I do not need gigabytes. Do not worry, let it be there, kids will figure it out, because the man I am talking to is in his 60s and he does not know how to use it. Give it to the kids and they will figure it out. So, we are talking to people who have no idea, what all this is and the people who need it do not get heard in the system. They have no voice in the Indian system. People who have the voice have no clue–that is the system we have created. How do we break this system? To me that is the larger challenge when you try to go from telecom to knowledge.

I have a vision, I have some wild ideas; we have a great team, we have some young associates, very capable, who work with us. The Prime Minister has been very supportive and so has been Mrs. Gandhi and we really need to take the next step forward. I know that Rajiv would have appreciated every bit of what we are trying to do today. He would have said, "Not 5000, but 10,000 locations to be connected Sam." It is that kind of leadership we need. We are fortunate that we can dream today, because the success of telecom in the past has given us the ability to dream a little better. And we really need to dream wild and create the whole new knowledge base where these 550 million people below 25 not only provide workforce to India but to the whole world. I was talking to some Italian friends and I said get ready, Indians are going to be there and there is nothing you can do about it, just accept it the way it is. We need to think in those terms that we are training the workforce of the world in the next few years.

How do we see the next 25 years down the road? That is where we look at all the successes in telecom, one by one, and try to connect and map with knowledge. With this telecom, how would a library look like, how would research look like and how would under-graduate studies look like? What could a five year old child learn? Three year olds know how to operate a computer, and at six years we are teaching them a, b, c! Whose idea was it that you can go to school only at six? How do you decide that you have passed the exam? Why do you have to pass an exam and why cannot you fail four times and learn? I think, it needs new thinking.

I want to leave with this last thought that the telecom revolution is giving us the ability to re-engineer all our processes, whether it is how do we get a birth certificate, land records, how do we apply for admission in a school or how do we learn mathematics and travel–all of this that we had mastered in the 20th century is completely wrong. All of this has to change. How do I get my travel reservation done? Why should I go to anybody–I should be able to do it over the phone, I do not need paper tickets, I do not need travel agents, I do not need any of that because telecom gives me a completely different set of tools. It is this connectivity between telecom and knowledge that I am excited about. I am dreaming something big with India, for India, and we need your support, your understanding, in going forward, and see if we can make a dent in the system.

J.S. VERMA

Jagdish Sharan Verma is the former Chief Justice of India. He has earlier served in various capacities including as the Chief Justice of Madhya Pradesh; Chief Justice of Rajasthan; Acting Governor of Rajasthan; Head of the Administrative Committee of Madhya Pradesh; Chairman of Advisory Boards constituted under the National Security Act and other preventive detention laws; and Company Judge in the High Court of Madhya Pradesh.

20

An Impartial, Trustworthy and People Friendly Judiciary

An Indispensable Pillar for Democracy

J.S Verma

This is a subject that is of great importance for all of us, and in the present democracies this is something which is a very important aspect irrespective of what discipline you belong to; even if you do not belong to a part of any government institution, as a citizen this is a matter of prime concern for all of us. So I hope I will be able to convey my perception to you not merely that we are experiencing in our country but also those belonging to this entire region and ultimately to the entire human family.

Since I have been in the judiciary quite long, I in a sense speak as an insider. I find this topic as something very well thought of as it uses all those words which together encompass the entire gamut of what I am supposed to talk to you about.

All of us know that the current measure of the progress of a nation and its standing amongst the comity of nations is judged by the human development index. Now the human development index depends on, and is directly linked to the quality or the degree of protection of human rights in any country. This linkage does not end there. We have to remember that, it ultimately depends on the quality of governance in the country. When we come to that, the next obvious question is: which is the kind of governance that is best suited for the protection of human rights and human development? And there is no dispute any longer that democracy, which is people-centred and also owned by the people, is the best form of governance. So, the next step is to look at the formula, the linkage between human rights and human development and the two depending ultimately on governance. So, that is the significance of democracy in the polity.

Democracy today means inclusive democracy so that every section of the society or the community participates in the process of governance, because in democracy people have a participatory role; and that does not mean the rule only by the majority. The majority today is for deciding the ruling party, but this does not mean that they are going to be the last word for everything; thereafter for its implementation all the sections of the society are expected to participate in all the decision-making processes and that is what is called inclusive democracy.

What are the most essential characteristics or the distinct foundation of democracy? The rule of law is the most fundamental and salient feature of democracy, the bedrock of democracy. If the rule of law has to be enforced, there has to be someone to ensure that rule of law prevails and that it is implemented properly in a fair manner; and it is here the role of the judiciary comes in.

The judiciary is fundamentally entrusted with the responsibility or the duty to ensure the proper implementation of the rule of law. Having stated so, the next step is to understand as to what is the nature of the judiciary that you must have in order to ensure that these end-results are achieved? Stated differently, what are the essential characteristics of the judiciary of the kind that is contemplated for the proper performance of this task?

The essential features of the judiciary are being impartial, trustworthy, and people-friendly; and these words are comprehensive enough to include within their ambit all that is required to ensure that proper measures are ensured for the rule of law. It has to be impartial because when there is an adjudication required between individuals regarding their rights, it has to be decided impartially irrespective of who the individuals are. Then there would be occasions necessarily where the conflict is between an individual and another individual or between an individual and the state itself, because very often the conflicts of individual rights or erosion of their rights, particularly in the area of human rights happen between the individual or individuals and the organs of the state. Such erosions are likely to be caused mainly by those who are in power. So, it has to be impartial whenever it is required to decide disputes not only between individuals but also between individual or individuals and the state or the different institutions of governance.

The judiciary has to be trustworthy. It must enjoy the credibility in the eyes of the public, that is to say that people must have faith in the decisions it ultimately gives, whether the person wins or loses. And finally, it has to be people-friendly: the judiciary has to be sensitive to the individual human rights.

In addition to these, of course that is also implicit in these three words, that the judiciary has to be competent—it has to be equal to the task it is entrusted with; it must be well-equipped to discharge these functions in such a manner that it remains updated itself with all that is required to discharge these functions properly. It must enjoy a level of integrity that is of the highest order. What is more important is that this integrity is not merely institutional but individual as well. Every member of the judiciary or every judge must enjoy a reputation for integrity not merely as a part of the institution but also personally as an individual.

The judiciary must also be independent. This independence should not merely be from extraneous factors but also from the internal infirmities or compulsions, so that a judge is not even subconsciously influenced by any such factor. The judgments or rulings should not in any way be influenced by even personal infirmities. So these are the broad characteristics needed of the judiciary.

I am not confining only to what is there in the Indian judiciary, which I will come to only towards the end of my talk. Here, I am dealing generally with the broad principles of the judiciary and the fundamental democratic principles involved in dealing with these issues.

Now what really is the basis for the distrust in the institution of judiciary? I will deal with this a little later. But to begin with, judiciary was considered and described by Alexander Hamilton, under the American Constitution while discussing the comparative roles and strengths of the three organs of democracy—the legislature, the executive and the judiciary. Hamilton, writing in the 78th Federalist described the judiciary as 'the least dangerous branch' amongst the three branches of the State. And those of you who are interested to know more about this, there is a book by Alexander Bickel titled "The Least Dangerous Branch"—the title is picked up from Hamilton's writing in the Federalist.

Judiciary is the least dangerous of the three organs. Why? Because it neither has the purse nor the sword; for finances it has to depend on the legislature and it does not have the power to implement its own decisions for which it has to depend on the executive. This was how Hamilton visualised and described the judiciary.

From above we see that judiciary everywhere has been rightly perceived, certainly not as the least dangerous branch but probably the most powerful arm of the State. This is happening everywhere in the world today, because it has the power to influence and reverse or change even the actions and decisions of both the legislature and the executive.

From where does the judiciary get its strength? The judiciary gets its strength from the public, because in a democracy it is ultimately the people with whom the ultimate political sovereignty vests. And it is the backing of the people or the public that gives judiciary its real strength or the needed power and inspiration. So long as the judiciary continues to perform the role it is entrusted with, which is to work for the public good, it will have public support. And, therefore, this is something that also ensures that the judiciary retains its credibility and strength in its own interest and continues to do what it is meant to do; and this really is a necessary corollary. The high status of the judiciary will continue only so long as it retains its credibility in the eyes of the public as an institution which is working for the good of the people.

Now, what is really significant to the history of the evolution of judiciary starting from the concept of being the least dangerous branch of democracy to what it is now. All of you know the original concept of a monarchy was that the king was the fountainhead of justice and therefore all power was vested in him. Then as time went by, the new concept of the rights of individuals began to be recognised and then the king only symbolised the fountainhead of justice. And we saw in England how the constitutional monarchy was developed along the lines of the Magna Carta; then you had the American Independence and also the French Revolution. The common feature of all these was that the rights of common man or the fundamental human rights were recognised or the concept of non-discrimination was accepted or the fact that men are born equal and free was universally acclaimed. Then the next logical step was to ensure that there was someone to monitor and ensure that those rights are respected and protected. And that is how the concept of judiciary of this kind was born and began to develop universally.

Mostly it is believed that the concept of judiciary, as it is conceived today as the essence of democracy, was developed even though it was conceived as the least dangerous branch initially. It became really so only after the famous judgement of the American Chief Justice Marshall in 1803 in the case of Marbury *versus* Madison in which he ruled that the judiciary had the authority and responsibility to verify whether a law made by the Congress was in accordance with the constitution or not, and if not, then to declare it invalid. Two centuries earlier that concept as the necessary corollary of the Magna Carta, started developing in what is known as Dr. Bonham's case in 1608 wherein Lord Coke had sowed the seed of this kind of the role which has reached today. In the American constitution, it was the Marbury *versus* Madison and some later cases that led to the development of the judiciary as we see it today, but now we have come to a stage where modern democracies have this provision of an all powerful judiciary which can even review any law made by Parliament and incorporated in the Constitution. India is one of them and there are many other countries with such provisions in their constitution; and that is so far as modern constitutions are concerned. So, this kind of judicial review at the time when it was spoken by Lord Coke more than two centuries before Marbury was almost considered a sacrilege and it had attracted a lot of harsh criticism. But today it is an accepted and respected principle that is being recognised by incorporating it into national constitutions.

This is the history of the evolution of judicial review that really gave the power to the judiciary to review the validity of all state actions including the laws made by legislatures. That is to say that the constitutional validity of all the laws made by the legislature and the validity of the actions of the executive or for that matter those of any public functionary, even the administrative acts of the judiciary itself, are subject to judicial review. The interesting part today is that even the chief justice's administrative orders are subject to judicial review by the judges of the same court. This is how the supremacy or the superior position for the power of judicial review has developed.

Now a few instances to illustrate these points further. Take the last US presidential election between Bush and Al Gore. It was ultimately the US Supreme Court which decided who was the winner. This is the effect of the judiciary on even the most powerful office in the world. And then it was the rule of law which led to the exit of the US President Nixon. One particular case in the US which I would like to mention here is the Brown case in 1954 that related to the desegregation of the schools. The Brown case clearly showed how the US apex court could influence the American education policy; and another such decision in Roe *versus* wages relates to abortion rights in the US. All this was done even without the express provisions of judicial reviews in as many words as in the modern constitutions. In England, we know that there is no written constitution; it is conventions that make up the British constitution; and there, the parliament is supreme. As a matter of fact, there is a famous aphorism of de lome, that the British Parliament can do anything except make a man a woman and a woman a man, to which a wit answered by saying that even that exception is not valid, for if parliament says that all men be called women and all women be called men, so be it! The doctrine of ultra vires in Britain has brought in judicial review even with the parliamentary supremacy.

More recently, of course you have the European Court and the impact of the Human Rights Act of 1998 which enables the judiciary to decide substantially to the same extent, as the judiciary in a country like India. Then take the instance of Israel, where the incumbent president has been investigated and he is now facing prosecution. Take the example of Australia. Though the freedom of speech and expression was not expressly guaranteed in the Australian constitution, that is to say there was no bill of rights in the Australian constitution, yet the Australian High Court, as the apex court is called there, has implied this power in the 1990s from the representative form of government which the constitution provides for. So, this is a good example of even without an express constitutional provision also, due to the result of judicial creativity these rights are being created. The South African constitutional court has given so many remarkable judgements which have expanded, as a result of judicial creativity, the scope for realisation and protection of human rights. Look at Pakistan. The most extraordinary event in the recent past in that country was that the ruling military dictator had to reinstate the chief justice he had sacked a few weeks before. You know Pakistan is not a democracy of the kind that we know; democracy exists there only on paper. Now the military dictator is scared everyday what the Supreme Court is going to do. So, from the least dangerous branch in a democracy, the judiciary is fast becoming the strongest branch even in Pakistan, is one thing, but to have that impact, the enforcement of the rule of law is required, even in a country ruled by the military—democracy is only in name and for all practical purposes in Pakistan it is a military dictatorship. Coming to India, the public interest litigation, which we are aware of, has also made a lot of difference.

Let us now talk about some particular international instruments of general application. Two declarations alone are enough; the Universal Declaration of Human Rights of 1948; it says in the preamble that human rights should be protected by the rule of law—and that is the fundamental objective of this entire exercise; and Article 10 says an independent judiciary is indispensable for the implementation of this right—this protection of the human rights is a statutory obligation on the part of the state. Therefore, the rule of law is a statutory obligation. These two expressions cover the entire gamut of these two vast topics—that is the universal declaration of human rights, the preamble and Article 10.

The ICCPR—the International Covenant on Civil and Political Rights—takes it further. It speaks of, in Article 14(1), that everyone shall be entitled to a public hearing by a competent, independent and impartial tribunal established by law. The responsibility of the state is spoken of clearly by the universal declaration recognised by the ICCPR and that really is the status of the judiciary, according to this international instrument on human rights protection. The net result, therefore, is that the state's responsibility for protection of human rights extends to everyone within its jurisdiction and that obligation is not merely to protect from the omission or commission of state agents alone, but also from non-state players so that it is ensured that there is no violation by anyone.

The state has to ensure that none of its agents violate within its jurisdiction, and it is also a corollary of the rule of law. It was on this principle, in the case of the 2002 communal violence in Gujarat, that the National Human Rights Commission held the state responsible for the carnage; regardless of who was the culprit—we asked them why did it happen? You not only have to see that you do not do it, but also must see that others also do not do it, as it is your constitutional responsibility to see that every citizen within your jurisdiction is protected. If so, why did it happen? Therefore, the initial presumption is that the thing speaks for itself—if it has happened and you are responsible unless you are able to explain that you did everything to protect and yet it was beyond human control. This is the extent of responsibility that the state has in protecting human rights.

Now we come to the next step; that is on the nature of the judiciary. For that too we have two international instruments to which I would like to draw your particular attention, for these two channels are of more relevance to our region because the majority of you hail from this region. One, is the Beijing Principles on the Independence of the Judiciary in the Asia-Pacific region. This process started in 1982 in the Asia-Pacific region and was continued in 1995 in Beijing at a conference of the chief justices of the Asia-Pacific region, which was ultimately finalised after amendments in 1997 at Manila in the Philippines. I was privileged, as the Chief Justice of India, to be a part of this in 1997 when it was finalised. This is significant because it lays down the basic principles of the nature of the judiciary which is required to be set up by every nation for the purpose of ensuring that the task entrusted to the judiciary is properly performed. The primary objective, as mentioned in this document, is to promote the administration of justice, the protection of the human rights and the maintenance of the rule of law within the region. Therefore, we see that all through, at every stage, in all these international instruments, in the basic concept of these principles, that is to say, there is a linkage between human rights and the rule of law and governance.

There are some particular provisions in the document that I would like to mention to you. The very first article in this document says the judiciary is an institution of the highest value in every society and that is what it is expected to be too, and when it is perceived to be so, it is the duty of every member of the judiciary to see that it remains so. Article 2 refers to Article 10 of the declaration of human rights and Article 14(1) of the ICCPR says setting up of a competent, independent and impartial tribunal established by law, which means that it is a statutory obligation of the state and that an independent judiciary is indispensable for the implementation of this right. And we said indispensable pillar of democracy: if the rule of law is the pillar of democracy, then the judiciary is entrusted with the task of ensuring that this is implemented and protected. Article 4 speaks of the importance of independence of judiciary as the essential feature for this and Article 7 says that the judges shall uphold the independence and impartiality of the judiciary by avoiding impropriety. Impropriety is not merely illegality; you see something may not be illegal but may be improper; and even appearance of impropriety in all their activities is to be avoided. All of you must have heard the saying that it is not enough that justice should be done but it should also be manifestly seen to be done. Therefore, the impropriety and even the appearance of impropriety should also be avoided by the judges. The objective in these documents clearly speaks once again and reiterates that all persons are able to live securely under the rule of law. It then deals with the appointment of judges to ensure that you have competent men with integrity holding the post of a judge that is to say that a judge is not only competent but also a person of integrity and independence. It also speaks of the tenure of judges so that their integrity and independence is maintained. What is significant is that Article 24 says that the parliamentary procedure for removal of a judge by vote of the people does not apply to the removal of a judge which would rest with the judiciary itself. This is the extent to which the provision on the importance of independence of the judiciary is made to ensure it. And any semblance of impropriety also needs to be avoided and it goes further and states in Article 39 that the highest position is given to it because the people who man it are expected to satisfy the highest standards of human behaviour then only we can expect them to uphold and execute these extraordinary tasks with utmost propriety and integrity. It says inducements or benefits should not be accepted or offered by the judges if they affect or may affect the performance of their judicial functions. This is why I always emphasise that—I was invited to deliver a speech on the fault-lines in our democracy last week at the Nehru Museum Library and one of the things I said was this—even post-retirement activities of a judge should conform to the standards required in service otherwise it can be misleading to those in service, lest someone may think that what you are doing now is influenced by what you did while in service. Therefore, once you have undertaken to be a judge, till the last day you must maintain that dignity and restraint. This document ensures that impartiality, trustworthiness, integrity etc will depend only on these principles being followed. It is adopted and accepted and practised not only in India but in the entire Asia-Pacific region and even the rest of the world.

The other document I would like to highlight is the Bangalore Principle's of Judicial Conduct. They deal with and further elaborate these requirements. Once again you find these three words—competent, independent and impartial in upholding constitutionalism and the rule of law. These are mentioned in the preambles itself. Then the second part of the preamble speaks of the public confidence in the judicial system and the moral authority and integrity of the judiciary is of utmost importance to the functioning of the judiciary in a modern democratic society—these are prominently mentioned in the preamble of the Bangalore principles. It then speaks of the values—independence, impartiality, integrity, propriety—once again anything improper has to be avoided and even the semblance of impropriety must be eschewed.

What is essential, therefore, is that it is alright to have all these in theory, but accountability must also be ensured. Judicial accountability must be ensured so that all these are practiced too. For this, you ought to have an effective mechanism in place to enforce judicial accountability, whenever needed. The mere presence of an effective mechanism for judicial accountability acts as an internal check or a possible deterrent against erosion of these values. But, there are bound to be aberrations how so ever well perfect may be the system in general, and for those aberrations, there must be an effective mechanism to deal with those aberrations, because you just cannot permit the system to get polluted even for a rare aberration. Therefore, it is the duty of the state also to ensure that there is an effective mechanism to deal with judicial accountability. The Bangalore principles speaks of this; it says by reason of the very nature of the judicial office, effective measures shall be adopted by the national judiciaries to provide mechanisms for implementing these principles for judicial accountability, if they are not in place within their jurisdiction.

I think these two international instruments cover the entire gamut and therefore these apply equally to everyone, it does not matter where you come from, because this is true for all democracies and all judicial systems wherever democracy and the rule of law prevails.

Let me now come to some specific things about India to illustrate my points further. In India, judicial review is a basic principle of the Constitution expressly provided when the Constitution was enacted. Article 13 clearly says any law made, even earlier and especially those made later, which are inconsistent with the Constitution, would be invalid. This is an express provision for judicial review. Not only that, the Fundamental Rights of individuals are guaranteed, which itself contains in Article 32 as part of the Fundamental Rights, a constitutional remedy for the enforcement of the Fundamental Rights. Therefore, Article 32 giving original jurisdiction to the Supreme Court itself is a Fundamental Right and imposes an obligation onto the Supreme Court to enforce Fundamental Rights of individuals whenever there is an occasion to do so. This is another express provision for judicial review. In addition to Article 32, there is Article 136 that deals with the special powers of the Supreme Court which enables the apex court to grant special leave against any determination which it thinks it must review or revise. This is with regard to the Supreme Court. So powers of the apex court under Articles 32 and 136 are wide enough to cover the entire gamut of the issues that I have been discussing here.

Then there is a corresponding power with the High Courts too. Within their jurisdictions corresponding to Article 32 is Article 226, which in its scope is much wider than Article 32 because Article 32 empowers the courts to issue the five prerogative powers such as the habeas corpus, prohibition, quo warranto etc. But Act 226 empowers the courts to issue—in addition to these—any other direction or order etc. Article 227 gives the power of superintendence to the high courts. Articles 13, 32, 136 for the Supreme Court and Articles 226 and 227 for the High Courts are enough to guarantee the power of judicial review. In the Kesavanda Bharati case in 1973 it was expressly held that Parliament's amending powers under Article 368 do not permit amendment of the basic structure and basic features of the Constitution. So that, even the amending powers of Parliament also cannot change that. Soon after this 1973 judgment, there came up the famous case of the then Prime Minister Indira Gandhi in 1975 where a law was enacted to provide that the election disputes relating to the Prime Minister and some other high dignitaries will not be subject to judicial review. But that part of the newly-enacted law was struck down by the apex court even though it was enacted after amending the Constitution, because judicial review is a basic feature of our Constitution. So that is the settled position of the provision of judicial review in this country. All state actions including the power of Parliament to amend the Constitution is not without limits.

The apex court recently also upheld judicial review even of executive actions taken under Article 356, which deals with the power of the Union government to impose president's rule in a state. And now even this power is subject to judicial review. This is the extent of judicial review not merely available, but exercised in this country.

We have in addition to these, the public interest litigation window, which you have heard of already.

Let me now come to judicial overreach. We need to segregate the two parts related to judicial overreach. One is the legitimate judicial intervention, which is now called judicial activism, and the other is the unwarranted judicial overreach, which is judicial intervention in areas that are not legitimate. But what is the test and how will you determine or how do we test the limit of unwarranted judicial overreach? Speaking extra-judicially in Manila, in 1997, I had said that the test is the action or the judicial intervention based on a settled or a newly-evolved juristic principle. If it is, then it is legitimate because then it becomes a part of the law that has a precedent value to be applied now and also in future similar situations. But if it does not have a precedent value, if it does not have a juristic value and principle, or if it dwells into area which is not a legitimate judicial function, then it is judicial overreach or judicial ad hocism, which may even tend to degenerate into judicial tyranny. Therefore, when the power of the judiciary is growing, that too very fast, this is an area which has to be vigilantly guarded by self-restraint of the judiciary itself, so that the doctrine of separation of powers as provided in the constitution between the three wings of the state is maintained and respected.

This is my perception of what is the role of the judiciary in a democracy. What it is meant to do is basically a great responsibility for which it must equip itself and constantly update its equipment and conform to the moral stature which will give it the moral authority institutionally and individually to retain that credibility in the public eye which ultimately is its real source of authority, strength and respect.

SONAL MANSINGH

SAEED NAQVI

SATISH NAMBIAR

SADIA DEHLVI

VARUN SAHNI

MYTHILI BHUSNURMATH

21 India at Sixty

Surendra Kumar

We are here to "Celebrate the 60th Year of our Independence." "Sixty" has different meanings for different persons. Sixty, for us civil servants, is the retirement age. Sixty, in the eyes of some, is the ripe age to join politics. Sixty years in the life of our nation is the ideal age to take off.

India is taking off, if one reads the headlines of the media, from Davos to New Delhi. Today we have gathered here to exchange views and brainstorm, but not to create a storm in a tea cup. We will share impressions and look back on what our country has achieved in the past 60 years. I would urge all the panellists to focus on four simple questions—What have been our three greatest achievements since Independence? What in your view were the three greatest failures, or blunders or near-misses? How do we obtain the twin objectives of marching forward economically, as we are doing now, and also creating a fair, just, equitable and inclusive society? And lastly, where do we see India after 10 years from now, taking into account all the factors from political to social, economical to technological developments?

During the early 50s, in a village when, in khaki uniform a postman came on a bicycle with a little envelope and pulled out pink colour paper, it used to be a telegram. It carried all kinds of messages.

This Chapter is based on India at Sixty: A Brainstorming session held at FSI on September 28, 2007.

Congratulations, on being blessed with a son and the parents went into jubilations. Sometimes, congratulations for being blessed with a daughter, but shoulders of some parents went down. And sometimes, sad news like mother passed away. The telegram brought messages, of sorrows and joy. We used to get postcards. If the corner was cut, it meant sad news. Now-a-days, it is rare that you get telegrams. It is still rarer to get postcards. It is the age of SMS. Your instant messages read like "Hey baby, are you meeting at 'Ghunaghroo' tonight?" If you want to make it spicier, you can add clips of lip-locking at bus stops or hugging in a public park!

We have televisions channels which ask whether the arrest of a journalist is right or wrong. You vote and after a few minutes they would announce that 80 per cent are against it. I am talking about technological advancement after the Independence. We used to listen to Amīn Sayani's melodious voice on the Vividh Bharati programme which was so popular, especially the requests for songs from the Defence forces. We used to wait to find out if our choice sent through the letters was included in the programme. Now, you have MP3 players and the most advanced gadgets in which you can store up to 5,000 songs and carry in your pocket.

We used to have telephones which were very sturdy and built in black colour. You could use it in your defence if an intruder came at the night. There was no cordless system; we used to have cables running for miles. Now we all know what is happening in the Indian telecom sector; we are selling 7 to 10 million cellular phones a month.

When I was in school, the usual mode of transport was bicycles. Even when I was studying in the Allahabad University, I was one of the three students in my GN Jha Hostel who had bicycles of their own. We were displaying them as if they were the Rolls Royce. People used to borrow it from us. Then we came to the age of Bajaj Chetak in the 70s. Even in the mid-70s, if you wanted to have a Fiat car, you required a recommendation letter from Ministers or MPs as there was a waiting time of over one year. Now you do not know how many brands are available in the car market. It is another kind of a change that you see here.

Times are changing and so is life and lifestyles. We do not get tired of telling about our $226 billion foreign exchange reserves and that we have been growing at the rate of 8.5 per cent for the last five years, and that we are the second largest economy in the world, we are home to the second largest pool of trained professionals in the world, and so on.

There was a time when many women joined national politics on a call from Mahatma Gandhi. Now there are a lot of them in all walks of lives from politics to industry; 33 per cent of our *panchayats* have women as *Pradhans*. There is, no doubt, a sea-change. Still, we keep on reading about foeticide in Punjab where three million baby girls never see the light of the day. In some remote areas, women are even paraded naked or are punished for marrying outside their caste. But we also have women like Mayawati who became the Chief Minister for the third time with a thumping majority.

On balance, I would say, we have achieved a lot. And I do feel proud of what we have achieved. At the same time, we must not gloss over the task which is left. Even if we have a middle class of 350 million who have the purchasing power as good as those in America or Europe, what about the majority who find themselves on the other side of the fence? More than 600 millions are far away from even the basic standard of living. They do not have electricity, drinking water, health clinics or schools. So we have come a long way, but we still have miles and miles to go ahead.

In my view, the first of the biggest three achievements we have had should be that we still continue to be a secular, functional parliamentary democracy. Secondly, it is the social transformation, notwithstanding all the occasional communal riots and atrocities. The social transformation in the past 30 years has been more significant than in the past 3,000 years! Third is the revolution in the telecom and IT sectors. It is the biggest leveller and the driving force for transformation of the economic development of our country.

About the failures, I cannot open my mouth as I am still serving in the government. You ask me this question after three years, and I will be happy to respond.

As for future, I see India as a front-runner and one of the three major economies in the world 10 years down the line. Our standard of living will be far better, we will have far better roads and airports. By all accounts, India will be far better than what it was when we got our Independence.

Sonal Mansingh*

The artistes in Independent India have been treated with respect but with gloved hands. They are lovely to be looked at and their performances are enjoyed. But they are then put away or packed away, and they remain on the periphery. So, rarely artistes are invited to speak and so I am doubly honoured. I have to repeat what almost every one has said already. First of the three things that we can be proud of, is of course hanging on to democracy. I say hanging on, because at times we have faced perils. There was a time when there was no democracy. But we came back to it right away. Indians in every corner realise the value of democracy. We see the world extolling our neighbour China and pointing fingers at us, but I think that has lessened somewhat in the past five years since the explosion of IT and some other factors. What people

Sonal Mansingh is a master of Odissi and Bharatnatyam, and has a background of decades of training in Chhau (martial dance from Orissa). In a career spanning almost half-century, she has danced in 82 countries of the world so far as well as extensively within India. In recognition of her enormous contribution in the field of classical dance, she was honoured with Padma Bhushan in 1992 and with Padma Vibhushan, the second highest civilian honour, in 2003. With this, she became the first woman dancer in independent India to receive this high honour. Her contributions have also been recognised with numerous other awards and a honorary degree of Doctor.

forget to add is the qualifying statement that China is not a democracy but it is easy to get things done there.

But in a democratic country, with such multiplicity and complex layers of existence, minds, attitudes, traditions, norms, manners, concepts and beliefs, it is not very easy to take everyone along. So hanging on to democracy is one single great achievement.

My second point, which you may agree or disagree with, is the very strong cultural roots we are blessed with. There are so many intrusions into private lives now. Krishna did not invite Radha to the Kadamba tree by sending an SMS. But now it is all different. It makes it so easy to sit in your drawing room and surf the channels or check the SMS. It is amazing to see that people of all ages are seen even crossing heavy traffic roads without looking at the vehicles but looking at their mobiles. God knows what message they have got there. So these are the things that take us away from our cultural roots, which come from centuries of unique cultural identity. Despite my cynicism, I can see that our cultural roots are still widespread either in large or small degree among all the people.

The third point I want to make is the acceptance of this multiplicity. It is one thing to have it and another to accept it. This acceptance is a very positive sign. Nobody needs to tell us that we have been secular for very many centuries. There are Hindus who fast with their Muslim neighbours during the Ramzan and there are Muslims who do not eat beef during the *Navaratras*. The story with the Sikhs, the Christians and the Jews is also not different. But given the changing times, and political, social, economic values and attitudes, it is becoming increasingly difficult. On the one hand communities are coming together and on the other, the divide and rule is getting larger and larger. To me, the achievement has been the open discussion, debates, discourses and disagreements and yet acceptance of this multiplicity.

Among the things that pain me, the first is about the state of our women. Even after many years of drafting a landmark legislation, the 33 per cent reservation for women in Parliament has not happened as yet. Almost 50 per cent of our population are women. Of course, we know about female foeticide. But the general attitude towards women is amazingly two divergent views: one is more and more visibility in public areas and on the other hand more and more aggression on them. When do we resolve this? I do not know. Has it got something to do with our education, something to do with imparting values in our homes and institutions? Here I would say that the role of media has been very disappointing. Where do we imbibe these values from? From our elders or our teachers? No longer is the system available to us, especially in the urban areas where it is only on the TV screen that you see *nana*, *nani*, or *guru*. The failure of our education system in training and imparting values is also responsible for the increasing aggression on women.

The other is the environment. It is nice to have seminars and debates on environmental imbalances in air-conditioned hotels. It is absolutely marvellous. It produces reels of papers which nobody reads. But do they try to do more? Do they worry about the decreasing number of glaciers? Do they worry about the dwindling number of tigers or other species? One of my students once told me that she had not seen sparrows for the last 20 years near her house in Safdurjung area. I asked many people about it. I found that terrific flow of electronic waves is causing terrible disturbances to birds. They become more fragile and lose sense of direction. The number of mobile phones is increasing by the day. Talk more for less money. As Amartya Sen puts it in his *Argumentative Indian*, we are truly talkative. We talk far too much. This is also something to be looked at. So there is woman, environment which is birds, air, nature, water, trees, etc, and we are not worried about them at all. There is more urbanisation and there are more buildings, fewer trees and depleting green cover. We have just 12 per cent green cover in the country, according to the latest available statistics. Who is bothered? One is bothered about bank balance, car, foreign trips, and farm house. It is a great failure of our society. It is said time and again that the Third World War is going to be about water. We will be begging, asking and fighting for a drop of water. What is the right way ahead? I would rather say it is right thinking, right attitude, right values and right balance as mentioned by Gandhiji. Mahatma Gandhi is a wonderful symbol for us. Right balance is difficult to achieve. The right way forward, for me, is to accept the multiplicity and the concern for the downtrodden. The right way forward is the genuine feelings beyond words. I will hope for an India with art, yoga and an India which is home to balanced people. I am confident that India will overtake China and the Indian Ganga of self-conscience and self-confidence will march on to rule the world.

Satish Nambiar*

Let me start by saying that I was 11 years old when we got Independence. I have seen the 60 years of our Independence right from that impressionable age. The second point I want to make in this context is what I would be saying. I would like to stress the fact that I am proud to be an Indian. Standing among all the inadequacies of over the past years, I am proud to be an Indian. There are three achievements that I have mentioned in my book. The first is that we have retained the basic democratic structure notwithstanding various inadequacies of which there are a large number. Secondly, I would like to stress that our impressive economic growth in the 15 years after economic reforms was initiated under real desperation

Satish Nambiar is the Director of the United Services Institution of India; former Advisor to the Government of Sri Lanka, Member of the Institute for Defence Studies & Analyses (New Delhi) and Member of the Advisory Council of the Folke Bernadotte Academy (Sandoverken). Awarded the Vir Chakra for bravery in battle during the Indo-Pak conflict in 1971, he is also the recipient of the Ati Vishisht Seva Medal in 1991 and the Param Vishisht Seva Medal in 1994, for distinguished service. Lieutenant General Nambiar served as the first Force Commander and Head of Mission of UN forces in the former Yugoslavia.

in 1992. Thirdly, not only because I am an ex-Army man, the major achievement has been the outstanding display of our armed forces not only in providing a security umbrella both within the country and outside, under which the country has moved forward in the last 60 years since Independence, but also providing assistance in times of national calamities and disasters, at the same time remaining totally apolitical. This is particularly relevant, not often mentioned, in the context of what we have in our neighbourhood. When we look to the East, the three countries—Thailand, Myanmar and Bangladesh—are under military regimes. Look to the West, Pakistan is also under a military regime. I think this is an important achievement.

I have also listed three failures, rather near-misses or blunders. A couple of them have been touched upon. Firstly, it is the inability of the establishment to provide basic education to our children particularly of the disadvantaged sections of the society. This is a, big failure and there is no excuse for it in my view. Secondly, our inability to provide basic health services to the needy and the poor including the children. And thirdly is the neglect of infrastructure development. These I think are the three big failures.

As the way forward, I have five points. First is to restore effective governance through probity in public life and by restructuring the civilian bureaucracy as the servants of the people, not the masters as they were in the colonial times. Secondly, ensure rule of law through implementation of police reforms and speedy judicial process. Thirdly, we have to accord top priority to basic education, health and infrastructure. Fourthly, introduce land reforms particularly in tribal areas. This assumes importance in the context of the growing problem of Naxalism. Lastly, remove the bureaucratic obstacles to economic growth. In so far as where we would be looking ahead 10 years from now, provided that we can get our economic act together, while ensuring that the benefits reach the poorer sections of the society and across the board in all regions of the country and if we are able to address the internal unrests, there can be little doubt that we will be a major regional power and player. If so India will be a global player of some significance both politically and economically. And this will take place, in my view, through sheer determination, innovation and the drive of our younger generation who will overcome the obstacles placed in their path by the sections of the political leadership and bureaucracy.

Saeed Naqvi*

In the 19th century, Sir Syed Ahmed Khan, a man of enlightenment in those times, wrote to the great poet Ghalib. And he sent him a translation called the "laws

---

Saeed Naqvi is a renowned writer, journalist and at present editor of the World Report, a syndication service on foreign affairs. His thought-provoking articles, reports, stories and features frequently appear in all the major national dailies of India and abroad. He has the distinction of having interviewed many world leaders and personalities in India and abroad. He has earlier worked as the Foreign Editor, Indian Express, Delhi; Editor, Indian Express, southern editions; with the Salem Evening News, Massachusetts; Sunday Times London; and the Statesman, Delhi. He has studied at Delhi University, Thomson School of Journalism, Wales, UK and Princeton University, USA.

by the emperor." He wanted him to write a preface to that. Ghalib had just been to Calcutta and seen things. He wrote back. And what he wrote led to the estrangement between them. He said, "forget these old and antique laws. Look where mankind is going." His one trip to Calcutta opened his eyes to the wireless and the new innovations he saw, which were way ahead of the times in the 19th century. Similarly, we can be nostalgic about the 60 years. But rather than making a blank statement on everything, I will restrict myself to one or two things which strike me as very important. One is that the difficulty with the cliché is that it embodies the essential truth. And since the cliché that sometimes the baby is thrown out with the water.

One of the great achievements of the past 60 years, I think, has been the width and depth of our democracy. Democracy has facilitated the upward mobility of classes. Today, we who could not be in the vicinity of the gates three-four years back, are sitting in the very sanctorum of power and we are wielding power. Naturally, when upward mobility of this scale takes place, it is accompanied by a social or status reversal of the other classes, hence the social turmoil we witness today.

Sometimes I believe that the political instability in the country is actually social turbulence. Because the elite are being replaced or being forced to give place to the non-elite. This seems to me a great achievement. It is remarkable that our democracy has reached so many people. Look at the nature of the debate that is going on, on the 1 2 3 agreement in the Indo-US nuclear deal. It is a good agreement but if people have not been involved in it, you are going to make heavy weather of it. It is shortsightedness to talk about this as an issue between the Right and Left or Buddhadeb or Karat. This is part of it. But basically, it is democracy giving the seal to it. So, you have to persuade the people and then things will be facilitated. This is very important.

Another big issue is about the Muslims. I really do believe that nowhere in the world, this I say with all responsibility, you would have a government of the day appointing a high-power committee to look into the socioeconomic conditions of the Muslims. First, it was entire minorities earlier, now, it is the Muslims in particular. And it comes out with a candid report which is so revealing. For instance, people think that all Muslims go to *madrasas*. But only less than four per cent of those school-going Muslim students go to the *madrasas*. No one knew there are only 33 Muslim members in the 543-member Parliament. No one knew that the constituencies with 62 or 55 per cent Muslims are in the reserved list. All these are realities. But the fact is that the report is out and is in the public domain and we are discussing it. I think it is a remarkable achievement of our democracy. In fact, nowhere in the world, do such a large number of Muslims have so much access to democracy. Their socioeconomic conditions may be different. I am saying it without any exceptions, unless you can argue that democracy is not a value. If electoral democracy has value, then this is an achievement of the last 60 years.

I should now touch upon the media, of which I have been a creature for the last 30 years. It is a mixed bag. The proliferation of the electronic media has been a very big disappointment to me personally. The manner in which electronic media has turned to the market for advertising trivia as the only incentive, leads to the following. There are four C's in our media.

1. First C is Cricket: It is wonderful. I love cricket and I have travelled around the world to see cricket. But I am a little bit old fashioned, and to me this Twenty20 seems to be in the globalisation era and soon we will have cricket in junkie stadiums with diamond bats and all. So you have three hours of cricket and five hours of discussion on it. When I was asked to be part of one discussion on cricket, I said no. But later it dawned on me that I should have been into it earlier. Because you see beautiful girls who do not know the elbows and knees of cricket, waxing eloquent on cricket. And that is nothing but frustrating five hours of dialogue.
2. Second C is Client. "*Bap ka beti ke saath balatkar*", *Aaj ki Khabar*. (Man rapes daughter, today's news.)
3. Third C is Cinema. News like Aishwarya Rai visits new temple.
4. Communication: Fatwa on Salman for attending Ganapathi pooja, and what do you say Mr. Naqvi? I said it was terrific. I was at Sholapur and all around Ganapati poojas were going on with cultural programmes and lectures. I was also invited to many and I had to do an *aarti* before Ganapati. This has been the culture of our country that my religion exudes something part of our culture.

The basic problem in the past 60 years has been that the media has not been able to communicate. This has been lost in transition.

Varun Sahni*

What have been the three major achievements? Firstly, I think it is the 60 years of genuine liberal democracy in a pluralist, multicultural, socio-economically deprived continental-size setting. Just look at the setting in which our democracy has been faring astonishingly well. It has been an achievement of historical importance and it is an achievement that deserves to be celebrated. The second great achievement, I think, is Non-alignment, though this is something we do not talk about any longer. But as a large, weak post-colonial state, evolving a

Varun Sahni is Professor in International Politics at the School of International Studies, Jawaharlal Nehru University (JNU), New Delhi. He has studied at St. Stephen's College (Delhi), JNU, and New College, Oxford. He has been "Personalite d'Avenir" at the French Foreign Ministry and Member of Mexico's Sistema Nacional de Investigadores (National System of Researchers). He teaches International Relations theory, and writes (in English and Spanish) on nuclear issues and border management, great powers and middle powers, and military politics in Latin America. He is a member of the guest faculty of the Foreign Service Institute (FSI) of India.

foreign policy that was both prudential from realistic standpoints and ethical from the normative perspective was a major achievement. The third achievement is that we as a nation successfully navigated through the perils of the 1990s, the most dangerous decade for us collectively. This was the decade when we were friendless externally and were beset with all imaginable domestic problems. Yet we managed to navigate successfully. These were the years of long perils when our long-incubating technological revolution was finally emerging. So to me, it has been an astonishing achievement.

What have been the three near-misses? For me the first near-miss was in the pre-Independence period. During the Second World War, our Army with 2.5 million men with arms, the largest all-military volunteer men in history, stood on the side of good. And despite that India was unable to secure a permanent UN Security Council seat at the central desk due to its colonial status. For me that is truly a near-miss. If some factors could themselves have played out differently, it could have gone completely the other way. We deserve that seat, therefore we ask for that now. I always add the traditional factor which is even by the 1945 criteria, we ought to get our place.

But let me just look at the post-Independence period which we are supposed to do. Now, the biggest near-miss is not going nuclear before July 1, 1968 even though we had the capability to do so. The second is our country's persistent failure to make the region coherent and peaceful. We have not presented a viable regional vision. We have not invested heavily in this regional vision, because it was a hard one. This has allowed other powers, especially China, to build alternative incentive structures for our neighbours. Therefore, we remain in a region that is fundamentally neither coherent nor peaceful. I think it is a huge failure.

The third, which some fellow panellists have already said and worth being emphasised again, is that even after 60 years of our Independence we lack an authentic public health and education system. Let us recognise that it is the direct result of our public policy that deprives basic health and education.

What about the way forward? I have five thoughts, and the most important is to invest heavily in public health and public education not just by the public exchequer but also through public-private partnerships. Building schools and hospitals that function must be really a national mission. It is just as telecom outreach mission that worked, just as oilseed that worked. It is literally to get some very capable people, empower them to build much like the way the Delhi Metro is being built today. Let them cut through everything else, just let them go and build hospitals and schools. The second most important thing is that of winning India relative peace for a decade, and here the armed forces have a huge role to play. Peace for us can never be absolute, it is always relative. But this is the time that our country needs to develop the capabilities and emerge as a system-shaping state. We are not there yet, but a decade plus we could be there. But for that we need a period of decade-plus relative peace.

The third point is seeing Naxalism for what it is, and which we are not doing now. It is a clear danger to our society and also to our democratic system. Naxalism should be dealt with a variety of state instruments, including politics, economics and the police force. Until we recognise it, we are creating a huge problem for us.

The fourth important element in the way forward is taking the HIV/AIDS crisis very seriously. I think we need to go the Brazilian way, not the South African way. The question was asked about our vision on what are we going to do for the world. I think that is the question the world is entitled to ask us as an emerging, system-shaping power. What are you bringing to the table? Are you just another large power-increasing state? China has already grasped this idea. China presents itself as a developing country mindful of the interests of other developing countries. Many countries in Africa see China protecting their interests. But why would any country welcome India's emergence? Here the idea we should begin to work on is Gandhi's idea of trusteeship. But Gandhi developed it obviously in a different context. Gandhi developed it to smoothen the rough edges of capitalism. Although this trusteeship is extremely difficult to put into practice, it holds the key to some of the most globally common concerns in the contemporary world. The central notion of the Gandhian concept of trusteeship is the value of non-possession. It goes hand in hand with the notion of we as individuals, groups and nations. The fragile global ecosystem in particular is crying for a new type of world politics. This has to be based, at least in parts, in the notion of the Gandhian trusteeship. We are either going to swim together or sink together. The notion of trusteeship is something that we need to begin to think seriously. There is a lot of work to be done on it, even theoretically and conceptually. But it needs to be done if we want to have a distinct voice in future.

Where is India going to be? I think the three big dangers that we could face over the next decade are mass social discontent, environmentally-induced conflicts and dynamics. Any of these, in isolation or in combination, could bring India's emergence as a system-shaping state to a grinding halt. But having said that, I feel that India will almost be a great power by 2017 or 2025. But the real question, I believe, is not about India's power, but the configuration of power around India. India will be powerful but those of us who studied international politics keep emphasising that absolute power is relative power. The Britain of Gordon Brown is definitely more powerful and richer than the Victorian Britain. The destructive power of the single trident submarine of the British navy is more powerful than all the fleet of the Victorian age at their peak. But that is in relative terms. The power is always going to be relative. So the question is not about how powerful we are going to be, but what about those around us. When we ask that question, a couple of other thoughts too emerge. Firstly the global centre of gravity would by then have firmly shifted to the Asia-Pacific from the Euro-Atlantic zone. And what we are going to confront is a bi-polar Asia-Pacific in a bi-polar world. This is going to pose a very tough choice potentially for us. Choosing between Washington and Beijing is not going to be something we can willingly do for two reasons. One, such a choice would divide us internally, which was one of the reasons for the first round of non-alignment. Being the weakest among the three, it is going to be a dilemma for India. Who would you choose? A declining global hegemony or a rising continental hegemony? It is not going to be an easy decision to be made at all, even if our public life has an opinion on it. There are compelling reasons for India to really fear an Asia of opposing axis and balances emerging. That will be really bad news for us. And I predict that if that would happen, what you would see will be a new bout of non-alignment, much more difficult non-alignment for India. And the reason is that this time one of the poles is going to be our next-door neighbour–China. Also, fence-sitting will be much more difficult for New Delhi, simply because we would like to see China and the US also having system-shaping capabilities. In other words, the non-alignment which we call as hiding strategy is possible when you are weak. Hiding strategy is difficult when you are one of the system-shaping powers. So the only option for us is to start working proactively in order to build a cooperative security architecture in the Asia-Pacific region. It is a process that needs to be unfolded, and surely will unfold slowly in the next 10-15 years. This is going to be an important time for us because we will probably see the American capabilities declining, again in relative terms, not in absolute terms. Therefore, we may begin imagining the US as enmeshed into a cooperative security process. So what India needs to do is to build robust economic and political links with both China and the US. India could end up playing a very important catalyst role in bringing these countries together and thereby creating a new cooperative Asia.

Mythili Bhusnurmath*

When I look at the past 60 years, to me there were three successes. Two successes come to my mind so easily and on the third we are having lot of debates in our office itself. The first major economic success in post-Independent India was most definitely the Green Revolution. I think very few of us remember today with all the talk of globalisation, that how terrible

Mythili Bhusnurmath is an economist-turned banker-turned journalist with an abiding interest in macro economics especially monetary economics, finance and banking. She has written extensively on these topics during her more than decade long stint as a journalist with both the Economic Times, the leading business daily in India and the Financial Express where she was the editor (the first woman to head a business paper in the country), for two years.

it was during the 50s and the 60s when we did not have food to feed the millions. It was really very, very difficult for us to leave our self-respect as a nation and go around with a begging bowl and ask for food from various countries, and that too not in very honourable terms perhaps. So, I think the Green Revolution was the first thing that gave us a great deal of self-respect. Today, we are not just able to feed our people but we are also exporting food items. Thus, the first major transition in the 60 years was the Green Revolution.

The second success to my mind is the huge jump we have seen in the growth rate of the economy. From a sedate growth rate of 4 per cent in the past, to a healthy 9 per cent today and we are talking about 10 per cent of growth in the near future. So it has been a huge, dramatic change and this is why we have suddenly become much more important in the eyes of the world. Because now they do realise our huge potential. Look at any international paper, be it the *Wall Street Journal* or the *Financial Times*, we are there. We have suddenly become much more important. That is purely because of our growing economic prowess. So that has been the second major transition we have achieved.

The population growth pressure has also eased and the per capita growth rate is close to seven per cent. This is a huge transition. Because it is not just enough that the GDP alone grows, it is also important that it translates into benefits to each one of us. Yes, per capita income is not an indication of the real individual prosperity. We do have a large number of people below the poverty line. But in the post-reform period, there has been a clear decline in the percentage of people living under the poverty line. This has been the second great achievement.

And on the third great achievement, we have lots of discussions. But as far as I could say, it was the combination of globalisation and IT and ITES revolution. When we talk about the IT and ITES revolution, there is a tendency to view it as a very huge one. But if you actually look at its numbers, the number of people employed in the IT and IT-enabled sector, it is very, very insignificant and even in terms of contributions to the GDP, it has not been that large. What it has done is that it has greatly raised the profile of the country in the world at large. To that extent, it has given us the ability to punch above our weight. But I would place globalisation as the third great achievement that has happened in the 60 years of our Independence. The moment we lowered our trade barriers, the moment we moved to a market economy, we became much more integrated with the world. The ratio of our export-import with the GDP has dramatically improved with 45 per cent growth and our forex reserves are much larger today. We have now the fifth largest foreign reserves in the world. So I would put globalisation as the third significant achievement so far.

So to my mind these are the three great achievements since Independence: globalisation, remarkable economic growth and the Green Revolution.

As far as failures are concerned, unfortunately we have a fair amount of failures. Perhaps the biggest failure to my mind is on the infrastructure front–both physical as well as social. On both these fronts we have failed pretty dismally. Despite the large amount of investment that was put in earlier, in the post-reforms period we could not invest as desired, especially in agriculture. The government could not invest sufficiently, particularly in agriculture, where public investment is the most important kind of investment. Education and health are two important areas of infrastructure where we lag behind badly. So poor infrastructure is one of the most significant failures and today we are paying for that.

The second failure I would cite is the slow pace of poverty reduction. It is certainly not a very happy state to see that we are a nation with close to 250 million living below the poverty line. If you go to other figures, it is still ok. We can have a dispute over numbers, but we certainly have a large number of people below the poverty line, much more than any self-respecting country would like to have. So we have not been able to do enough for a variety of reasons to reduce the number of the poor.

The third biggest failure I see is not strictly economical but it has serious repercussions on the economy. And this is poor governance–corruption and the poor delivery of governance as a result of which whatever we spend, does not reach the poor. Rajiv Gandhi's figures have been quoted *ad infinitum*. And no scientific study was done to establish how much of a rupee went to the poor. But it is a fact that delivery has been an abysmal failure in our country.

As far as challenges are concerned, the biggest challenge we face is that of regional imbalance. I do not think we really realise how important it is going to be. We really cannot have, in a democracy, a twin-speed economy. You cannot have one part of the country growing at 12-14 per cent and another part literarily struggling with poverty. So the regional imbalance is going to hit us very hard. And the growing spread of Naxalism is surely a reflection of the fact which we do not realise that in a democracy you cannot have two parts growing at two diametrically different growth rates–one in the 21st century and one in the 16th or 17th century. So, to my mind, the growing regional imbalance is a big challenge for us.

Another problem is that employment generation is not catching up with the growth of the economy. There is a dramatic transformation in the structure of the economy. When we became Independent, we had close to 50 per cent of our GDP coming in from agriculture. But today, it is less than 20 per cent. But the population dependent on agriculture has not shown any significant decline—even today over 60 per cent of the population is dependent on agriculture. So unfortunately, what has happened is that over a period of time, we have the same share of population depending on a shrinking share of the GDP pie. This has created huge problems for the country. Therefore, we should find alternate employment for all those living in rural areas and this could be non-agriculture also. Non-farm employment must be found for the 60 per cent of the people who are increasingly trying to fend for themselves on a smaller and smaller share of the pie. In the past when we did not have enough communication, the people were content with their lot sadly. Today, that is not the case. They are empowered and they know they can and they will protest. So, unless we address the issue of growing unemployment at the earliest, I think we are going in for a very sorry time.

We have outlined some failures and challenges and also how to we address the infrastructure issue. As far as opportunities are concerned, the biggest opportunity that we have is that of the demographic dividend. I think it is a huge opportunity to which we have not woken up yet. But this opportunity will materialise only if we are able to empower our youth. Unless we are going to give them the skill sets with which they can look for opportunities, the entire demographic dividend will turn out to be a demographic liability rather than an asset. Today there is great support as the Western world would not have recourse but to turn to Indians, not India. Though India is not able to emerge as an economic power as it would want to be, Indians across the world will be a very powerful force. Evidently, this opportunity of demographic dividend is a huge opportunity.

The second opportunity is the tremendous change in mindsets. Gone are the defeated days, gone are the days of scarcity, gone are the days when we were content with just what we have. We did not look for alternatives everywhere then. Now look at the youngsters around us, they have a huge gung-ho force, epitomised in the Twenty20 cricket. It epitomised a new India which can stand up on its feet and give back as good as it gets. Because they knew that they are as good as anybody else in the world. With that change in mindset, we can do anything. There is nothing that we cannot do. It is a huge achievement. To my mind, it is a huge transition.

And the third thing as the opportunity to cash upon is the peace dividend. Ever since the Second World War, there have been problems all around–be it Kashmir or Palestine. Ten years from now, we will be a $2-trillion economy. We will punch much above our weight. There is more urbanisation as a result of which there is more prosperity. But it also poses tremendous challenges. How do we address the issues of urbanisation without adequate infrastructure. Social security issues will also be there. By and large, we are a much more empowered India and an empowered population today.

Sadia Dehlvi*

Since most of what needed to be said has been already said, I would like to speak on two areas of my main concern—women and minorities. I would really like to see India where we do not have pogroms like Gujarats or any other form of terror. Let us work towards an India where minorities and women are secure and can walk with their heads held high.

It is unfortunate that the story of Indian Muslims has been scripted by the broader Hindutva agenda. The myth of Muslim appeasement has been propagated to such an extent that the ordinary Indian has actually begun to believe these lies. If these were true, the social and political realities of the minority would speak differently. Muslims are sitting on the edge of the Indian framework and if communal agendas go unchecked and secular tempers not developed, India's largest single minority will fall out of the picture completely. In 1961, in an address to the AICC, Nehru held that communalism of the majority is far more dangerous than the communalism of the minority. Not condoning the latter he stated, "majority communalism is apt to be taken for nationalism."

At a recent seminar on secularism, the topic was "The desirability of treating Muslims with constitutional safeguards." I was shocked when they started speaking about Hindutva as the perfect ideology for India and the blatant outright anti Muslim comments. I spoke on the need to integrate minority rights in the development policies of India and the dangers of the Hindutva ideology as being practiced in Gujarat. My comments provoked mayhem and the participants refrained me from speaking further, calling me anti-national. It is disturbing that Hindutva forces have infiltrated the intellectual discourse in our country. A healthy nation is about healthy communities and if India has to progress, the Muslim community must walk aside with the rest of India.

Another disturbing trend is that the so-called war against terror is seen as a war against Islam and Muslims. This is terrible for the Muslims as they now face religious discrimination along with being socially underprivileged. There seems to be a global media strategy on showing Muslims in a negative light and often we see the worst types of stereo representation of the community. On media debates that seeming address Muslim concerns, we see incompetent self styled television created leaders who are invited to voice their opinion. To a large extent the media creates Muslim devils and then beats the community with them.

Another area of serious concern is the status of women in India. The growing statistics on female foeticide are pointers to the fact that women in India are being denied the very basic right to life. Indian

* Sadia Dehlvi comes from one of the oldest media houses of Delhi, "Shama Group of Publications". She has been the editor of "Bano", an Urdu monthly for women. As an activist Ms. Dehlvi has been working with women and minorities for over a decade and continues to write for various magazines and newspapers in English and Urdu.

women have progressed but the development is more visible in the cities and women empowerment has yet to trickle to rural India.

I know little of foreign policy but am deeply concerned about the nuclear deal and cannot comprehend why our government is in such a hurry to push the deal through. India has made a paradigm shift in its foreign policy and the reason for aligning with America need to be debated and explained to the public.

It has been 60 years since India's Independence and surely she will soon be a super power and will hopefully act with the responsibility that comes with being an influential global power.

J.S. Verma

I will just speak on a few things which all the speakers have agreed upon. The first thing which every one said is our democratic ethos. Let me say, it is not only our observation, but it is an observation of the historians too. It is the distinct feature of the Constitution, deep-rooted in democratic ethos. In spite of all cacophonies, differences and diversities, the power of the people to decide is more significant, when we compare it with our neighbours. The empowerment of the people is a real success story. And there has to be more, if we want to get more advanced.

Another aspect is that it is an inclusive democracy that we have. It is not just really a rule of the majority. All sections of the society have a role to play and they are involved in the decision-making and the governance process. According to me, the greatest assurance of secularism is: whenever there are atrocities against a minority community, those who do not belong to the minorities come forward to denounce these acts. Having said so, I have to admit that there are aberrations also. There are fundamentalists around us all the time. But the fact is, this is the culture which has developed and this is true assurance of our democracy.

The other thing I wish to mention, as others have said, is that we have a vast pool of knowledge-makers. As result of this, developed countries are outsourcing knowledge from here. The British National Health Service will collapse if Indian doctors are not there. Indian doctors, engineers and technicians are everywhere in the US. That is another success story.

In the near-miss or blunders side, there is economic growth but we do not have distributive justice. We have many billionaires, but we also have a vast section of our people who are living under the poverty line. This is likely to lead to social and political unrests. Naxalism is only one of the manifestations of this kind of inequality. I do not think there is any Naxalite who is not a brilliant mind. It is a reaction to the inequality. That is what we need to tackle.

Another near-miss is education. Sometime back there was news that there are 34,000 schools without a single student and a teacher. Article 45 of our Constitution is the directive principle which promises total literacy within 10 years of Independence. What have we been able to do? Article 21 was enacted as a fundamental right and added as a fundamental duty of citizens under Clause K of Article 51(A). Thus, 6 to 14 years education is parents' responsibility. If fundamental rights alone was a sufficient guarantee, there would not have been exploitation either as child labour or bonded labour. We had Article 23 and 24 right from the beginning of our journey as a democratic nation.

The affirmative actions, and the methods chosen have unfortunately led to more divisions and creating more fissures. What is needed is a pragmatic approach and empowerment in the right way. The recent results of the Central Services and CBSE have shown that wherever opportunities are given, persons from the economically and socially weaker sections have come to the top. So what we need is a pragmatic approach and some imagination and not measures which are merely for the purpose of seeking votes.

Another area is population explosion. Our population has doubled from what it was in 1951. Whatever is our economic growth, unless such measures are taken, which are accepted by the people, we will not reach the desired target.

I would also like to add a couple of other things. One is in the political sphere—the erosion of the Prime Ministerial authority. The Parliamentary form of government depends on the strength of the Cabinet led by the Prime Minister. Our Prime Minister mentioned three things—the prime ministerial authority is not eroded, a political party that would ensure that political problems are not treated as law and order problems and third is an efficient and incorruptible civil service.

I would add two more things. First is a strong and objective media, and the second is an independent and credible judiciary.

Corruption is eating into the vitals of every institution. This is an area which should be addressed. For that, everyone should start from oneself. We are very good at telling people what they should do, but we are not doing it ourselves. I think, charity should begin at home and the fight against corruption should be led by everyone of us.

What do I visualise about India of tomorrow? I have absolutely no doubt and I am a great optimist. India has a great future and this faith lies in our vibrant youth. The only thing left is that we must ensure that right values are inculcated in them. Ethical values, therefore, should be an essential component of education at every level. This is more so especially today as professions are becoming too mechanical. Everywhere it is money that counts. These trends need to be arrested.

SURENDRA KUMAR

Surendra Kumar is a historian by education, diplomat by profession and a sensitive author and poet. He has represented India in a dozen countries in the last three and a half decades in various capacities as: Ambassador to Mozambique, Libya, Eritrea and Democratic Republic of Congo; High Commissioner to Kenya, Swaziland and Malta; Consul General in Chicago, Minister (Press, Information and Culture) London; PR of India to UNEP & UN-HABITAT; Secretary, Ministry of External Affairs, Government of India; and Dean, Foreign Service Institute, New Delhi.

22

India of My Dreams

SURENDRA KUMAR

"*Sare jehan se achha hindostan hamara...*" best in the world is my India, thus paid tribute to India of his dreams Alamma Iqbal some 80 years back! It is a different matter that years later, he was not too keen to take credit for having penned such stirring tribute to India (by that time he was already espousing the idea of Pakistan). No other lyric has come anywhere near this simple but emotionally touching description of the quintessential essence of what India meant to millions over the years. If Rabindra Nath Tagore's "*jana gana mana adhinayak jai hey*" is the national anthem, Iqbal's "*qaumi ekta tarana*" has been sung at countless commemorative events in India for the last 60 years as the closing finale. It encapsulated dreams of millions of men, women and children of India when it was first rendered; it still strikes that passionate national fervour decades later.

For Wipro Chairman, Dr. Azim Premji, the highest dream for India is enshrined in Tagore's those unforgettable lines: "where the head is held high..." It is an inspiring ideal which we still have to work hard to achieve.

For Gandhiji political freedom alone was not enough; for him, true democracy would be realised only when the tears have been wiped off the cheeks of each and every poor in India...

For Jawaharlal Nehru, who called dams and factories as modern day temples and who helped set up IITs and Research Labs and gave the call of "*aaram hai haraam*" (down with rest), India should not only progress economically but remain a secular parliamentary democracy which should remain connected with the rest of the world and help less developed countries in every possible way to see them move forward.

The young, youthful Prime Minister Rajiv Gandhi whose entry in politics was a quirk of destiny rather than of cool calculated planning and who tried to introduce the youth of India to the 21st century gave the slogan of "*Mera Bharat Mahaan*" (My country India is great). Unfortunately, his life was cut short in his prime by a suicide bomber. The country is reaping the harvest of the seeds which were sown in the Telecom and IT sectors during Rajiv Gandhi's regime.

The coalition government headed by Shri Atal Bihari Vajpeyee, the first non-Congress government, to complete six years in the saddle, was blamed in the media to have been carried away by the upturn in economy and undertaken a blitzkrieg campaign of "India Shining" slogan which backfired; they lost the election defying all forecasts.

But today, the world is sitting up and taking note of India Incredible, India surging ahead at its own pace in its own manner creating history. After all, the Indian economy has grown at an average rate of over eight per cent for five consecutive years!

Thus, flows on the eternal river called India disproving all doomsday forecasts and overcoming all adversities stringing along the thread of unity in its bewildering ethnic, cultural, lingual, religious, social diversity, Dr. Iqbal was right when he said:

> *Kuch baat hai ki hasti mitati nahin humari,*
> *Sadion raha hai dushman, daur-e jahan humara!*
>
> (There is something unique about India;
> It has survived for centuries even when the whole world turns hostile!)

Mahatma Gandhi dreamt of *Rama Rajya:* the ideal reign of king Rama who is still revered by millions of Hindus as the ideal king, ideal son, ideal brother and ideal husband. But this concept is alleged to have created a sense of unease among the Muslims. And many feminine activists disapprove of Lord Rama's decision to force Sita to walk on fire to prove her innocence on return from Sri Lanka and then exile her just on account of a comment of an ordinary washerman!

For thousands of years, Indians have been worshipping women in the form of powerful deities: Lakshmi—the goddess of wealth, Saraswati—the goddess of learning, Durga—the goddess of energy and mother goddess. There can be no higher tribute to the greatness of woman than the concept of *ardhanariswara* i.e. the God is half woman! India was run by a woman Prime Minister called Indira Gandhi for 16 years. A few years back in an "India Today" poll, she was voted the best PM of India since Independence. But in the same India, foeticide is rampant; in Punjab, economically and educationally the most advanced state of India, around 2.3 million female children are never allowed to be born, they are aborted by their own parents! Frequent reports in the media about stripping a helpless woman and parading her naked through the streets in the presence of scores of indifferent passive spectators reminds one of the scene from *Mahabharata* when the Kauravas tried to disrobe Draupadi in the court in front of her husbands, the five warriors Pandavas! It is nothing short of a national shame as is the rate of 53 rapes a day.

While the upper middle class, the neo-rich class in India is thrilled every time a new shopping mall boasting and offering a host of international brand names is opened, outside these gleaming shopping malls, live hundreds of workers involved in the construction of these malls, not one or two but the entire family, in a tiny makeshift canvas/plastic tent pitched on the ground!

Some stinkingly rich individuals have gold plated taps and showers in their bathrooms but a few million slum dwellers in Mumbai wait for as long as 14 hours to defecate on railway lines running the risk of getting cut into pieces by coming trains!

While we never get tired of pronouncing our secular traditions from the roof tops, we do not hesitate to fan communal hatred to extract electoral victories. Some are hailed as nationalists and patriots but others are castigated as pseudo-secularists!

We have some of the brightest scientists in the world whose day begins with the recitation of *Hanuman Chalisa*, apoem in praise of Lord Hanuman, god of wind. Their professional scientific temper and personal religious faith do not pose any intellectual conflict in their minds. This is India, our Bharat where contradictions abound in every nook and corner of our daily lives and coexist simultaneously, representing different decades and centuries at the same time.

Though Finance Minister Shri P. Chidambaram saw no reason why abject poverty could not be eradicated in India in 20 years, if our economy continued to grow at the current rate, for his Cabinet colleague Mani Shankar Aiyar, Minister of Panchayati Raj, Youth Affairs and Sports and Development of North Eastern Region, India of today where more than 826 million people (Dr. Arjun Sen Gupta Report) still live on Rs. 12 a day is not the India of his Dreams.

While Railways Minister Shri Lalu Prasadji's turn-around of the railways was an inspiring story for other public sector undertakings, Dr. Dipak C. Jain, Dean of Kellogg School of Management, Northwestern University, strongly felt that Indian values, family *samskaras* and professional ethics were as important as leadership, vision for future, innovation and team spirit for the success of any organisation. His ideas about creating an ideal brand equity for India in today's globalised world were interesting as well as practical.

We are known to be a tolerant people. We have welcomed foreigners for centuries; Jews persecuted in Mesopotamia in the 6th century BC found shelter in

India. Parsis so few in number exercise huge influence in the field of trade and industry. We embraced Mother Teresa, an Albanian Nun, and honoured her with a Bharat Ratna. When she died her mortal remains were carried on the same carriage, which had carried the body of Mahatma Gandhi after his assassination. But it is baffling that such a tolerant people surprisingly deprived a large number of their own brethren of the most basic human rights for so long. And communal riots do flare up from time to time causing loss of many innocent lives and huge damage to public property, though the majority of Indians are essentially secular.

What do I wish to see in India of my dreams? Of course, an economically advanced India where millions of men, women and children would not live in abject poverty and squalor. They will have reasonably nutritious meals everyday, hygienic sanitation, safe drinking water, affordable and reliable health care facilities, decent accommodation to live, access to road, railways and airports, pollution free environment, school to send their children, a sensitive, responsive, caring, efficient and people friendly administration and police force. Is it too much to ask for? These are the most basic needs which all human beings should be entitled to. This is not asking for the Moon!

In India of my dreams there must be no discrimination on the basis of caste, creed, language, religion or gender. Yes, all these protections are provided for in the directive principles of our constitution but the fact remains that discrimination does take place on these counts, no matter at how a small scale.

In India of my dreams, we would not have educated unemployed youth or neglected older people. Education imparted will not only expand horizons of knowledge, understanding and appreciation of India's diversity, but also connect us with the rest of the world and appreciate what they have to offer. Above all, it should change our mindset and rid us of all outdated rigidities, prejudices, biases, and self-righteousness; and make us humble enough to listen to arguments contrary to ours, and create a caring and sharing, inclusive society. In today's jet paced life, and relentless pursuit of success and riches, we must not lose our cultural, civilisational and spiritual moorings and not get sucked in and consumed by ruthless materialism. Such an India will be at ease with itself and with the rest of the world.

"If I were asked under what sky the human mind has most fully developed some of its choicest gifts, has most deeply pondered on the greatest problems of life, and has found solutions, I should point to India."

— Max Mueller

M.J. AKBAR

M.J. Akbar is a former editor of Sunday magazine. He launched The Telegraph in 1982. He has worked as an Advisor in the Ministry of Human Resources and helped policy planning in the key areas of education, the National Literacy Mission and protection of heritage. In 1994, he launched India's first global newspaper, The Asian Age, which has grown into a major media presence nationally and internationally. In 2005, M.J. Akbar was invited by King Abdullah Bin Abdul Aziz A-Saud, custodian of the Two Holy Mosques, to become a member of the Forum for Islamic Scholars and Intellectuals. In 2007, he joined the Brookings Institution in Washington as a Visiting Fellow in the Brookings project on US Policy Towards the Islamic World. Simultaneous with a career in journalism and politics, he has also been a prolific author.

23

Islam, Jehad and Global War on Terrorism

M.J. Akbar

Islam, Jehad and the Global War on Terrorism is the topic of concern across substantial parts of the world. There is so much misunderstanding today, because death and violence are inherently complicated, complex and controversial.

The last formal call to jehad, which means one legally tenable by the laws of the Shariat, was given by the Caliph during World War I when Turkey went to war. The Caliph was head of a state, he had an army, and there was a genuine reason to go to war. I may also add that the first person to give a call for a holy war in 1914 was not the Muslim Caliph. The first people to declare a holy war were the Russians led by the Tsar. Holy war is not an exclusive Islamic concept. We often get this impression that the concept of holy war did not exist before the arrival of Islam.

The first call for jehad after World War II in the contemporary phase of history was given by Pakistan in Kashmir in October 1947, when the Pakistani raiders crossed into the state of Jammu and Kashmir. This is on record, but of course nobody understood then what it meant. The world's understanding of this problem improved only when it reached the Western world.

I have a problem with the title: Islam, Jehad and the Global War on Terrorism. Very often we do not fully understand the terms we use in discourse. This has also become a problem in the relationship between the West and Muslim nations and peoples.

Let me try and illuminate my dilemma with an illustration or two.

On the fifth anniversary of 9/11, I was at the Brookings. George Bush had used a phrase in a speech: "Islmo-fascism." CNN asked me to come for a discussion on this, to which I agreed, and it turned out to be a useful interview on television. I began with a poser: Islam is 1,400 years old; how old is fascism? Fascism did not enter our dictionary before 1920, when Mussolini came to power in Italy. So, whatever, else fascism might or might not be, it cannot be Islamic. On the other hand, there are many Muslims who are fascists. But why do you blame Islam for the sins of Muslims? We do not blame Christianity for Hitler or the Vatican for Mussolini. So let us begin to address a problem accurately.

Take the phrase: Islam and the West. There have been a large number of seminars on Islam and the West and there are plenty of tracts, pamphlets and books on this subject. The last book I saw was a speech made by Britain's Prince Charles in 1993. But Islam is a faith and the West is geography; how can you compare a faith with geography? Why cannot we have discussion on South Asia and the West? In any meaningful dialogue we must discuss like with like.

Similarly, Islam and democracy. How old is Islam? The answer is 1,400 years. Now, how old is democracy? In a practical sense, it is 50-60 years old. The US is the oldest practicing democracy. The American Constitution is the genuine model and a guide for the modern world when it comes to democracy. But even in the US, which gave the concept of democracy as a practical model of governance to the world, the Blacks got genuine voting rights only after Lyndon Johnson's reforms in 1965. All I am suggesting is that democracy itself is an evolving concept. If so, what has it got to do with Islam? If anything, the basic values of Islam—equality, charity and justice—are more egalitarian, and therefore more democratic, than other faiths.

I was speaking on this topic in Jakarta recently. I noted that a billion and half people— The Chinese—just to the north of India have never ever heard of democracy. How many conferences have we had on Confucianism and democracy? So, where is the question of dragging Islam into a discussion on nation states and democracy?

The headscarf is an integral part of the cultural Islamic world. It has now been turned into the standard symbol of the barbaric and backward. I told some French friends that the Virgin Mary would have never got into a French school. Each icon of the Virgin Mary shows her wearing a hijab, a headscarf. Who wears the perfect hijab in the world? The Roman Catholic nuns. Headwear is part of traditional culture in some parts of the East; it represents a form of modesty. How many of you know that if a woman wants to visit the Pope she has to cover her head? I respect the Pope's right to respect.

In any case, this is the first time in the history of civilisation that a piece of cloth, a scarf, has come to be considered as the symbol of a backward, and the nudist thong is considered civilised. I may add that the full veil is nothing but disgrace for many Muslim societies today, as it is forced on women and is restrictive and regressive. It is a denial of gender equality. I ask the conservatives who insist upon it a simple question. Do their wives wear the full veil when they are in front of the Kaba? No. There is nothing in Islamic practice that demands the full *burqa*.

There is no text without a context. And the subtext in the "West vs. Islam" formulation is that the West represents everything that is forward-looking, scientific, civilised, modern, technological etc, etc, and Islam is now the embodiment of the backward, the barbaric, the spiteful and the medieval.

The behaviour of the Muslim radical fringe of course encourages such a negative image of Muslims. There are those whose are now talking about the revival of a caliphate. This is an absurd concept propagated by Osama bin Laden. The Caliphate was an empire idea, a pre-nation-state idea. It is like the Holy Roman Empire, which had relevance and validity when it existed. Kemal Ataturk destroyed the Caliphate because it had become an irrelevant institution in the era of nation states.

Pakistan was created in 1947 in the name of Islam; within 30 years, it could not bear the pressure of language. An Islamic identity was not sufficient to preserve Pakistan's unity, and Bangladesh was born.

Another familiar accusation is that Islam does not tolerate minorities.

I am going to an incontrovertible source, for the Muslims at least, the Koran. Let us see what the Koran says about Christians. The Koran considers Jesus as perhaps the second most important prophet after Mohammad. It mentions the name of Mary far more times than in the New Testament—34 times in the Koran against 19 times in the Bible.

The Koran was revealed at a time when there were many communities in Mecca and Medina: the Arabs who had become idol-worshippers, Jews, Christians, and the growing band of Muslims. The last three could be said to belong to the same source faith of Abraham.

The one substantive difference was on the question of the last prophet. We cannot expect the church to accept Mohammad as the last prophet, because that would make Christianity a 600-year-old religion. So, the church had to fight the new faith, which claimed a prophet in the same tradition but beyond Jesus. The Jews too refused Mohammad's assertion to be the last prophet. So there had to be conflict. Yes, while the Koran does say that all non-Muslims will oppose Islam and the prophet, the Koran also accepts the legitimacy of Jesus, but not his divinity. The doctrine of tauhid is the unity of God. But why does the Koran accept the virginity of Mary and not the divinity of Jesus? The explanation it offers is very interesting. The Koran cites Adam, who was born from neither man nor woman. If Adam is not called divine, how can Jesus be? It is up to Allah to create man he wishes. The Koran accepts there will be a theological conflict with Jews and Christians. But what does it say after that? When it comes to living together, it says, let God be the judge of who is faithful and who is not.

In terms of your behaviour, says the Koran, towards Jews, Christians and the Sabians, "on them shall be no fear nor shall they grieve." And therefore the people of the Book are given space in a Muslim country. Which is why when the Jews were expelled by the Spanish Inquisition, the one place where they found succour, the only place in which they found shelter, was the Ottoman Empire. When the British reached Baghdad in 1918 the most powerful community in the Iraqi capital was not the Muslims but the Jews. Iraqi Jews controlled commerce and the chambers of commerce and industry and they were flourishing untrammeled, unquestioned by anyone. I might also add that the Jews in the Ottoman Empire did not demand Israel because their holy land was already freely accessible to them.

The Koran is very explicit: let there be no compulsion in religion. Nothing could be more explicit than this. So, the whole mythology about the spread of Islam through the sword is baseless. There is no Koranic sanctity for spreading faith with the sword. Of course, a few Muslims might have done it, but they did not have sanction from the Koran. The Koran says, emphatically, "Your religion for you, and my religion for me."

The Koran is multicultural. I remember a statement made by the RSS chief that if Indian Muslims accept Lord Krishna as a prophet, then Hindus would have no more conflicts with Muslims. I wrote a piece stating why Lord Krishna could easily be a prophet of Islam, as Krishna came to the earth much before Mohammad (PBUH). I will explain. The Koran says that to every people was sent a messenger and Allah revealed it through one way or other. If that message or messenger is neglected, rejected or misused, then the day of the reckoning will come. Another verse says that Allah assuredly sent amongst every people a messenger, but will not tell name every messenger. And, most importantly, the messenger came in every language or thought. There is no reason why a messenger speaking Sanskrit should not have been sent. Mohammad is the last prophet—this is non-negotiable in Islam. Lord Krishna preceded Mohammad.

According to some scholars, Verse 85:21 of the Koran is a reference to a dweller of Kapil or Kapilavasthu, and refers to the Buddha. All I am trying to suggest is that the Koran did not become the message of the billion and a half people because it is narrow, because it is restrictive. It became so because it is an open message. That the Koran may have been misused by a number of Muslims is not a true reflection on the Koran or Islam. It is the reflection on those Muslims.

And finally to jehad. We all know that the greater jehad is the struggle to cleanse oneself from within; this is the Jehad-I-Akbar. But the troublesome jehad is the Jehad-e-Asghar, the call to war.

The first Caliph, Abu Bakr outlined the 10 rules before the first armies went out. Let me put this proposition first: every jehad is fought by Muslims, but every war fought by Muslims is not a Jehad. Why? Because the 10 rules of jehad are clearly defined, and the most important of these rules state that it can be declared only by an established or recognised authority. Again, Rules 7 and 8 are very clear: you cannot kill innocents, you cannot kill bystander, you cannot even destroy a palm trees. A scorched earth policy is very familiar war tactic. But a Jehadi cannot do it. Jehad is a war for justice. The prophet's life is divided into three stages—571 when he was born, 610 when he received the message, and 622, when he migrated to Medina. Between 610 and 622, or the first 12 years of his public life, when he was spreading the message, was a period of heavy persecution—his life was always under threat and he was severely harassed during that period. Not a single war verse of the Koran was sent during the Mecca period. All the war verses came to him in Medina. Why? Because in Medina, he became head of a government and a state, and war became a necessary part of state policy.

In Christianity, the greatest values are love and martyrdom—after all Jesus gave his life for others, washing away their sins with his own life and thus redeeming them. But this is not the case with Islam. In Islam, the greatest virtues are equality, charity and justice. The moment a Muslim sees inequality, he will respond, irrespective of where he is and what he is.

The prophet was once asked what made him think that he was the last prophet. His reply was fascinating: "My brother Moses, he said, had only one eye—it was the eye of the law." Moses is the great law-giver and his law is as valid for Muslims as it is by Christians and Jews. "And God", said the prophet, "gave my brother Jesus only one eye—the eye of love. God has given me two eyes—law and love." You cannot run a society and a nation without the combination of law and love.

I consider one of the finest descriptions of jehad to be Krishna's sermon to Arjuna, wherein Krishna says there comes a time when war is obligatory, and it does not matter if you have to fight your brother. The restoration of order over rides emotions. If you do not go to war against the unjust then injustice will prevail. There will be no order. Though in the end only one person in left alive in the *Mahabharta*, the restoration of order and justice has been achieved. It is a powerful metaphor.

There is a case for a just war, in almost all religions, in all ideologies. Religious or secular Jehad is the Islamic theory of just war.

There are no non-violent people or nations. We, in India, like to believe that we are a non-violent nation. Hinduism cannot be a non-violent religion if its two operative epics are war epics—both, the *Mahabharta* and the *Ramanyana* deal with war; they deal with actual realities. Non-violence is an ideal, but reality demands more practical measures.

And now, how global is global?

If you look at what is called the global war or conflict, it is global essentially within the geographies of the last two Muslim empires somewhat less than the range of the war area is Ottoman empire and the areas of the Mughal empire. In 1918 something very, very interesting happened to the Muslim world. Every single Muslim nation was colonised. With the defeat of the Ottoman empire there was not a single Muslim nation in the world which was not under European rule.

From the colonies, three kinds of nations emerged. One was the Indian model, the model from which finally emerged democracy and Gandhian nationalism. The second model was Kemal Ataturk's nationalism in Turkey. Ataturk's achievement is often grossly underestimated. If Ataturk had not protected the integrity of Turkey—we think of the war ending in 1918; rubbish, the war did not end in 1918 for half of the world—there would not have been a Turkey as you see it today. Lloyd George armed and encouraged Greek troops into Turkish land, and wanted the Turkish border at somewhere near Ankara. Lloyd George failed for two reasons. The Turks fought magnificently. And in 1922, Australia, New Zealand and Canada told Lloyd George that they had enough of war. They refused to fight against Turkey to achieve Lloyd George's Machiavellian ambitions. That was a big turning point for the British Empire, because for the first time the dominions rejected a call from the mother country. If Ataturk had not succeeded, what would have been the state of Turkey today? The region from Izmir to Istanbul and Edrine would have been in Greece, from where the Muslims would have been pushed out, just as Muslims had been pushed out from Bulgaria, Hungary and elsewhere. What would have been the consequences? Turks would have been fighting for their country for decades. This conflict would have made the Palestine issue look like peanuts, or a sideshow.

A third model became the pattern for Muslim world that emerged out of the Ottoman Empire in the Arab world: neo-colonisation. The principal neo-colony was Iraq, created in 1921. The first rulers of Iraq were the Hashemites, with clear instructions from London as to who gave the orders.

It is not my view that the conflicts of nationalism and neo-colonisation will not be resolved, they will be resolved; and they will be resolved in their own way and in their own time. Those imposing their will eventually will recognise that the world will spin on an axis of equals. But it will take time. One of the mistakes we tend to make is to confuse the calendar of history with our lifetimes. History has a different measure.

Whatever be the rights and wrongs, perplexities and complexities, the one rationale that sanctions jehad is when a nation is invaded and occupied. There is no confusion on this score.

The days of war with regular armies are probably over. There is a new dynamic at work in the Arab world, the Arab street. For a long while, the Arabs were trapped in what I call the Myth of 1956. The Arabs actually believed that in 1956 Nasser stood up and turned back the Anglo-French-Israeli invasion with Arab strength and military power. All that happened then was that America pulled the plug on the invasion. But that led to so much complacency in the Arab world that 1967 was inevitable. In 1967, complacency was shattered. But the Americans fell into the trap of 1967. They, and Israel, began to believe that any people who had left their shoes behind the outside walls of Jerusalem would never fight. Today, the Arabs of Iraq have shown that they can fight.

We should not, in any case, confuse Arab governments with the Arab people. You can take on Arab governments and you can destroy their armies, but dealing with the Arab people is a different matter. Once the street rises, and this is a street with a memory, with a history, with a passion and with a cause, you will have to fight the war of the shadows. We saw that war in Afghanistan in the 19th and 20th centuries. Britain and Russia were defeated by shadow arrives in Afghanistan. There are no Victoria crosses and medals for those who fight you from the shadows. But you cannot frighten anyone with death if he is ready to die.